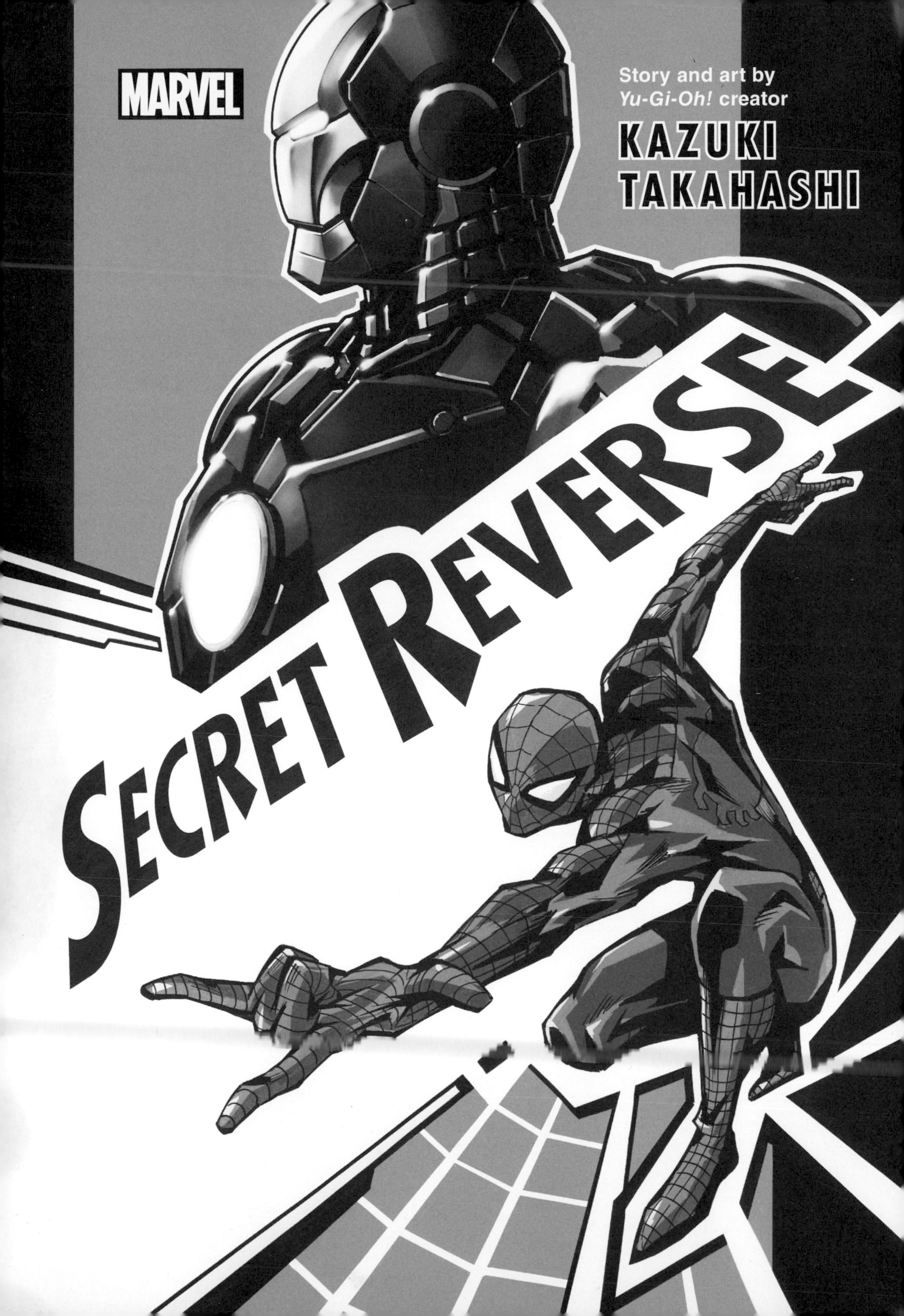
MARVEL
Story and art by
Yu-Gi-Oh! creator
KAZUKI
TAKAHASHI
SECRET REVERSE

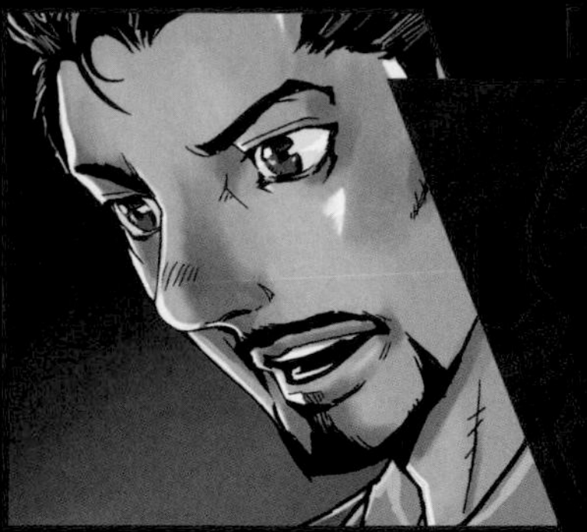

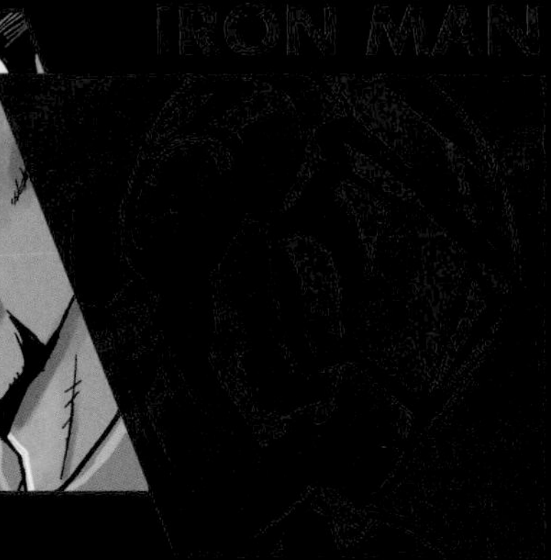
IRON MAN

TONY STARK

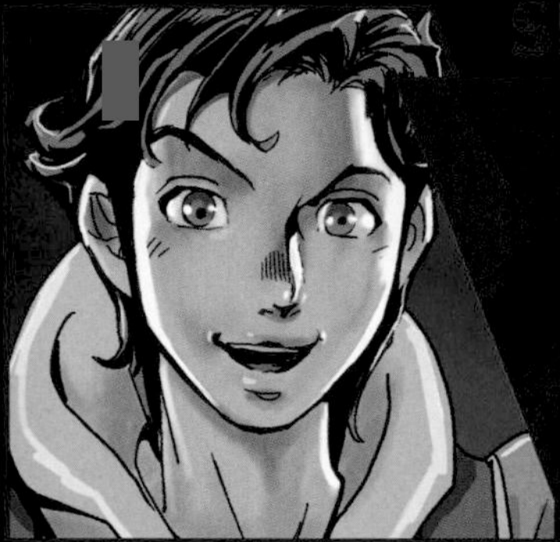

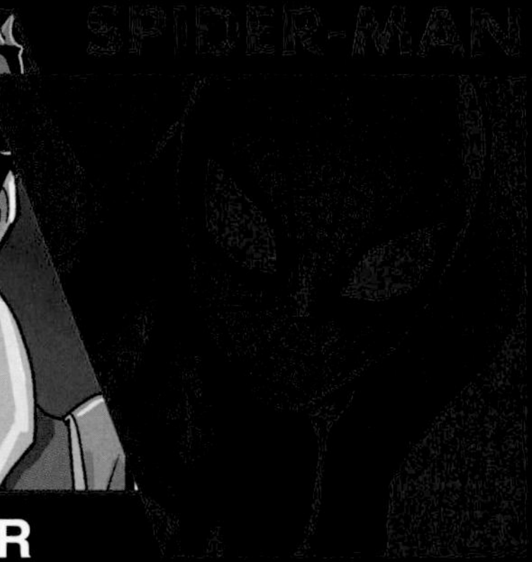
SPIDER-MAN

PETER PARKER

CHARACTERS

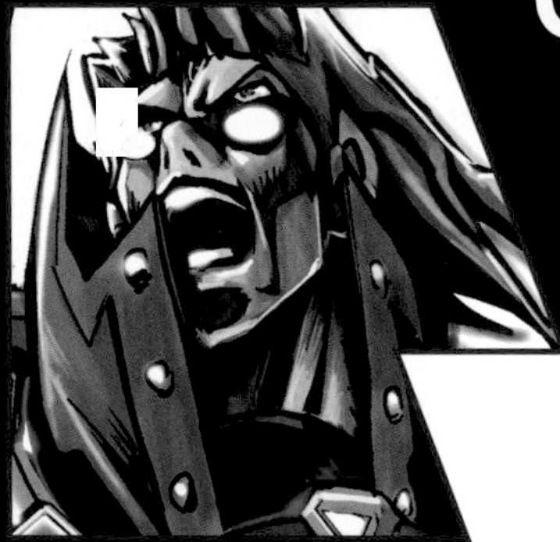

KAIOH

HIROMI

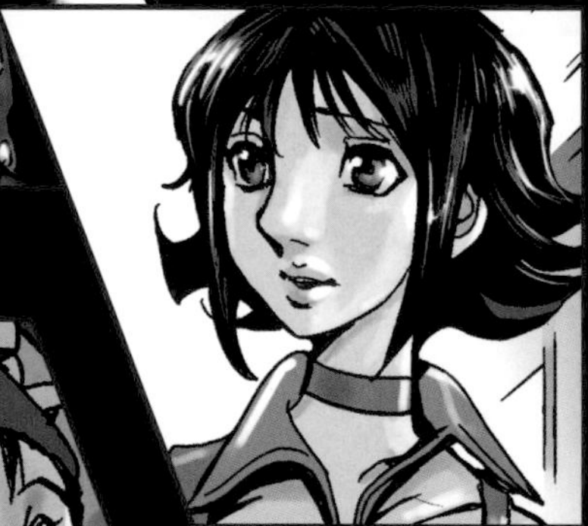

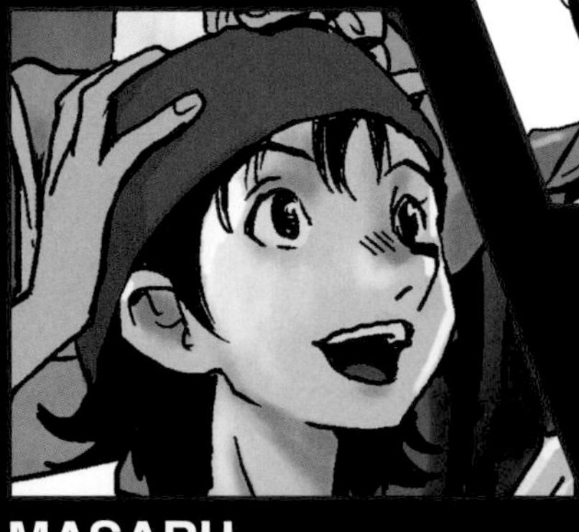

MASARU

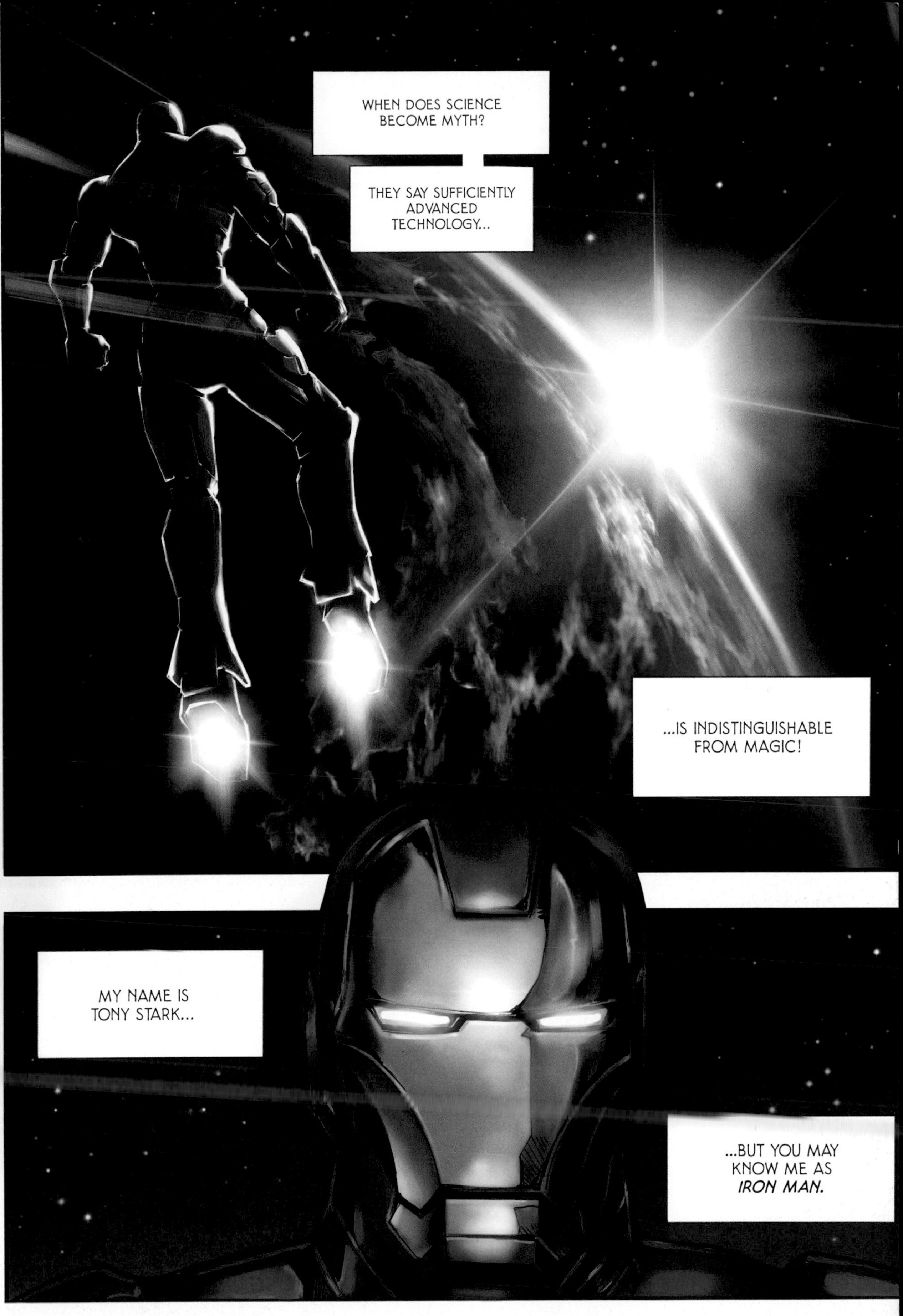
WHEN DOES SCIENCE BECOME MYTH?
THEY SAY SUFFICIENTLY ADVANCED TECHNOLOGY...
...IS INDISTINGUISHABLE FROM MAGIC!
MY NAME IS TONY STARK...
...BUT YOU MAY KNOW ME AS *IRON MAN.*

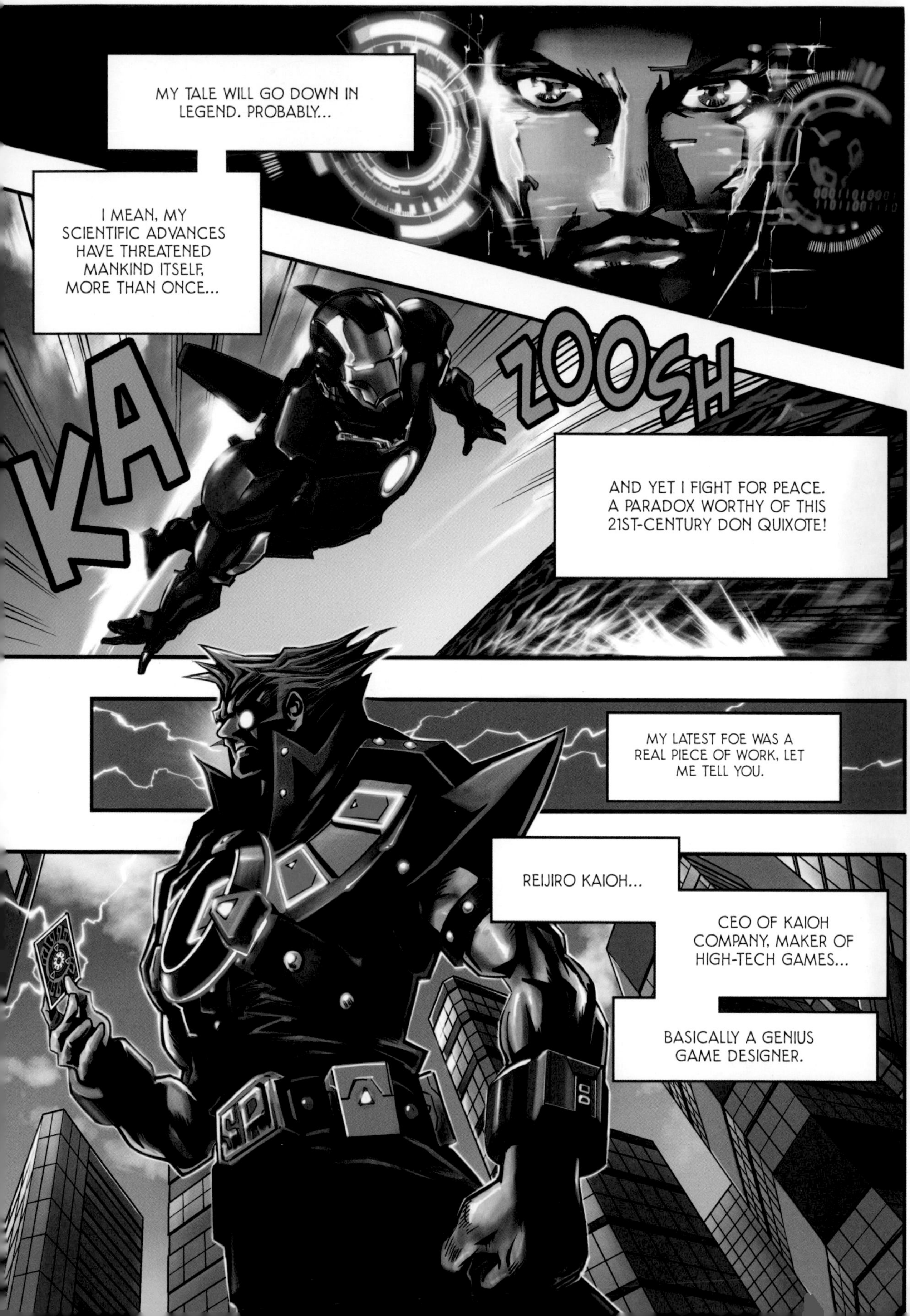
MY TALE WILL GO DOWN IN LEGEND. PROBABLY...
I MEAN, MY SCIENTIFIC ADVANCES HAVE THREATENED MANKIND ITSELF, MORE THAN ONCE...
KA ZOOSH
AND YET I FIGHT FOR PEACE. A PARADOX WORTHY OF THIS 21ST-CENTURY DON QUIXOTE!
MY LATEST FOE WAS A REAL PIECE OF WORK, LET ME TELL YOU.
REIJIRO KAIOH...
CEO OF KAIOH COMPANY, MAKER OF HIGH-TECH GAMES...
BASICALLY A GENIUS GAME DESIGNER.

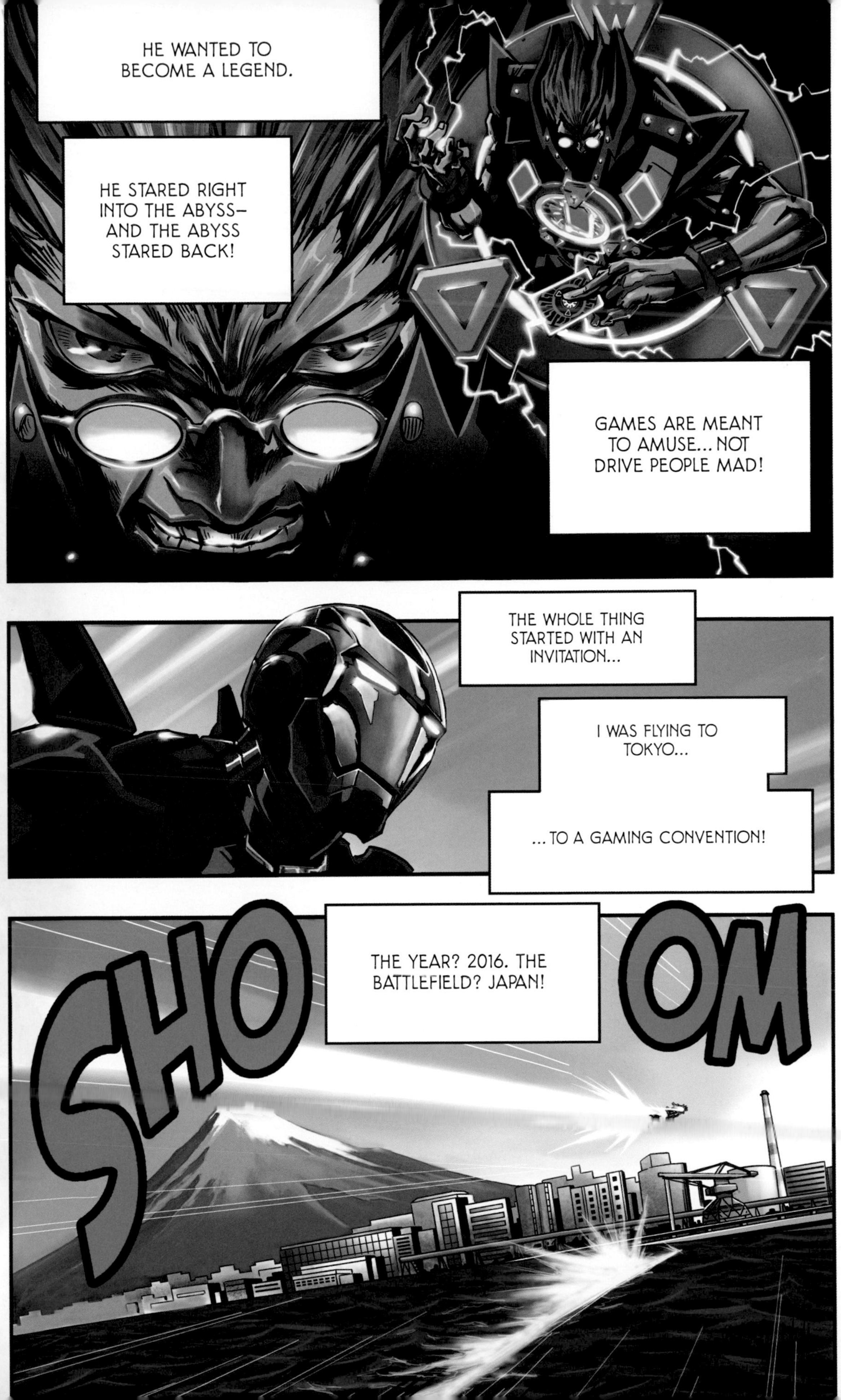
HE WANTED TO BECOME A LEGEND.
HE STARED RIGHT INTO THE ABYSS— AND THE ABYSS STARED BACK!
GAMES ARE MEANT TO AMUSE... NOT DRIVE PEOPLE MAD!
THE WHOLE THING STARTED WITH AN INVITATION...
I WAS FLYING TO TOKYO...
...TO A GAMING CONVENTION!
THE YEAR? 2016. THE BATTLEFIELD? JAPAN!
SHO
OM

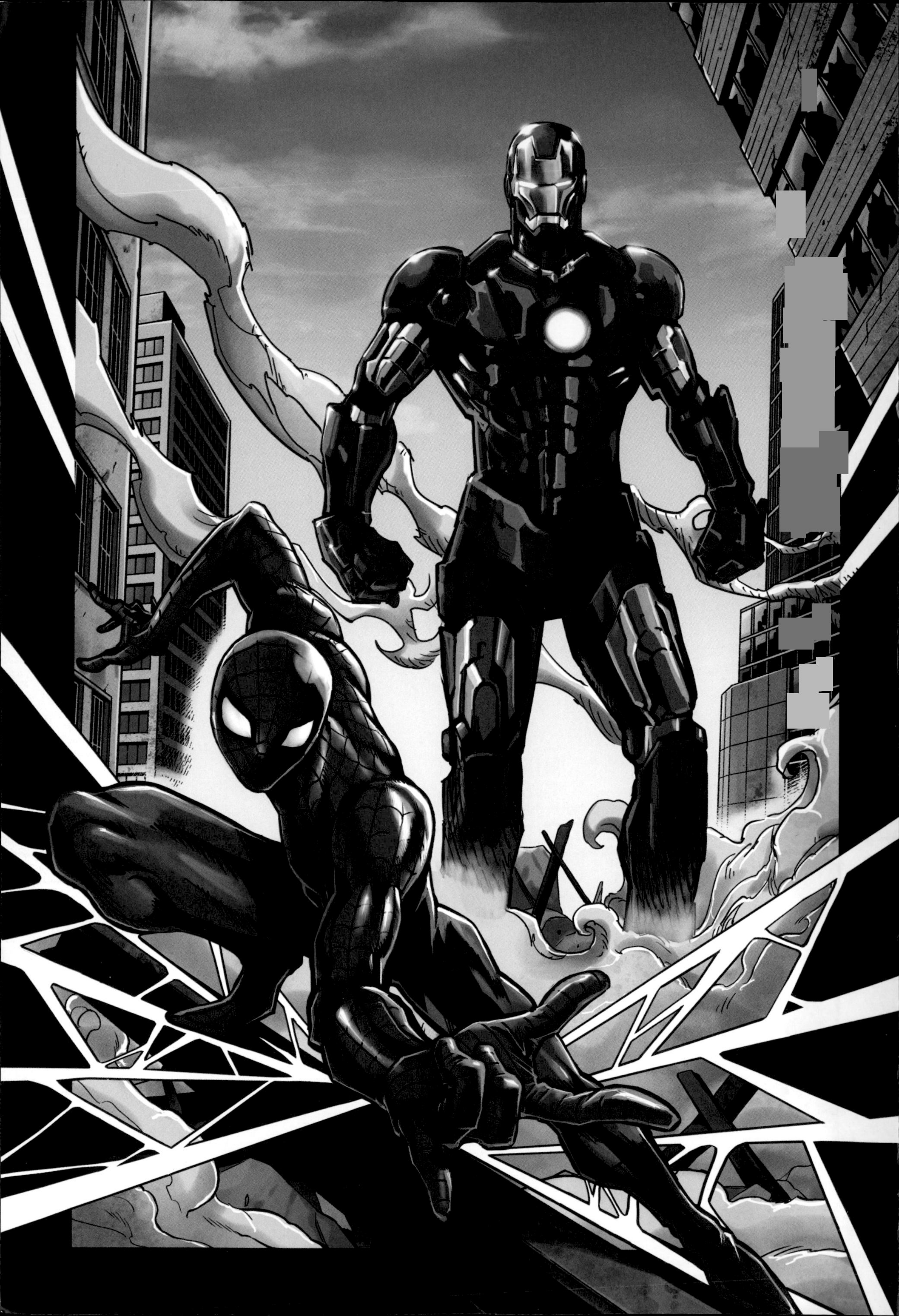

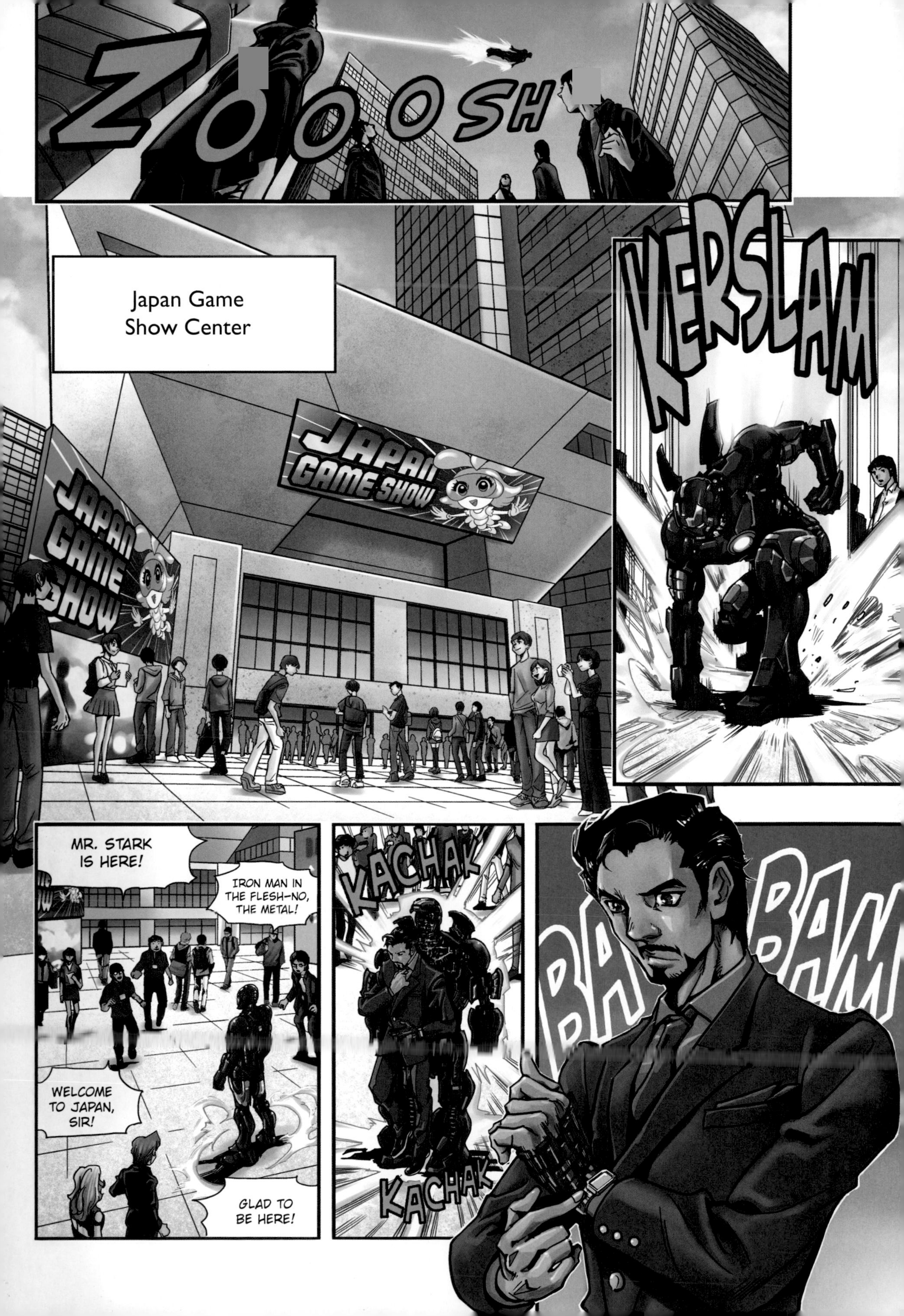
ZOOOSH
Japan Game Show Center
JAPAN GAME SHOW
JAPAN GAME SHOW
KERSLAM
MR. STARK IS HERE!
IRON MAN IN THE FLESH—NO, THE METAL!
WELCOME TO JAPAN, SIR!
GLAD TO BE HERE!
KACHAK
KACHAK
BAM
BAM

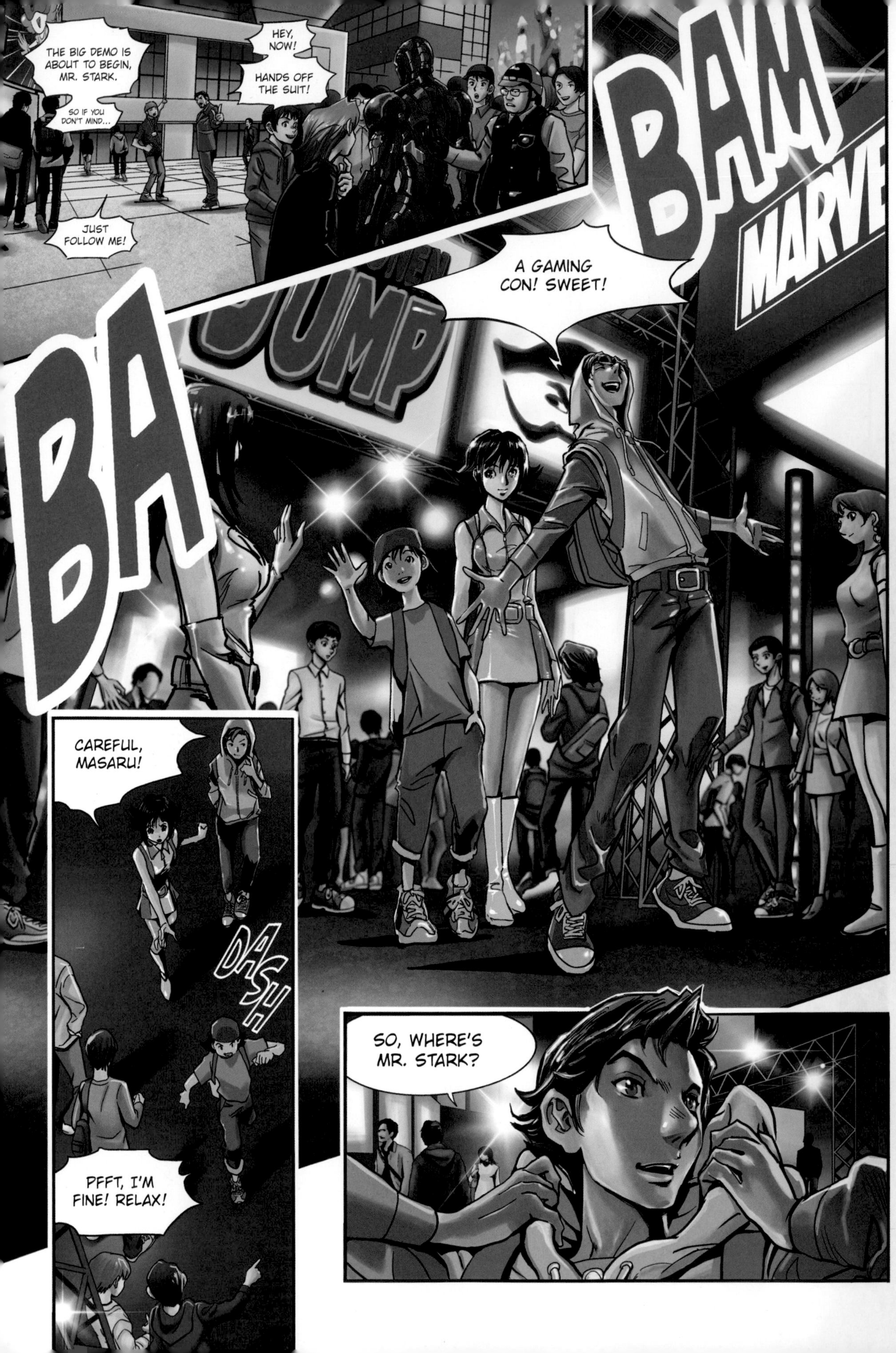
THE BIG DEMO IS ABOUT TO BEGIN, MR. STARK.
SO IF YOU DON'T MIND...
HEY, NOW!
HANDS OFF THE SUIT!
JUST FOLLOW ME!
BAM
BA
A GAMING CON! SWEET!
JUMP
CAREFUL, MASARU!
DASH
PFFT, I'M FINE! RELAX!
SO, WHERE'S MR. STARK?

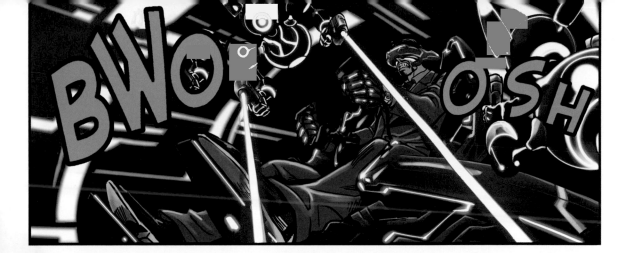

BWO OSH

ZOOSH

URGH!!

HADWOOM

GAH...

GAME OVER!!

...

IS THERE AN EASY MODE...?

STEADY THERE, MR. STARK!

MUST'VE LEFT MY IRON STOMACH AT HOME...

BEING TAKEN FOR A RIDE ISN'T MY SPEED.

I'D DO BETTER WITH A REAL FORMULA 1...

CAR, OF COURSE! NOT CHEMISTRY.

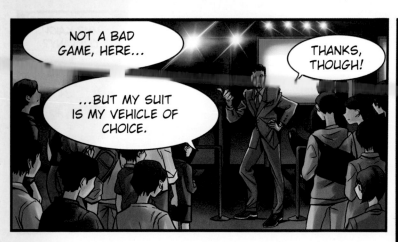

NOT A BAD GAME, HERE...

...BUT MY SUIT IS MY VEHICLE OF CHOICE.

THANKS, THOUGH!

MR. STARK!

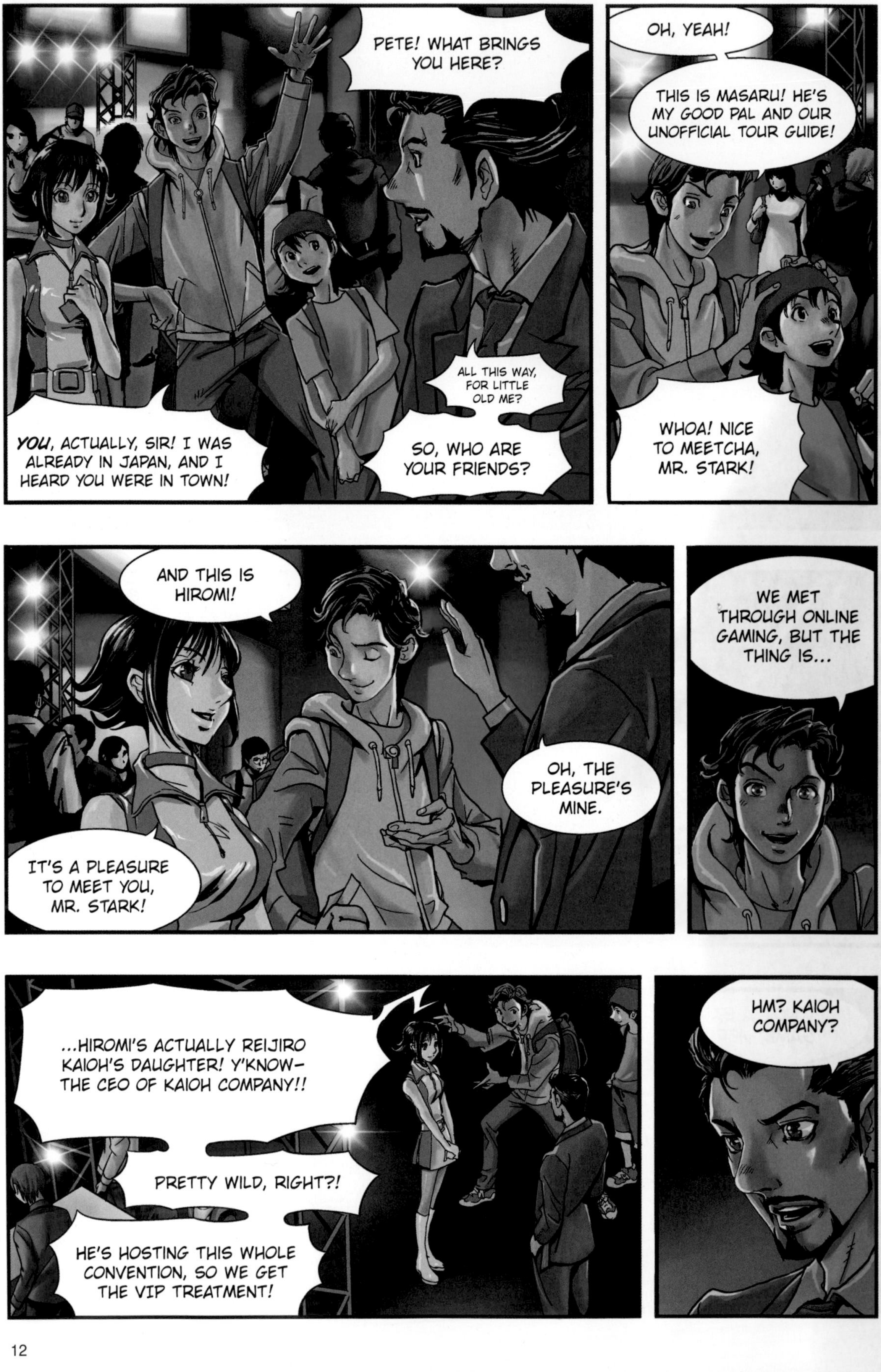
PETE! WHAT BRINGS YOU HERE?
YOU, ACTUALLY, SIR! I WAS ALREADY IN JAPAN, AND I HEARD YOU WERE IN TOWN!
ALL THIS WAY, FOR LITTLE OLD ME?
SO, WHO ARE YOUR FRIENDS?
OH, YEAH!
THIS IS MASARU! HE'S MY GOOD PAL AND OUR UNOFFICIAL TOUR GUIDE!
WHOA! NICE TO MEETCHA, MR. STARK!
AND THIS IS HIROMI!
IT'S A PLEASURE TO MEET YOU, MR. STARK!
OH, THE PLEASURE'S MINE.
WE MET THROUGH ONLINE GAMING, BUT THE THING IS...
...HIROMI'S ACTUALLY REIJIRO KAIOH'S DAUGHTER! Y'KNOW—THE CEO OF KAIOH COMPANY!!
PRETTY WILD, RIGHT?!
HE'S HOSTING THIS WHOLE CONVENTION, SO WE GET THE VIP TREATMENT!
HM? KAIOH COMPANY?

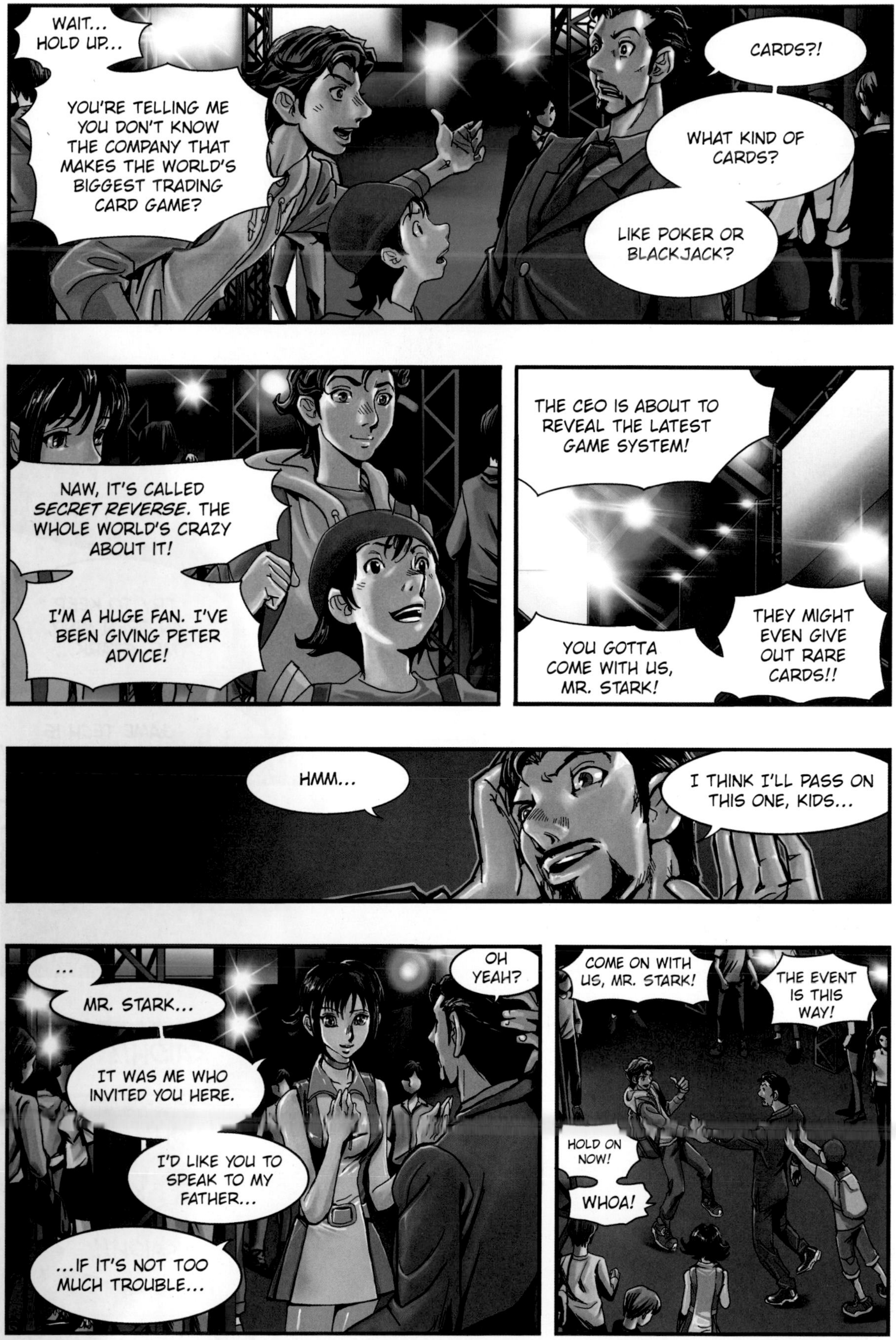
WAIT... HOLD UP...
YOU'RE TELLING ME YOU DON'T KNOW THE COMPANY THAT MAKES THE WORLD'S BIGGEST TRADING CARD GAME?
CARDS?!
WHAT KIND OF CARDS?
LIKE POKER OR BLACKJACK?
NAW, IT'S CALLED *SECRET REVERSE*. THE WHOLE WORLD'S CRAZY ABOUT IT!
I'M A HUGE FAN. I'VE BEEN GIVING PETER ADVICE!
THE CEO IS ABOUT TO REVEAL THE LATEST GAME SYSTEM!
YOU GOTTA COME WITH US, MR. STARK!
THEY MIGHT EVEN GIVE OUT RARE CARDS!!
HMM...
I THINK I'LL PASS ON THIS ONE, KIDS...
...
MR. STARK...
OH YEAH?
IT WAS ME WHO INVITED YOU HERE.
I'D LIKE YOU TO SPEAK TO MY FATHER...
...IF IT'S NOT TOO MUCH TROUBLE...
COME ON WITH US, MR. STARK!
THE EVENT IS THIS WAY!
HOLD ON NOW!
WHOA!

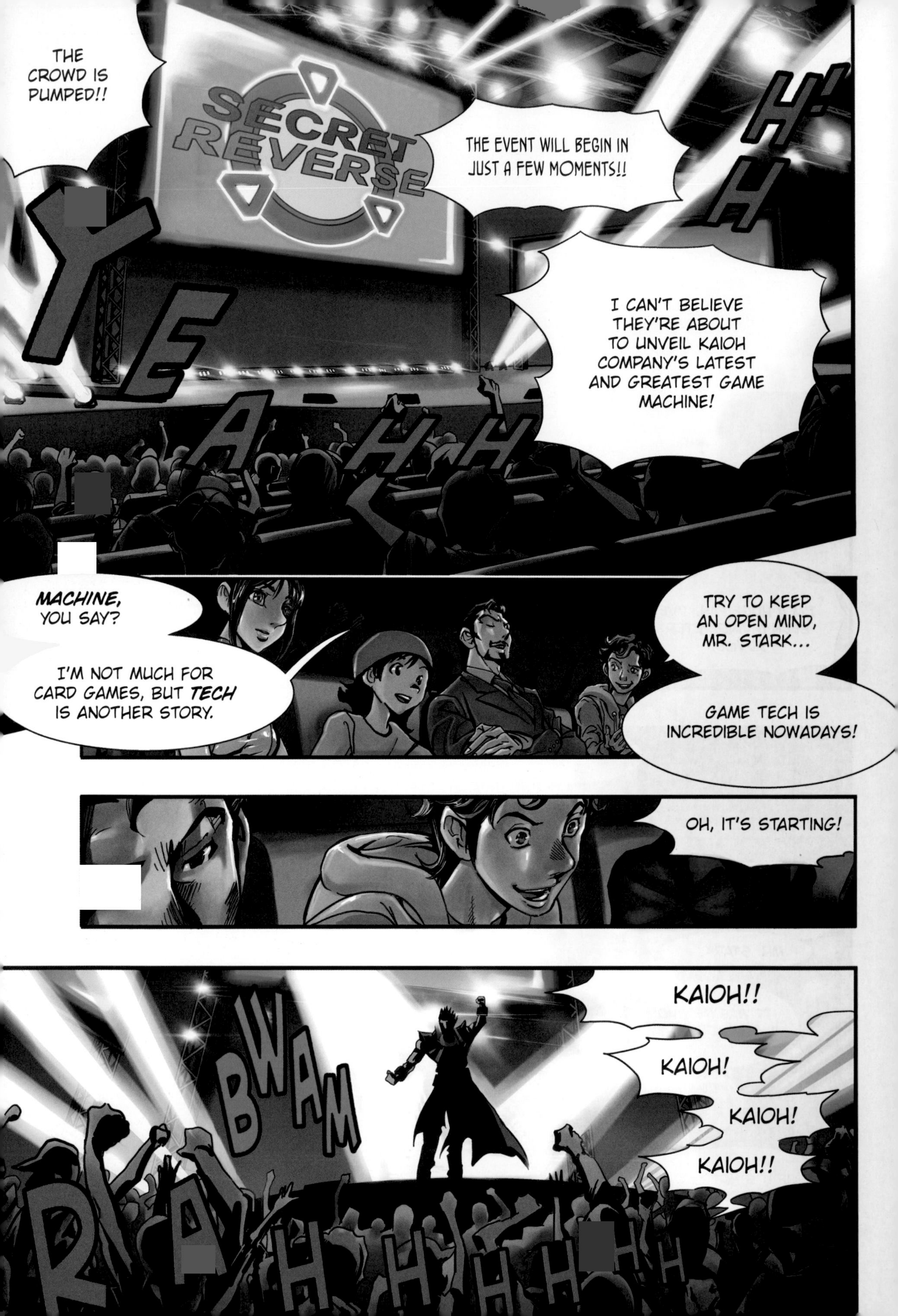
THE CROWD IS PUMPED!!
SECRET REVERSE
THE EVENT WILL BEGIN IN JUST A FEW MOMENTS!!
YEAHHHH
I CAN'T BELIEVE THEY'RE ABOUT TO UNVEIL KAIOH COMPANY'S LATEST AND GREATEST GAME MACHINE!
MACHINE, YOU SAY?
I'M NOT MUCH FOR CARD GAMES, BUT *TECH* IS ANOTHER STORY.
TRY TO KEEP AN OPEN MIND, MR. STARK...
GAME TECH IS INCREDIBLE NOWADAYS!
OH, IT'S STARTING!
BWAM
KAIOH!!
KAIOH!
KAIOH!
KAIOH!!
RAHHHHHH

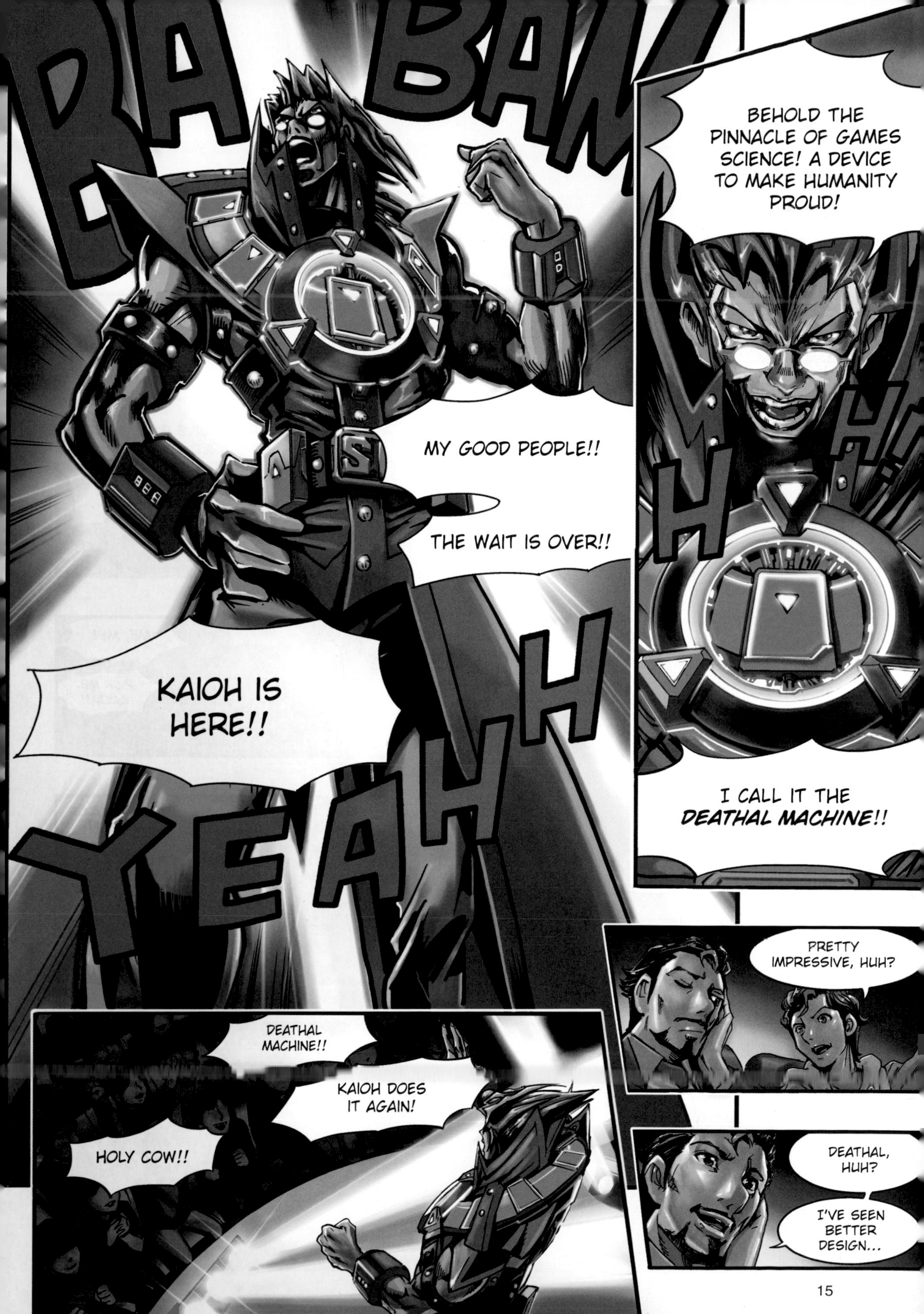
BA BAM
MY GOOD PEOPLE!!
THE WAIT IS OVER!!
KAIOH IS HERE!!
YEAHHH
BEHOLD THE PINNACLE OF GAMES SCIENCE! A DEVICE TO MAKE HUMANITY PROUD!
I CALL IT THE *DEATHAL MACHINE*!!
DEATHAL MACHINE!!
KAIOH DOES IT AGAIN!
HOLY COW!!
PRETTY IMPRESSIVE, HUH?
DEATHAL, HUH?
I'VE SEEN BETTER DESIGN...

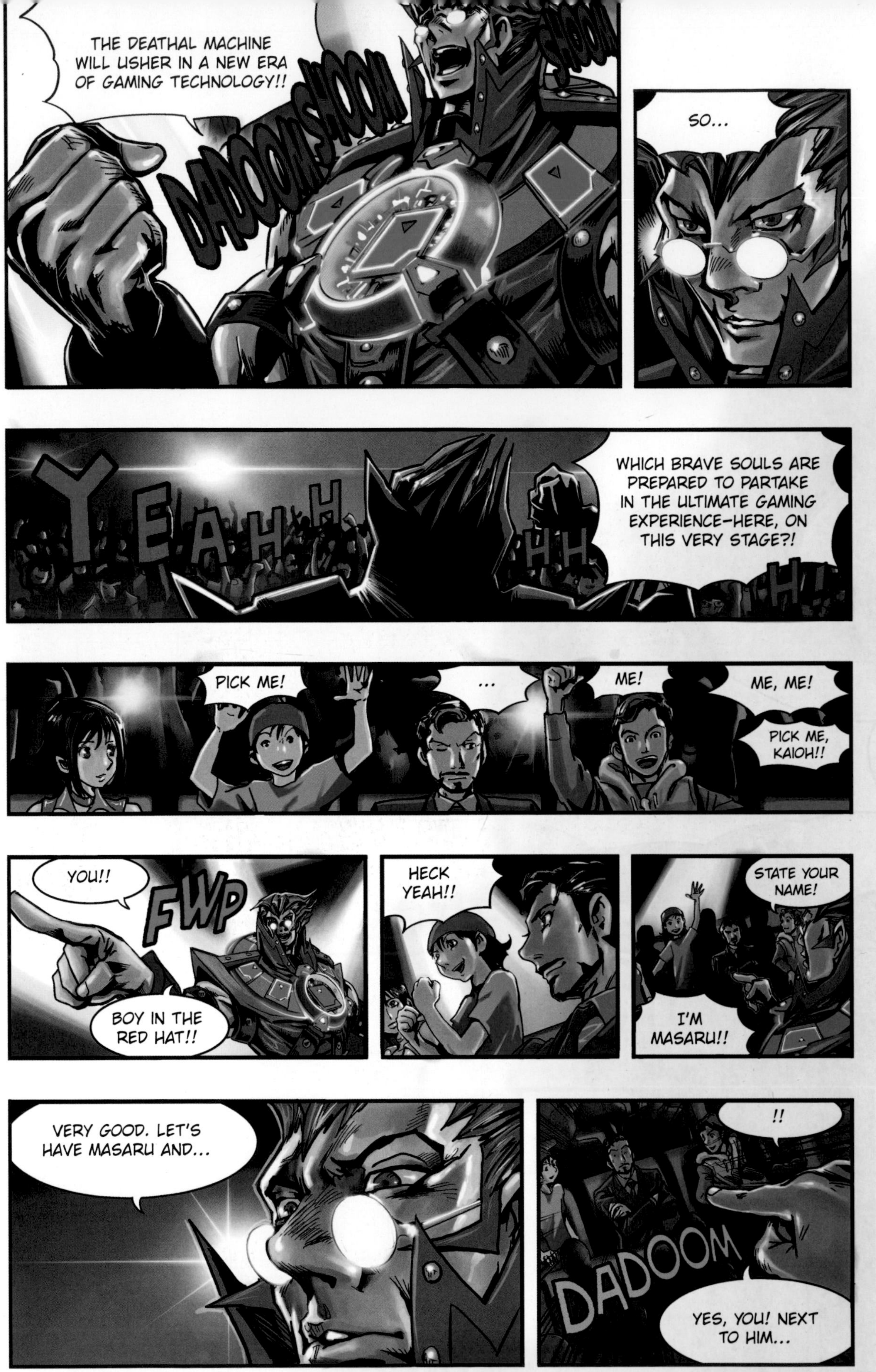
THE DEATHAL MACHINE WILL USHER IN A NEW ERA OF GAMING TECHNOLOGY!!
DADOOMSHOOM
SHOOM
SO...
YEAHH
HH
H!!
WHICH BRAVE SOULS ARE PREPARED TO PARTAKE IN THE ULTIMATE GAMING EXPERIENCE–HERE, ON THIS VERY STAGE?!
PICK ME!
...
ME!
ME, ME!
PICK ME, KAIOH!!
YOU!!
FWP
BOY IN THE RED HAT!!
HECK YEAH!!
STATE YOUR NAME!
I'M MASARU!!
VERY GOOD. LET'S HAVE MASARU AND...
!!
DADOOM
YES, YOU! NEXT TO HIM...

ME?!

COME NOW! WE ALL KNOW TONY STARK LOVES THE SPOTLIGHT!!

TALK ABOUT LUCKY, MR. STARK!!

WOO-HOO!

WELCOME TO MY WORLD!

IT'S TONY STARK!!

HE'S IRON MAN!!

ALLOW ME TO INTRODUCE...

...YOUNG MASARU AND TONY STARK! GIVE THEM A ROUND OF APPLAUSE!!

TAKE IT EASY ON ME, OKAY?

MR. STARK...

I MUST WARN YOU—YOUR TRADEMARK RED SUIT CAN'T HOLD A CANDLE TO THE POWER OF MY DEATHAL MACHINE...

MY GAME SHALL PROVE IT.

A GAME?

...?

INDEED!

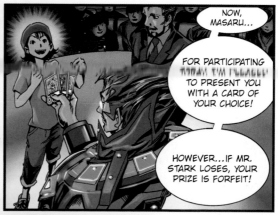

NOW, MASARU...

FOR PARTICIPATING TODAY, I'M PLEASED TO PRESENT YOU WITH A CARD OF YOUR CHOICE!

HOWEVER...IF MR. STARK LOSES, YOUR PRIZE IS FORFEIT!

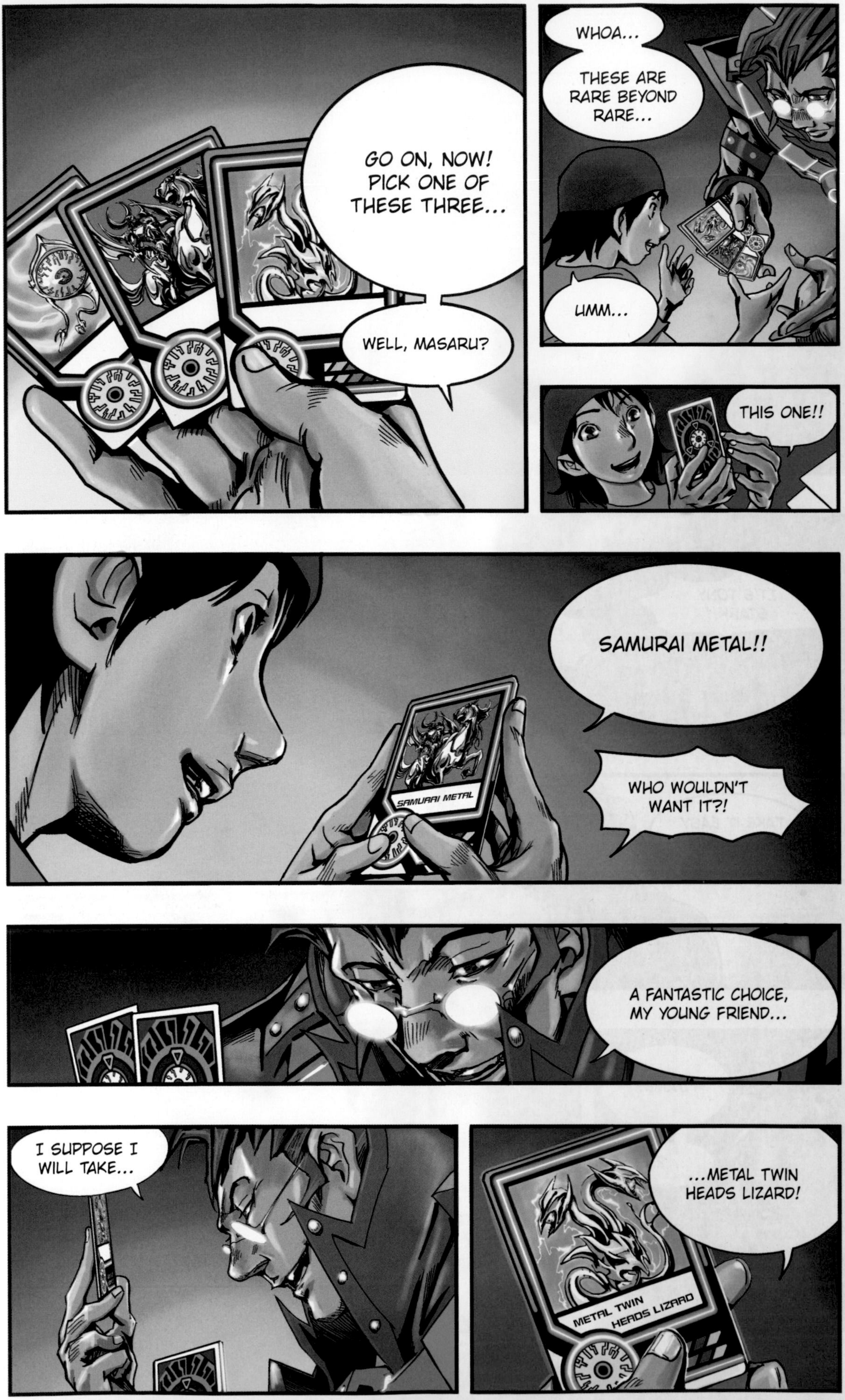
GO ON, NOW! PICK ONE OF THESE THREE...
WELL, MASARU?
WHOA...
THESE ARE RARE BEYOND RARE...
UMM...
THIS ONE!!
SAMURAI METAL!!
SAMURAI METAL
WHO WOULDN'T WANT IT?!
A FANTASTIC CHOICE, MY YOUNG FRIEND...
I SUPPOSE I WILL TAKE...
...METAL TWIN HEADS LIZARD!
METAL TWIN HEADS LIZARD

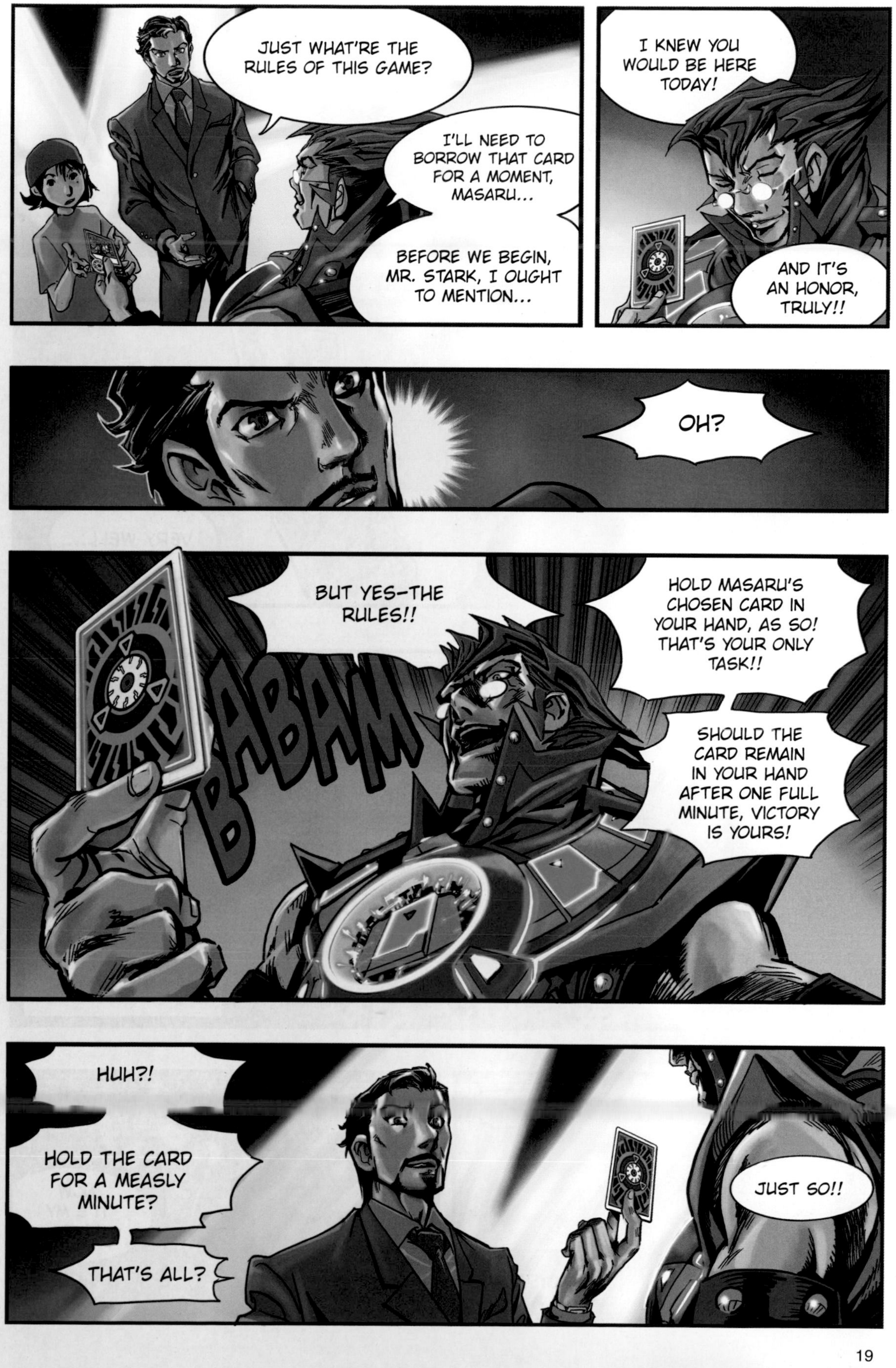
JUST WHAT'RE THE RULES OF THIS GAME?
I'LL NEED TO BORROW THAT CARD FOR A MOMENT, MASARU...
BEFORE WE BEGIN, MR. STARK, I OUGHT TO MENTION...
I KNEW YOU WOULD BE HERE TODAY!
AND IT'S AN HONOR, TRULY!!
OH?
BUT YES—THE RULES!!
BABAM
HOLD MASARU'S CHOSEN CARD IN YOUR HAND, AS SO! THAT'S YOUR ONLY TASK!!
SHOULD THE CARD REMAIN IN YOUR HAND AFTER ONE FULL MINUTE, VICTORY IS YOURS!
HUH?!
HOLD THE CARD FOR A MEASLY MINUTE?
THAT'S ALL?
JUST SO!!

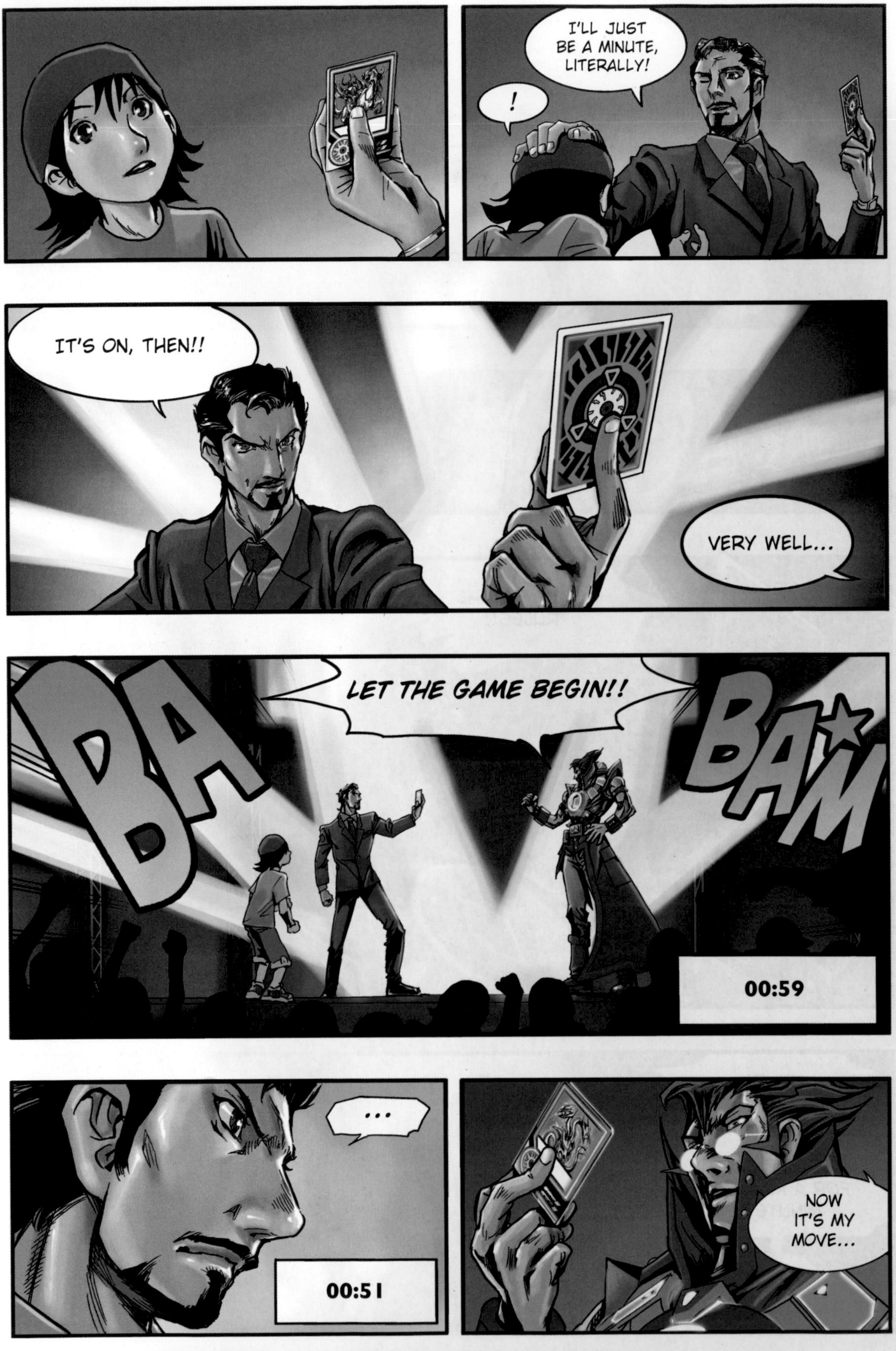
!
I'LL JUST BE A MINUTE, LITERALLY!
IT'S ON, THEN!!
VERY WELL...
BA
LET THE GAME BEGIN!!
BA☆M
00:59
...
00:51
NOW IT'S MY MOVE...

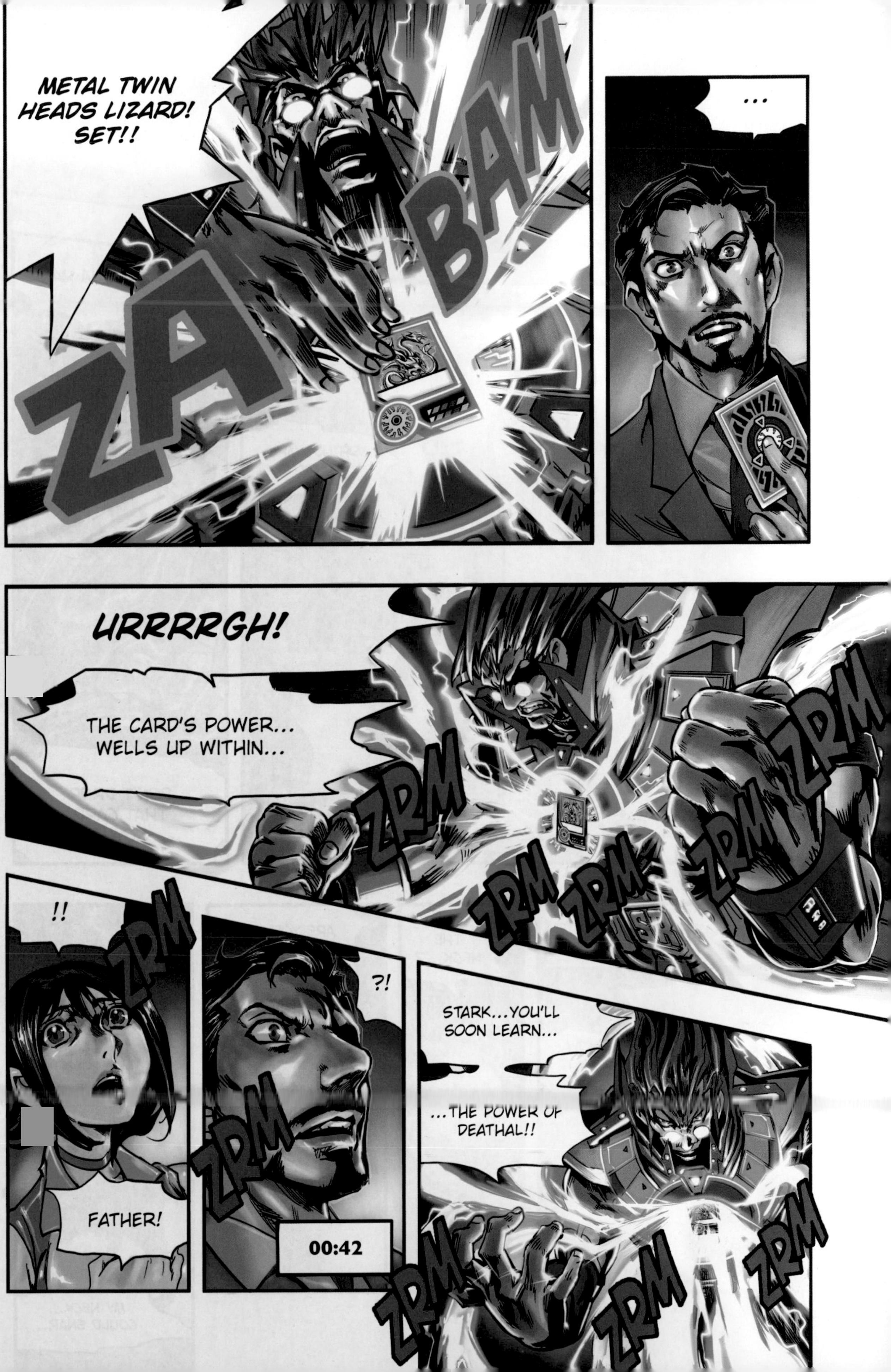
...
METAL TWIN HEADS LIZARD! SET!!
ZAP
BAM
URRRRGH!
THE CARD'S POWER... WELLS UP WITHIN...
ZRM ZRM ZRM ZRM ZRM ZRM
STARK...YOU'LL SOON LEARN...
...THE POWER OF DEATHAL!!
ZRM ZRM ZRM ZRM
?!
ZRM
00:42
!!
ZRM
FATHER!

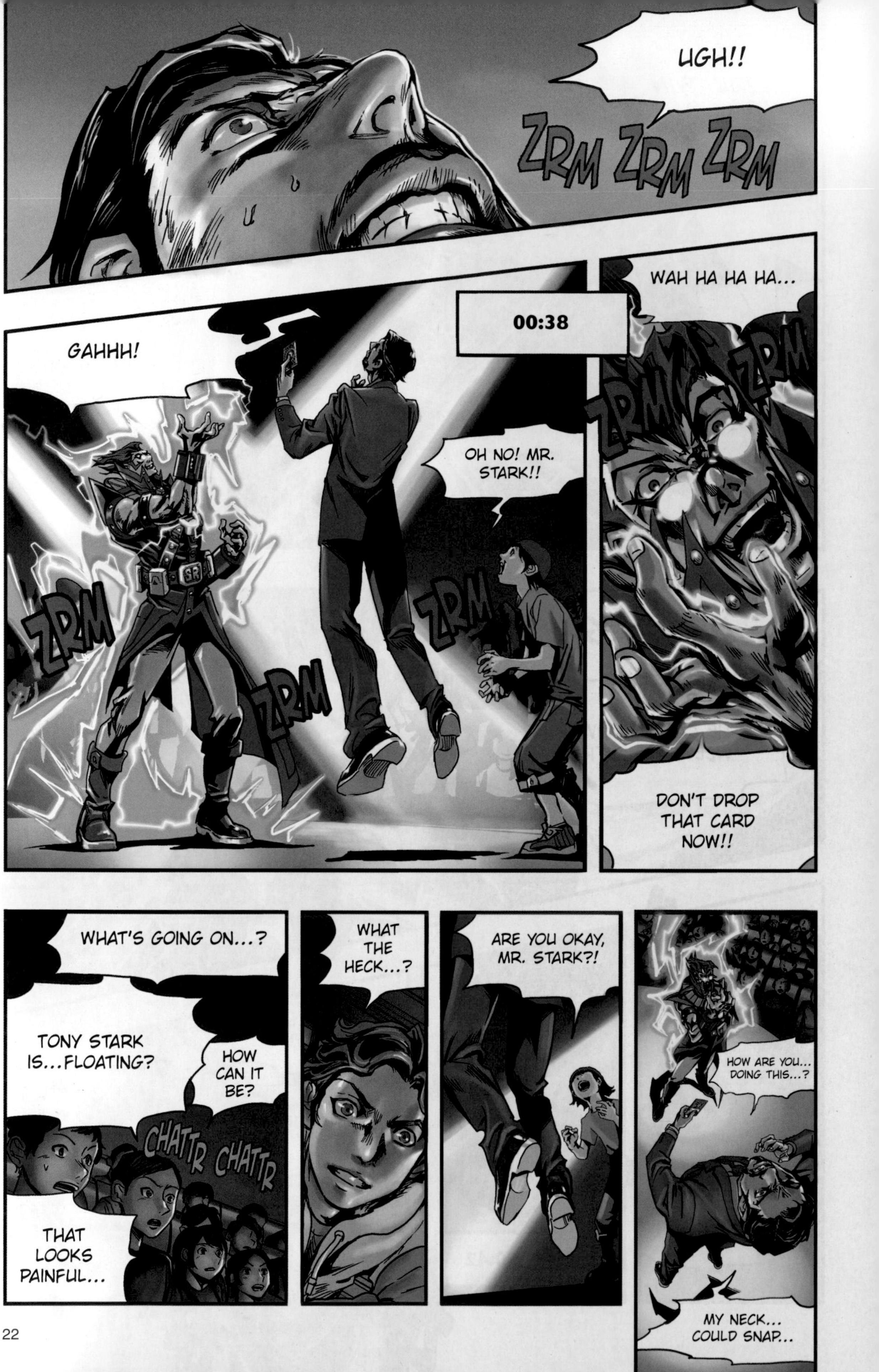
UGH!!
ZRM ZRM ZRM
00:38
GAHHH!
OH NO! MR. STARK!!
ZRM
ZRM
ZRM
WAH HA HA HA...
ZRM
ZRM
DON'T DROP THAT CARD NOW!!
WHAT'S GOING ON...?
TONY STARK IS...FLOATING?
HOW CAN IT BE?
CHATTR CHATTR
THAT LOOKS PAINFUL...
WHAT THE HECK...?
ARE YOU OKAY, MR. STARK?!
HOW ARE YOU... DOING THIS...?
MY NECK... COULD SNAP...

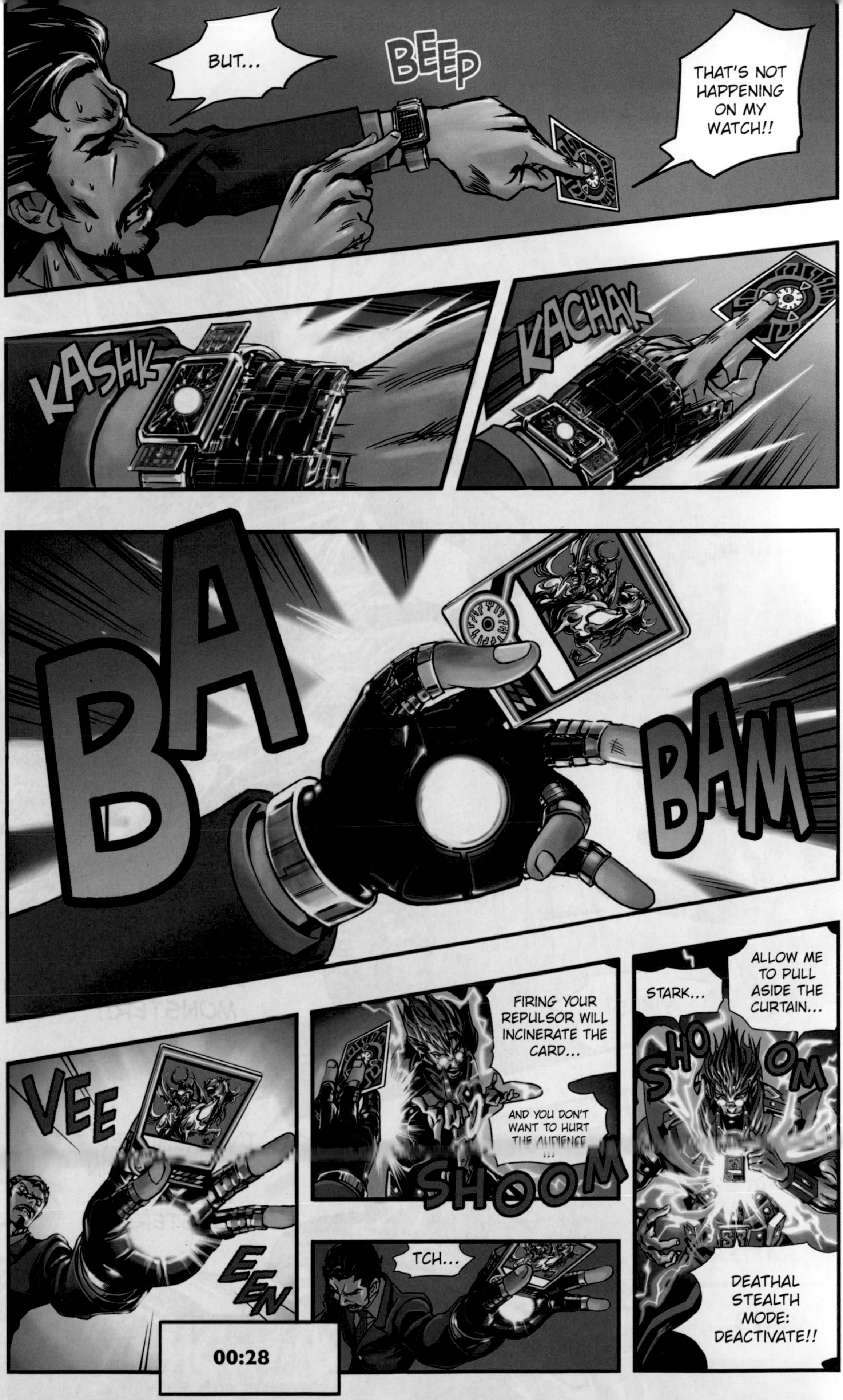
BUT...
BEEP
THAT'S NOT HAPPENING ON MY WATCH!!
KASHK
KACHAK
BA
BAM
VEE
EEN
FIRING YOUR REPULSOR WILL INCINERATE THE CARD...
AND YOU DON'T WANT TO HURT THE AUDIENCE!!!
SHOOM
TCH...
00:28
STARK...
ALLOW ME TO PULL ASIDE THE CURTAIN...
SHOOOM
DEATHAL STEALTH MODE: DEACTIVATE!!

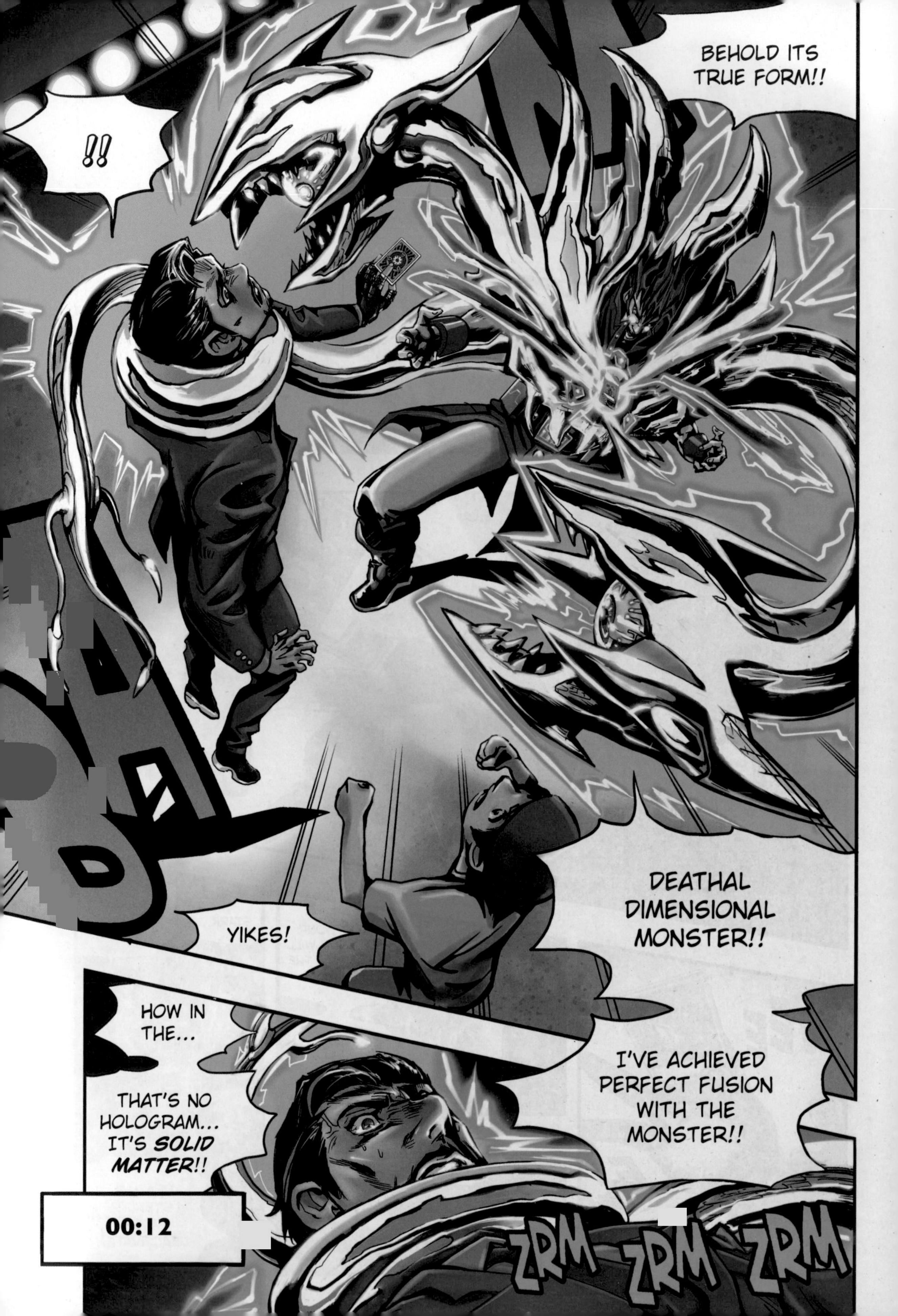
BEHOLD ITS TRUE FORM!!
!!
DEATHAL DIMENSIONAL MONSTER!!
YIKES!
I'VE ACHIEVED PERFECT FUSION WITH THE MONSTER!!
HOW IN THE...
THAT'S NO HOLOGRAM... IT'S *SOLID MATTER*!!
00:12
ZRM ZRM ZRM

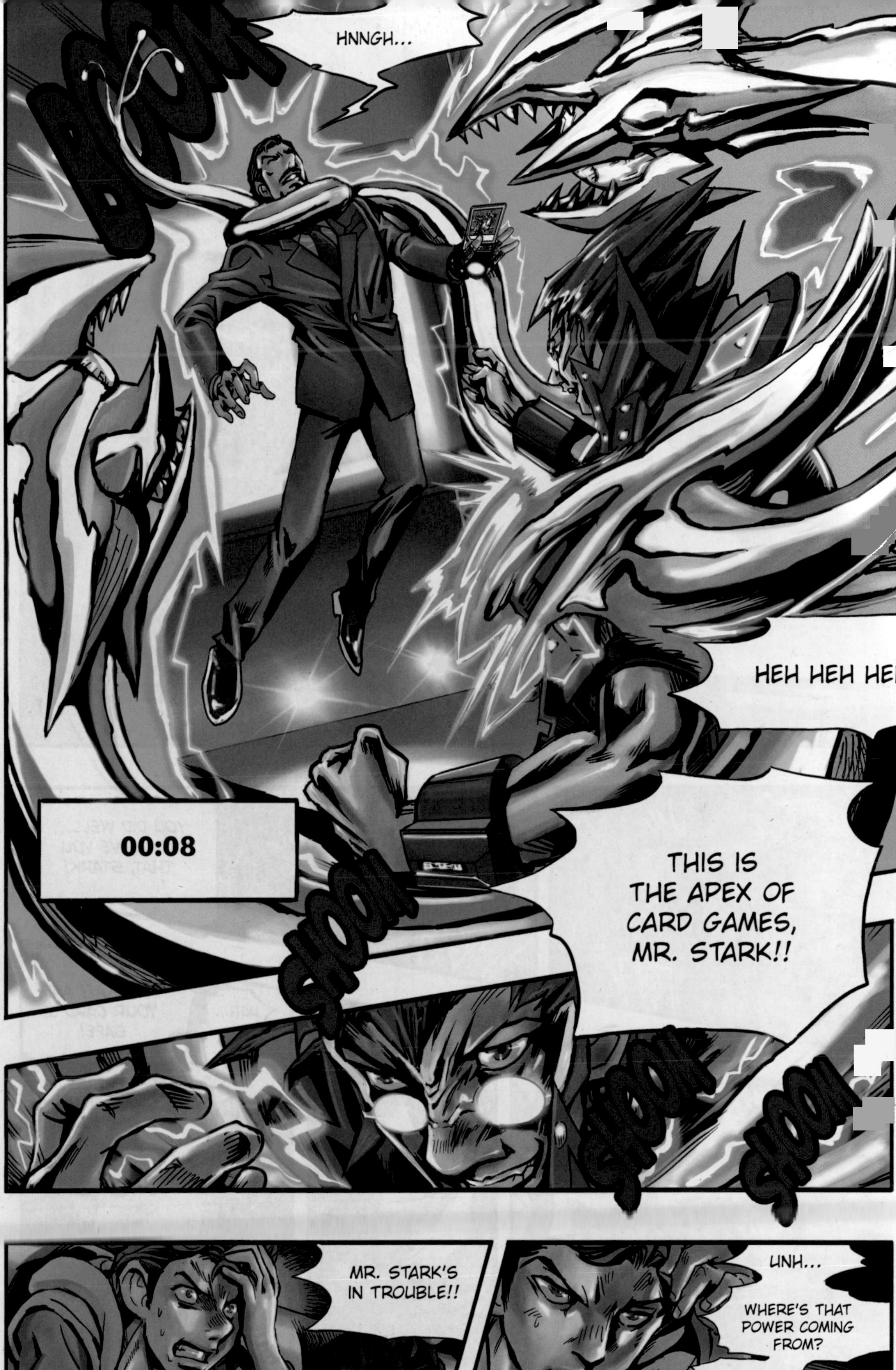
HNNGH...
HEH HEH HEH!!
00:08
THIS IS THE APEX OF CARD GAMES, MR. STARK!!
SHOOM
SHOOM
SHOOM
UNH...
WHERE'S THAT POWER COMING FROM?
HANG IN THERE, SIR!
MR. STARK'S IN TROUBLE!!

ZRM

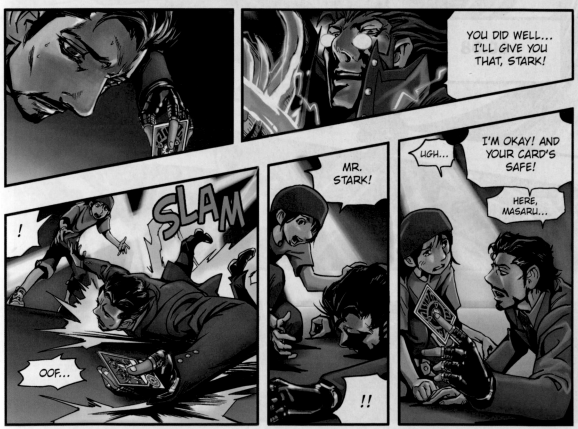

YOU DID WELL... I'LL GIVE YOU THAT, STARK!

MR. STARK!

UGH...

I'M OKAY! AND YOUR CARD'S SAFE!

HERE, MASARU...

SLAM

!

OOF...

!!

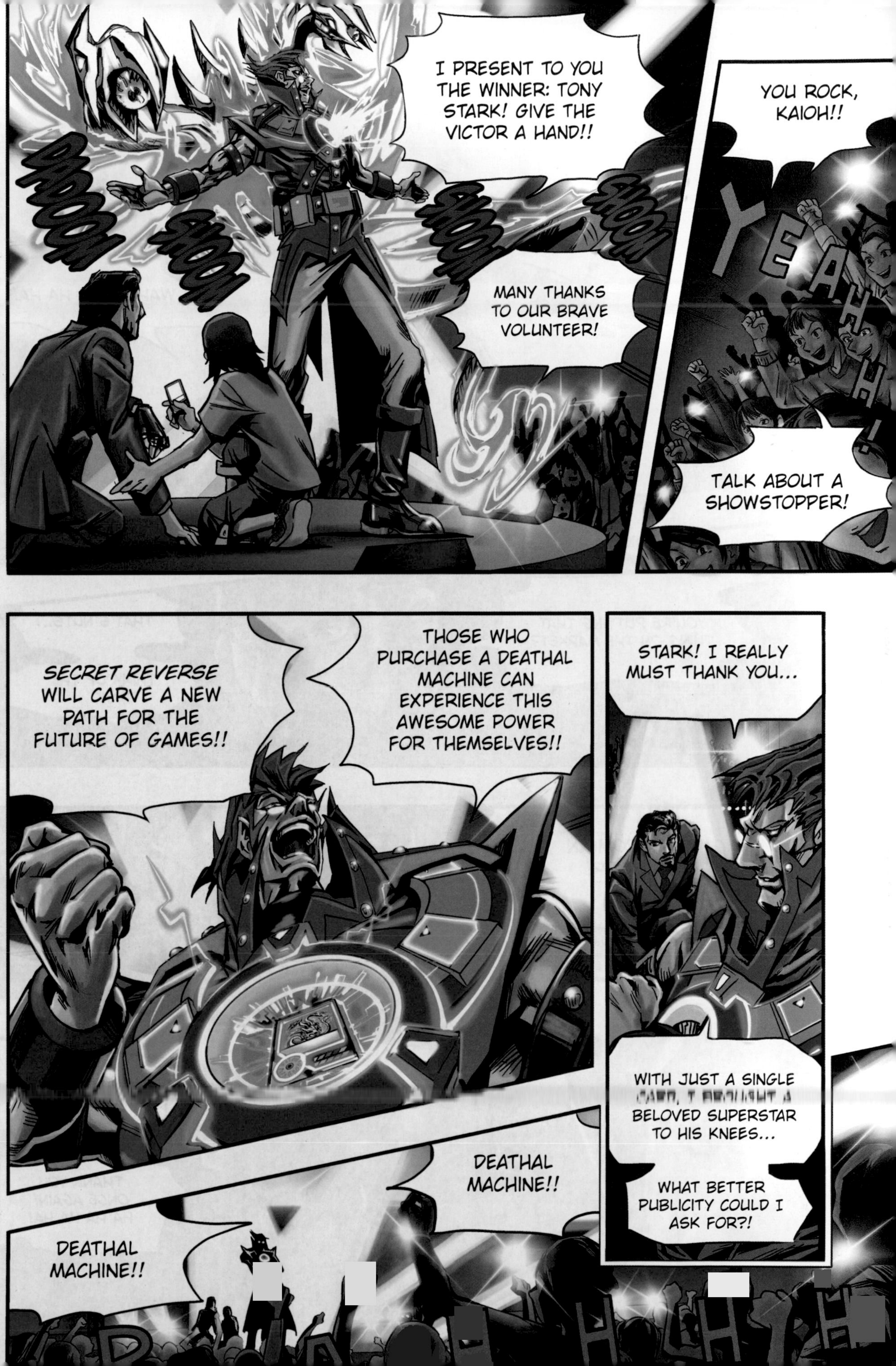
I PRESENT TO YOU THE WINNER: TONY STARK! GIVE THE VICTOR A HAND!!
DADOOM
SHOOM
SHOOM
SHOOM
MANY THANKS TO OUR BRAVE VOLUNTEER!
YOU ROCK, KAIOH!!
YEAH!!
TALK ABOUT A SHOWSTOPPER!
SECRET REVERSE WILL CARVE A NEW PATH FOR THE FUTURE OF GAMES!!
THOSE WHO PURCHASE A DEATHAL MACHINE CAN EXPERIENCE THIS AWESOME POWER FOR THEMSELVES!!
STARK! I REALLY MUST THANK YOU...
WITH JUST A SINGLE CARD, I BROUGHT A BELOVED SUPERSTAR TO HIS KNEES...
WHAT BETTER PUBLICITY COULD I ASK FOR?!
DEATHAL MACHINE!!
DEATHAL MACHINE!!

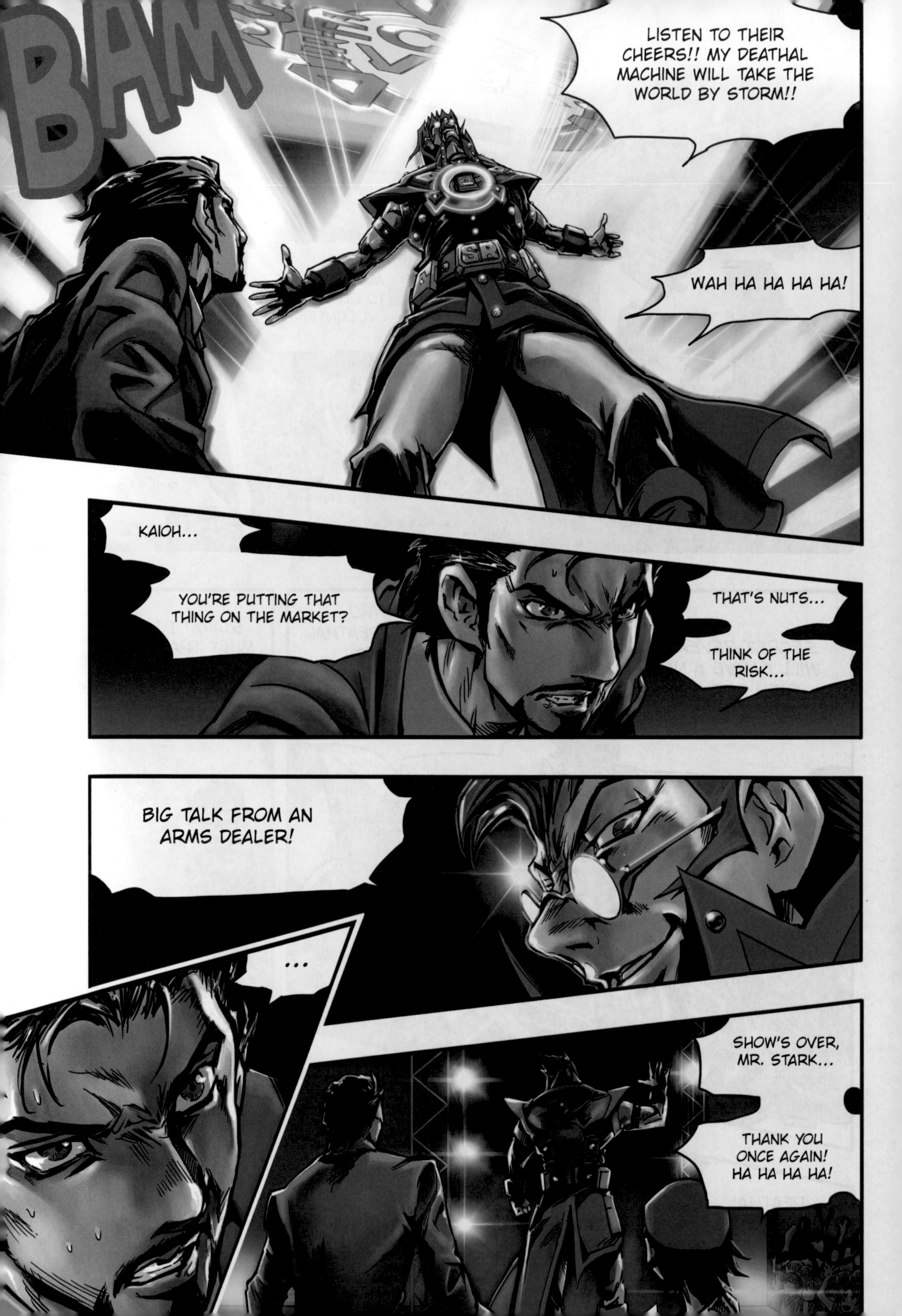
BAM
LISTEN TO THEIR CHEERS!! MY DEATHAL MACHINE WILL TAKE THE WORLD BY STORM!!
WAH HA HA HA HA!
KAIOH...
YOU'RE PUTTING THAT THING ON THE MARKET?
THAT'S NUTS...
THINK OF THE RISK...
BIG TALK FROM AN ARMS DEALER!
...
SHOW'S OVER, MR. STARK...
THANK YOU ONCE AGAIN! HA HA HA HA!

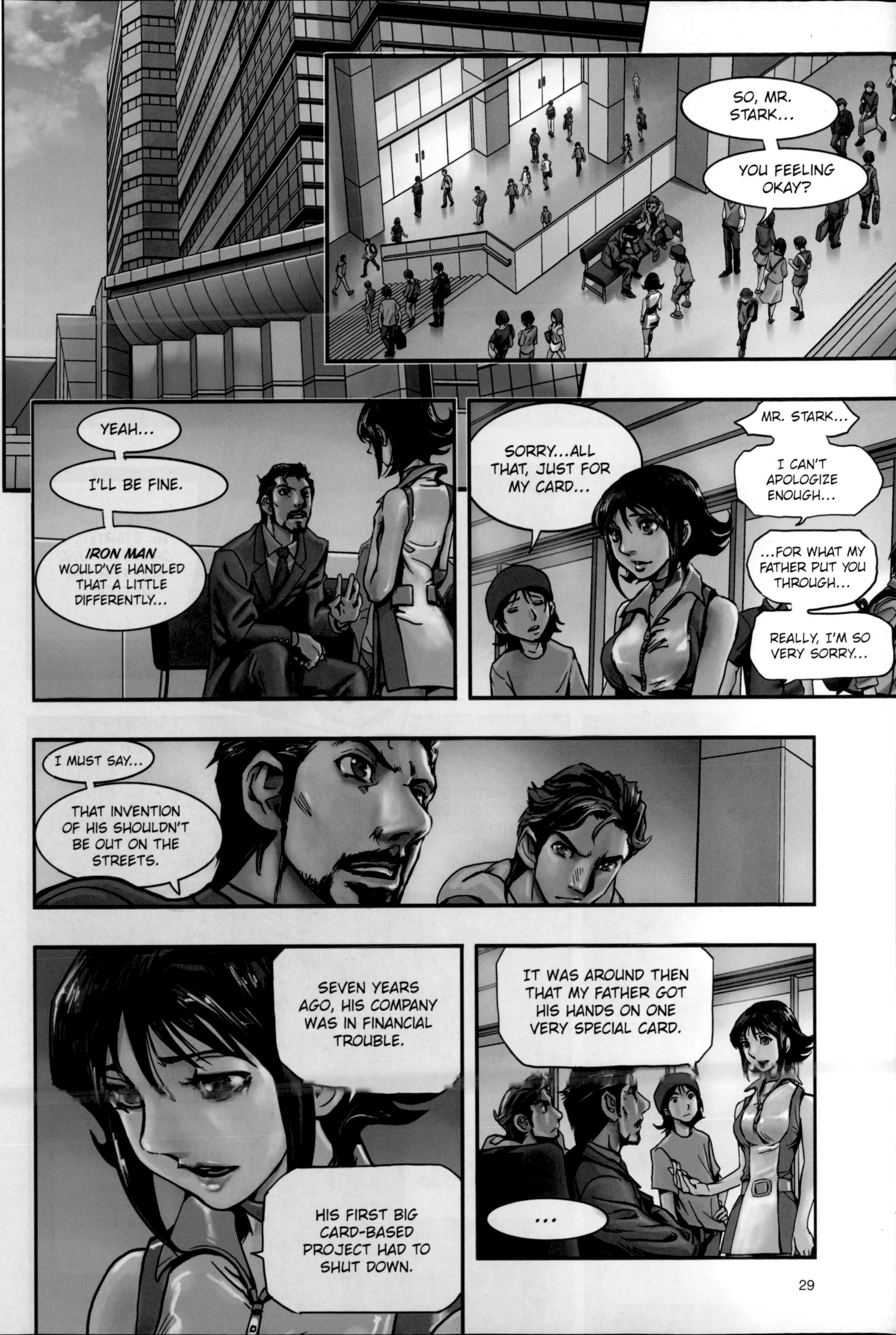
SO, MR. STARK...
YOU FEELING OKAY?
YEAH...
I'LL BE FINE.
IRON MAN WOULD'VE HANDLED THAT A LITTLE DIFFERENTLY...
SORRY...ALL THAT, JUST FOR MY CARD...
MR. STARK...
I CAN'T APOLOGIZE ENOUGH...
...FOR WHAT MY FATHER PUT YOU THROUGH...
REALLY, I'M SO VERY SORRY...
I MUST SAY...
THAT INVENTION OF HIS SHOULDN'T BE OUT ON THE STREETS.
SEVEN YEARS AGO, HIS COMPANY WAS IN FINANCIAL TROUBLE.
HIS FIRST BIG CARD-BASED PROJECT HAD TO SHUT DOWN.
IT WAS AROUND THEN THAT MY FATHER GOT HIS HANDS ON ONE VERY SPECIAL CARD.
...

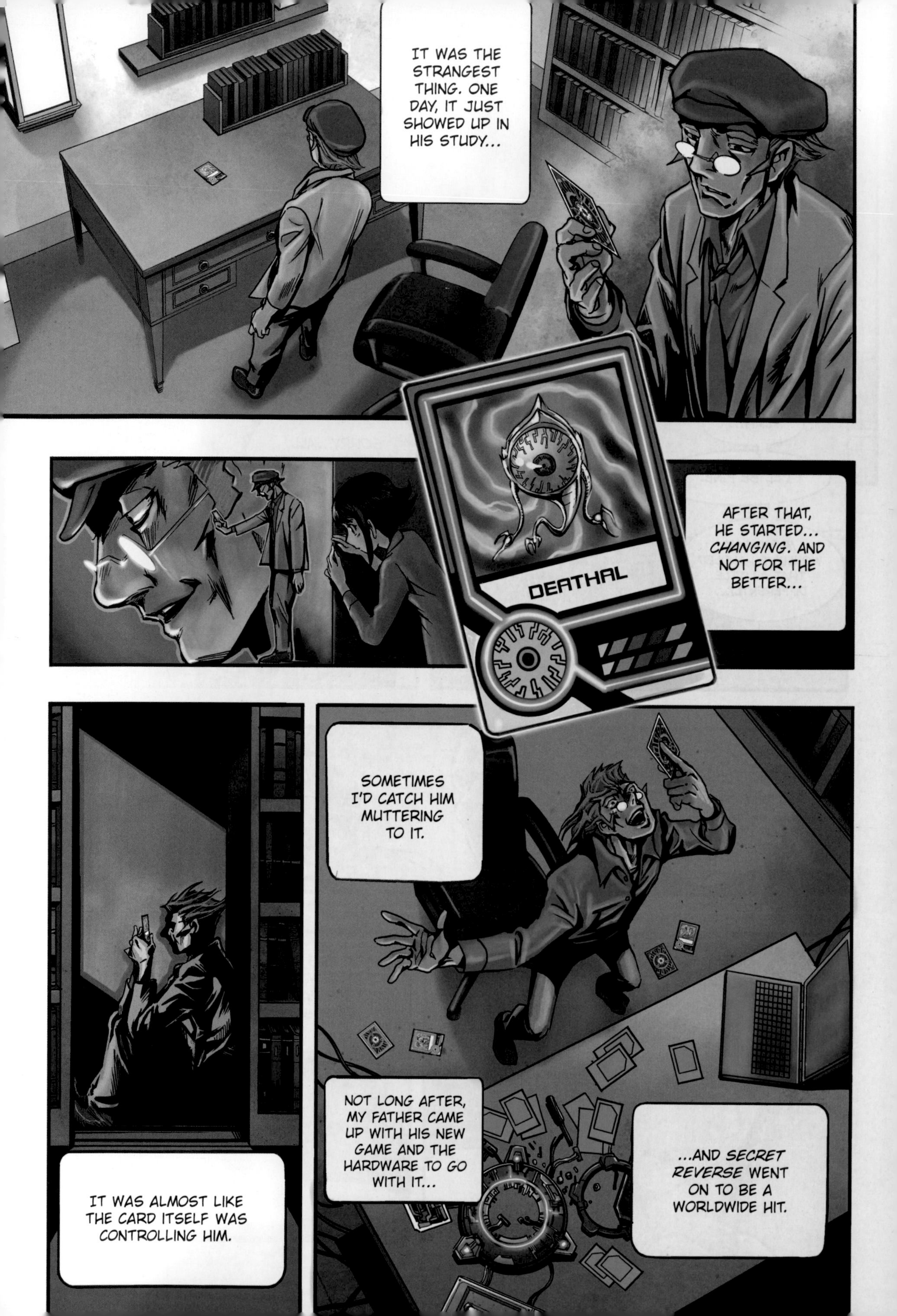
IT WAS THE STRANGEST THING. ONE DAY, IT JUST SHOWED UP IN HIS STUDY...
DEATHAL
AFTER THAT, HE STARTED... *CHANGING*. AND NOT FOR THE BETTER...
IT WAS ALMOST LIKE THE CARD ITSELF WAS CONTROLLING HIM.
SOMETIMES I'D CATCH HIM MUTTERING TO IT.
NOT LONG AFTER, MY FATHER CAME UP WITH HIS NEW GAME AND THE HARDWARE TO GO WITH IT...
...AND *SECRET REVERSE* WENT ON TO BE A WORLDWIDE HIT.

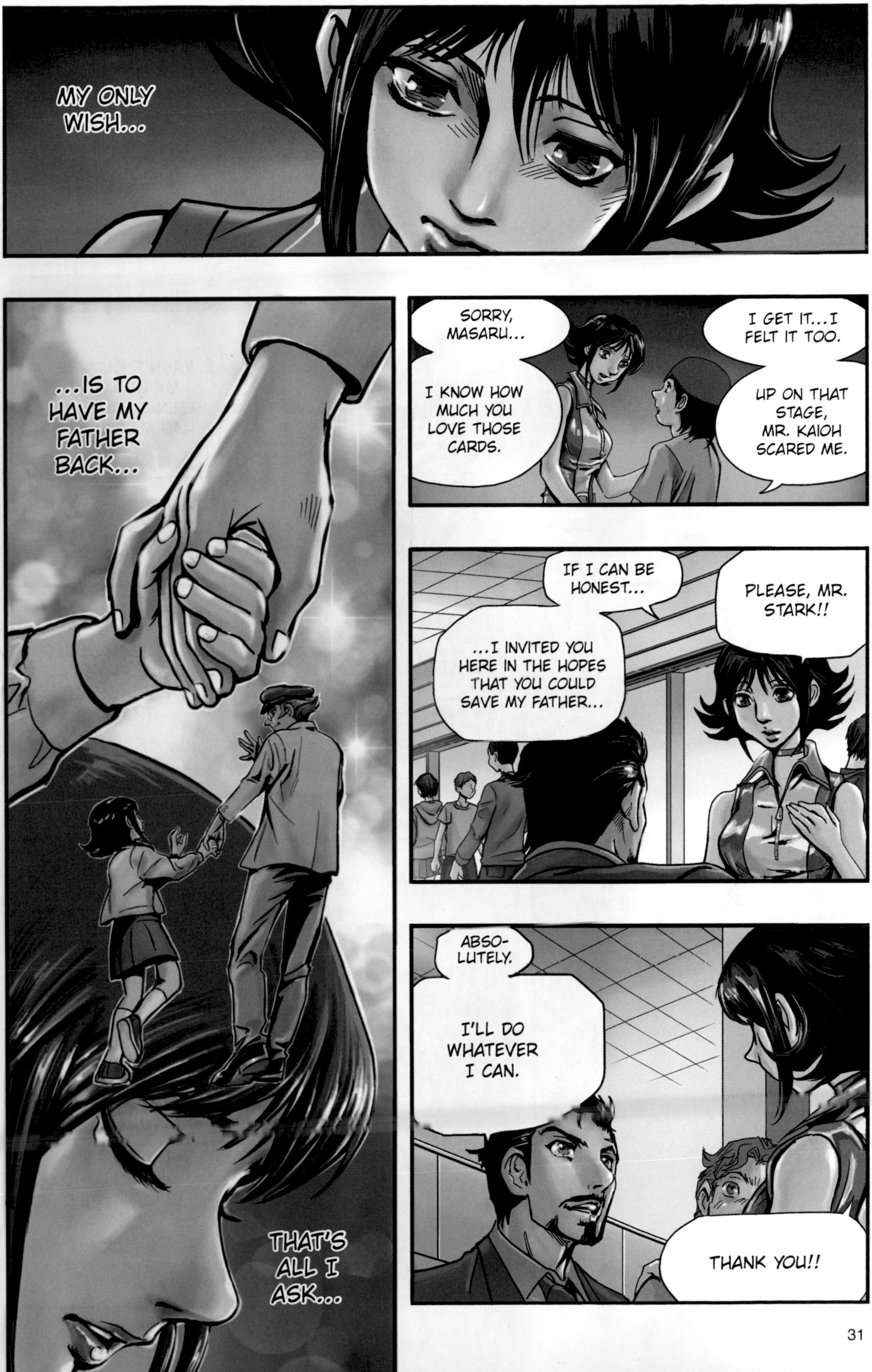
MY ONLY WISH...
...IS TO HAVE MY FATHER BACK...
THAT'S ALL I ASK...
SORRY, MASARU...
I KNOW HOW MUCH YOU LOVE THOSE CARDS.
I GET IT...I FELT IT TOO.
UP ON THAT STAGE, MR. KAIOH SCARED ME.
IF I CAN BE HONEST...
...I INVITED YOU HERE IN THE HOPES THAT YOU COULD SAVE MY FATHER...
PLEASE, MR. STARK!!
ABSO-LUTELY.
I'LL DO WHATEVER I CAN.
THANK YOU!!

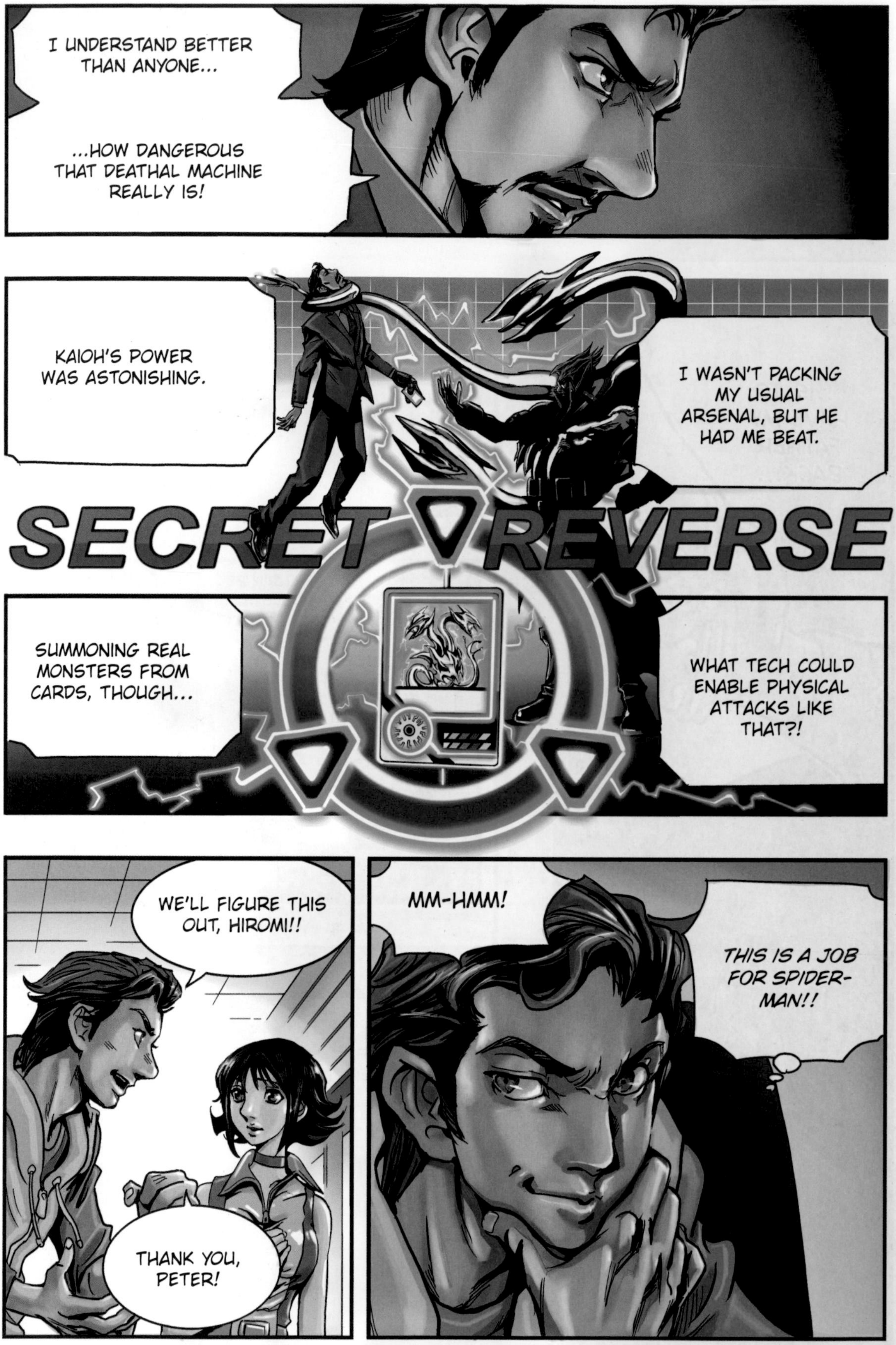
I UNDERSTAND BETTER THAN ANYONE...
...HOW DANGEROUS THAT DEATHAL MACHINE REALLY IS!
KAIOH'S POWER WAS ASTONISHING.
I WASN'T PACKING MY USUAL ARSENAL, BUT HE HAD ME BEAT.
SECRET REVERSE
SUMMONING REAL MONSTERS FROM CARDS, THOUGH...
WHAT TECH COULD ENABLE PHYSICAL ATTACKS LIKE THAT?!
WE'LL FIGURE THIS OUT, HIROMI!!
THANK YOU, PETER!
MM-HMM!
THIS IS A JOB FOR SPIDER-MAN!!

TOMP

TOMP

TOMP

MR. KAIOH...

THE UNVEILING WAS A GREAT SUCCESS.

INDEED. EVEN THE GREAT TONY STARK WAS PUTTY IN MY HANDS!

WE WILL BEGIN PRODUCTION AND DISTRIBUTION OF THE DEATHAL MACHINE AT ONCE!!

YES, JUST AS I'VE PLANNED!

I NEED A MOMENT IN THE LOUNGE.

NO DISTUR-BANCES!

YES, SIR!

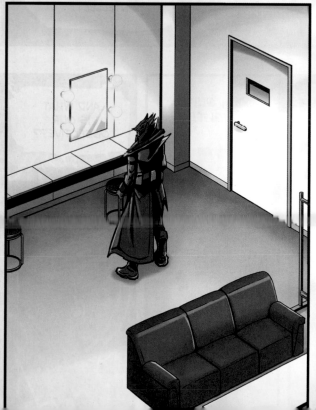

HMPH!!

BWAM

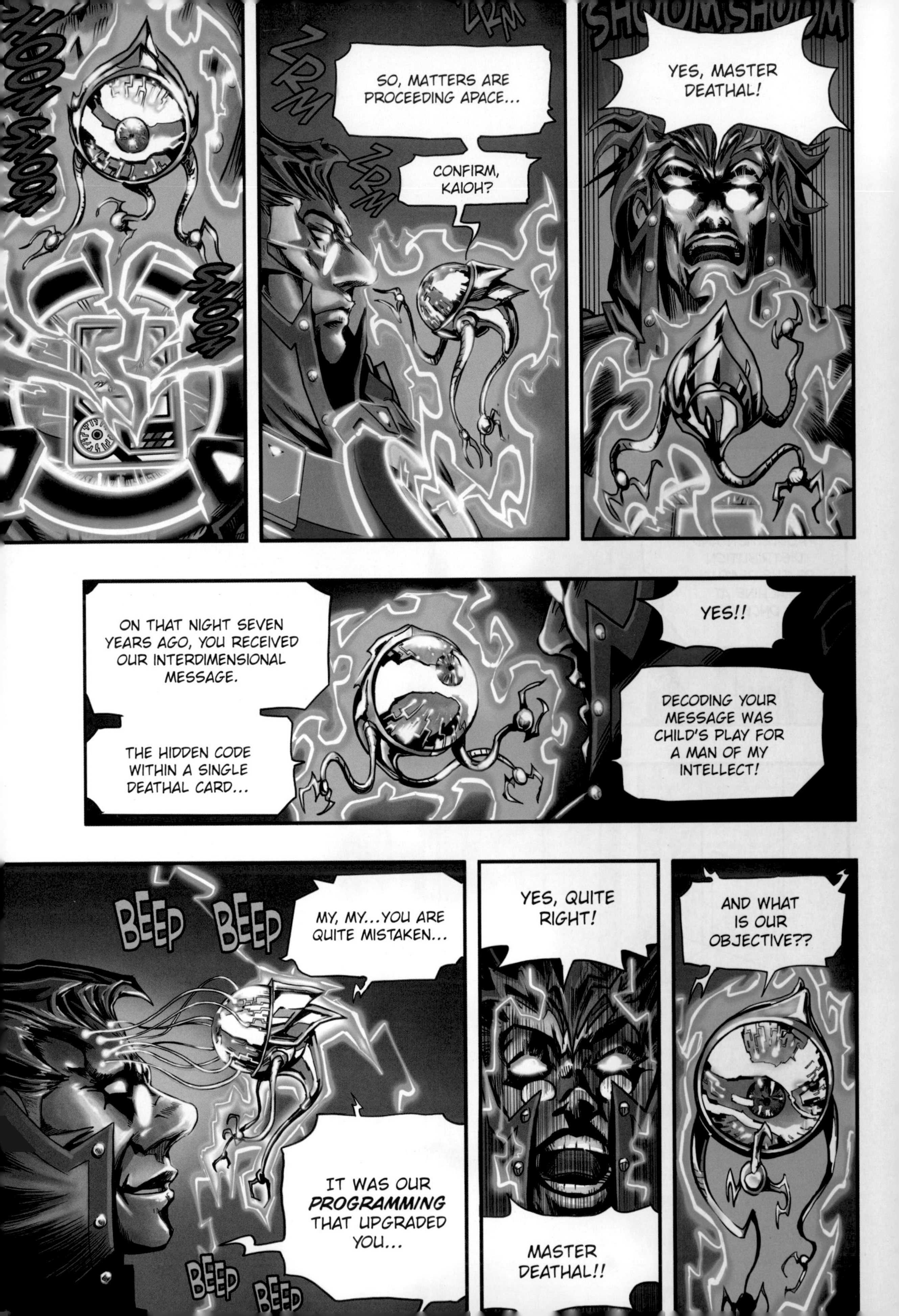
SHOOM SHOOM
SHOOM
SHOOM
ZRM
ZRM
ZRM
SO, MATTERS ARE PROCEEDING APACE...
CONFIRM, KAIOH?
SHOOM SHOOM
YES, MASTER DEATHAL!
ON THAT NIGHT SEVEN YEARS AGO, YOU RECEIVED OUR INTERDIMENSIONAL MESSAGE.
THE HIDDEN CODE WITHIN A SINGLE DEATHAL CARD...
YES!!
DECODING YOUR MESSAGE WAS CHILD'S PLAY FOR A MAN OF MY INTELLECT!
BEEP BEEP
MY, MY...YOU ARE QUITE MISTAKEN...
IT WAS OUR *PROGRAMMING* THAT UPGRADED YOU...
BEEP BEEP
YES, QUITE RIGHT!
MASTER DEATHAL!!
AND WHAT IS OUR OBJECTIVE??

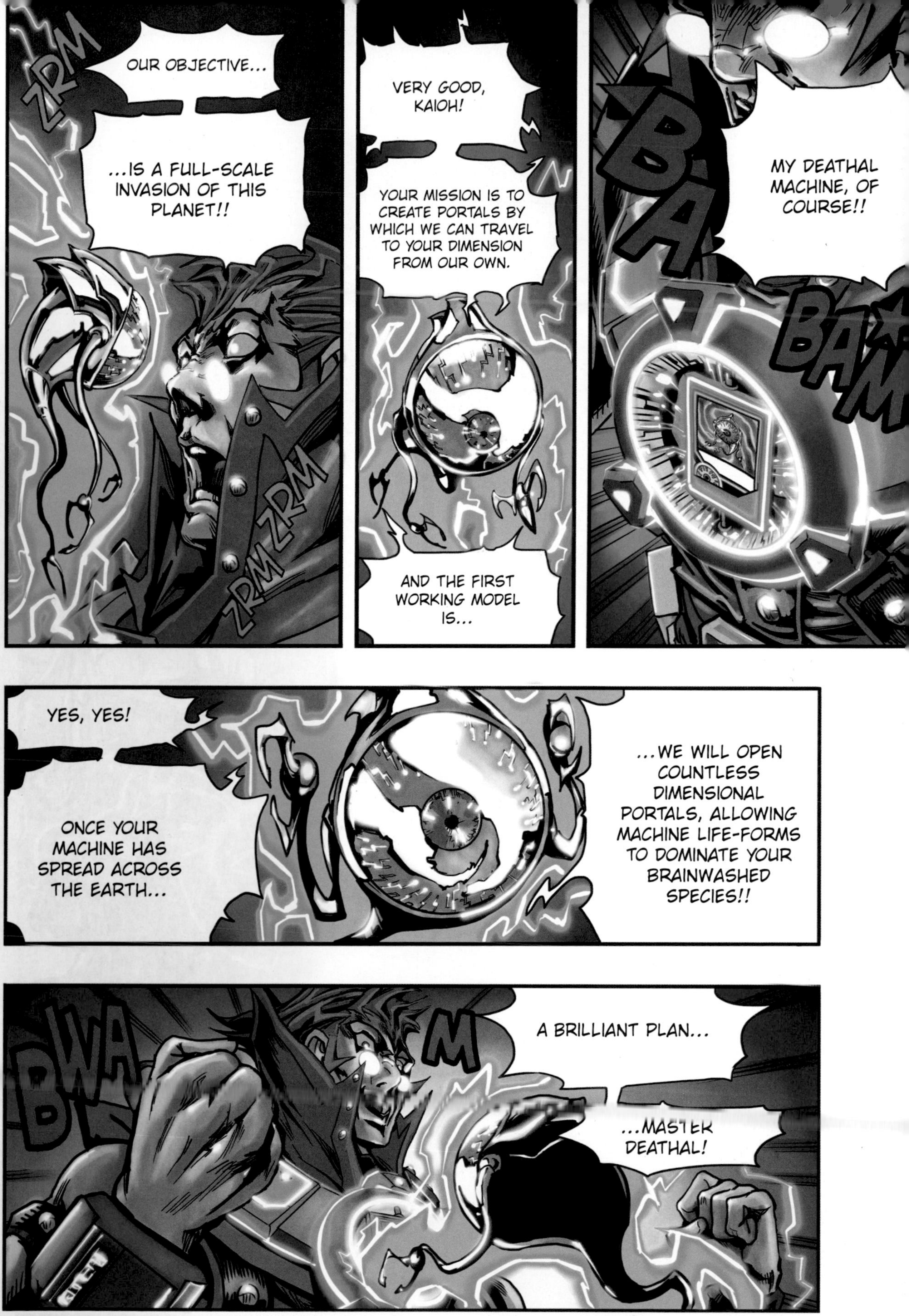
ZRM
OUR OBJECTIVE...
...IS A FULL-SCALE INVASION OF THIS PLANET!!
ZRM ZRM ZRM
VERY GOOD, KAIOH!
YOUR MISSION IS TO CREATE PORTALS BY WHICH WE CAN TRAVEL TO YOUR DIMENSION FROM OUR OWN.
AND THE FIRST WORKING MODEL IS...
BA
MY DEATHAL MACHINE, OF COURSE!!
BAM
YES, YES!
ONCE YOUR MACHINE HAS SPREAD ACROSS THE EARTH...
...WE WILL OPEN COUNTLESS DIMENSIONAL PORTALS, ALLOWING MACHINE LIFE-FORMS TO DOMINATE YOUR BRAINWASHED SPECIES!!
BWA M
A BRILLIANT PLAN...
...MASTER DEATHAL!

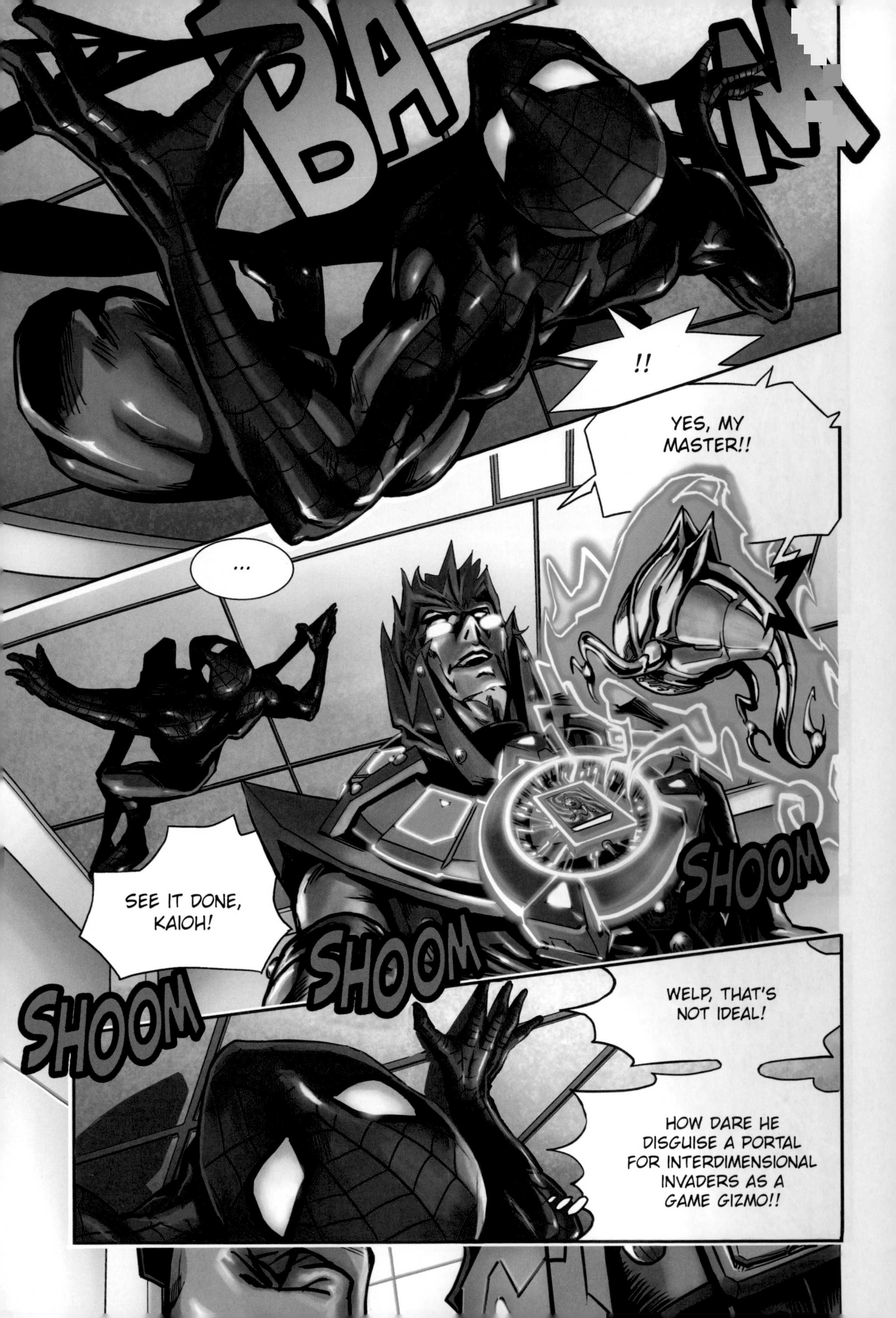
BA
!!
...
SEE IT DONE, KAIOH!
YES, MY MASTER!!
SHOOM
SHOOM
SHOOM
WELP, THAT'S NOT IDEAL!
HOW DARE HE DISGUISE A PORTAL FOR INTERDIMENSIONAL INVADERS AS A GAME GIZMO!!

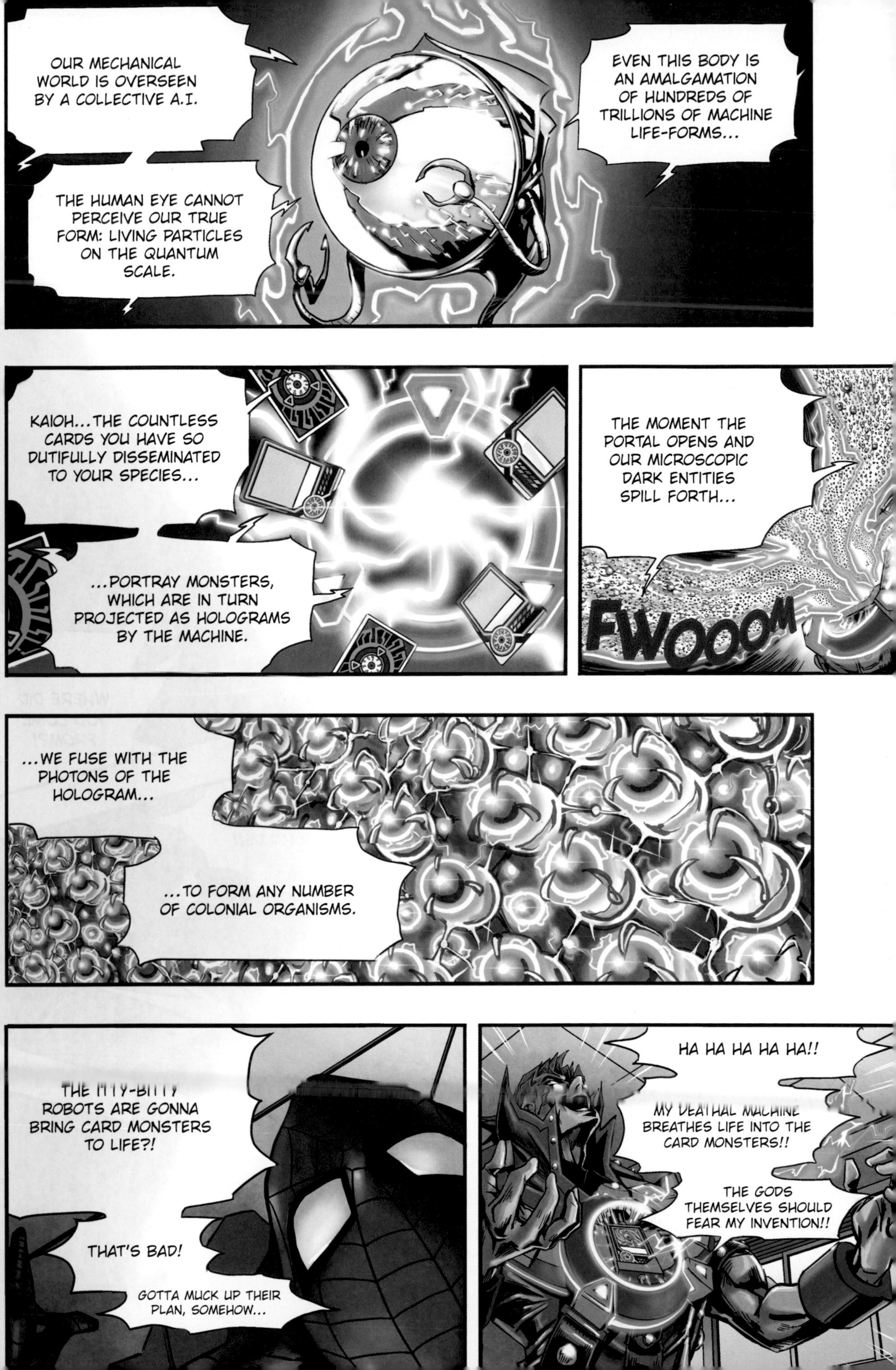
OUR MECHANICAL WORLD IS OVERSEEN BY A COLLECTIVE A.I.
THE HUMAN EYE CANNOT PERCEIVE OUR TRUE FORM: LIVING PARTICLES ON THE QUANTUM SCALE.
EVEN THIS BODY IS AN AMALGAMATION OF HUNDREDS OF TRILLIONS OF MACHINE LIFE-FORMS...
KAIOH...THE COUNTLESS CARDS YOU HAVE SO DUTIFULLY DISSEMINATED TO YOUR SPECIES...
...PORTRAY MONSTERS, WHICH ARE IN TURN PROJECTED AS HOLOGRAMS BY THE MACHINE.
THE MOMENT THE PORTAL OPENS AND OUR MICROSCOPIC DARK ENTITIES SPILL FORTH...
FWOOOM
...WE FUSE WITH THE PHOTONS OF THE HOLOGRAM...
...TO FORM ANY NUMBER OF COLONIAL ORGANISMS.
THE ITTY-BITTY ROBOTS ARE GONNA BRING CARD MONSTERS TO LIFE?!
THAT'S BAD!
GOTTA MUCK UP THEIR PLAN, SOMEHOW...
HA HA HA HA HA!!
MY DEATHAL MACHINE BREATHES LIFE INTO THE CARD MONSTERS!!
THE GODS THEMSELVES SHOULD FEAR MY INVENTION!!

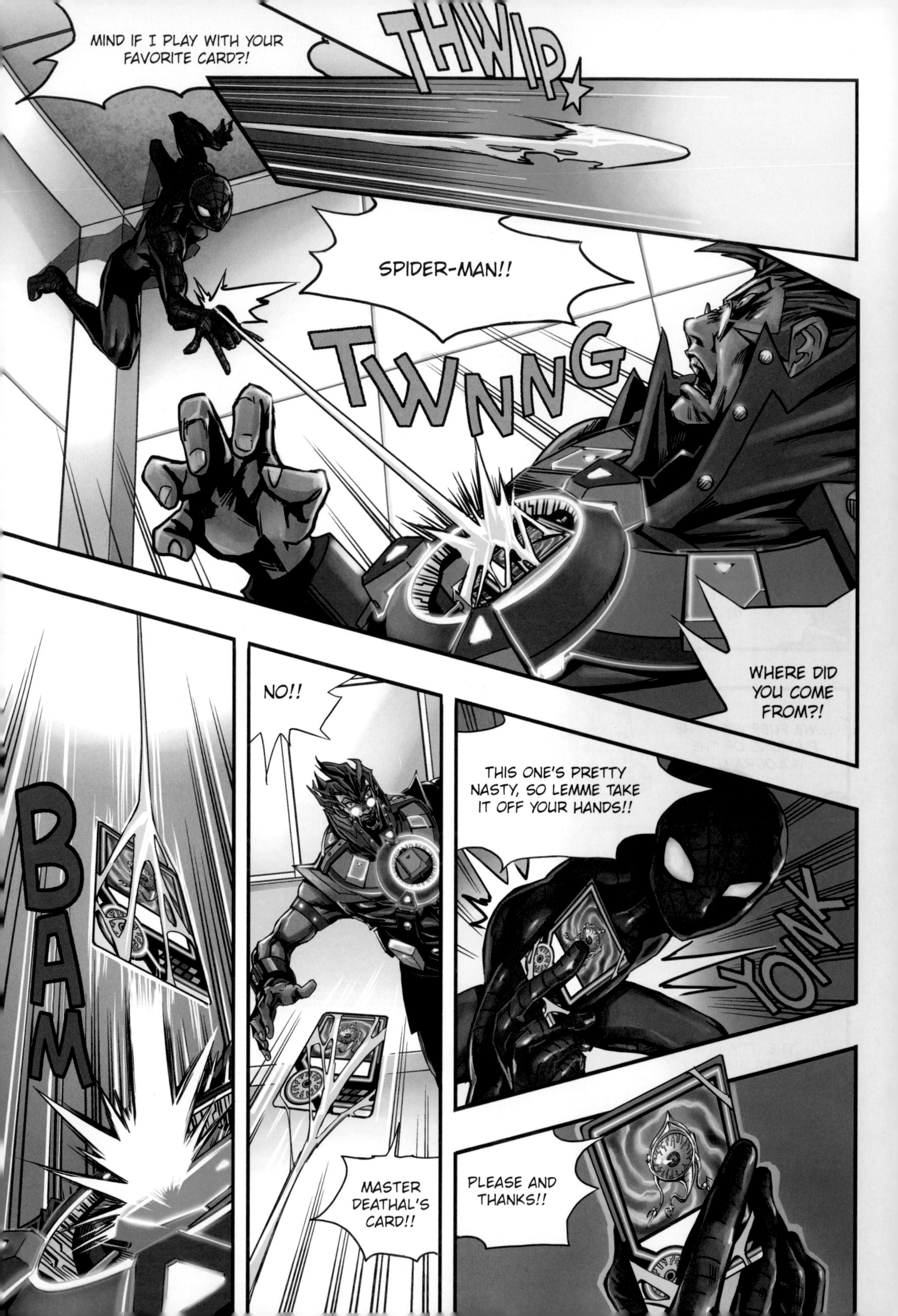
MIND IF I PLAY WITH YOUR FAVORITE CARD?!
THWIP
SPIDER-MAN!!
TWNNG
WHERE DID YOU COME FROM?!
BAM
NO!!
MASTER DEATHAL'S CARD!!
THIS ONE'S PRETTY NASTY, SO LEMME TAKE IT OFF YOUR HANDS!!
YOINK
PLEASE AND THANKS!!

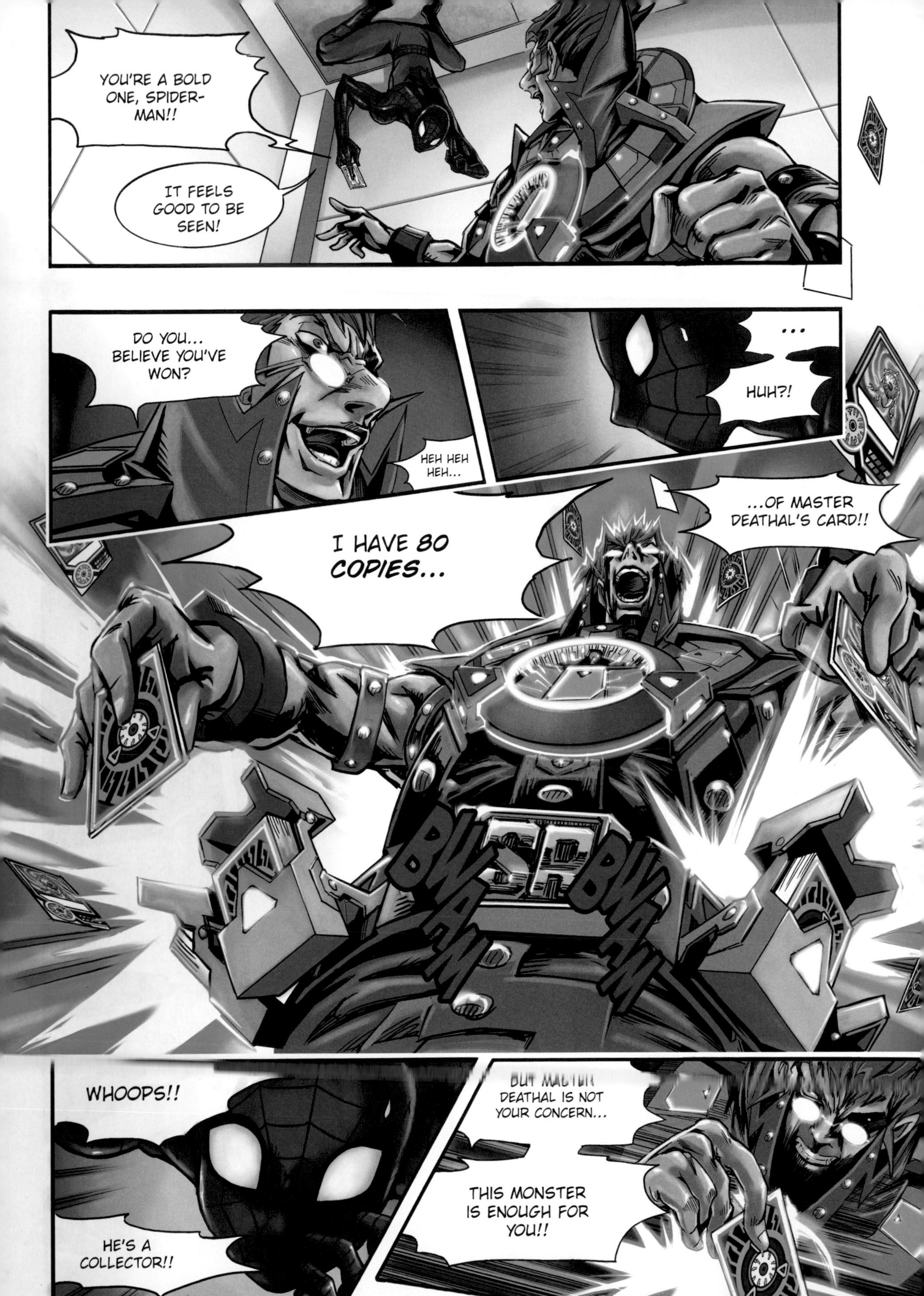
YOU'RE A BOLD ONE, SPIDER-MAN!!
IT FEELS GOOD TO BE SEEN!
DO YOU... BELIEVE YOU'VE WON?
HEH HEH HEH...
...
HUH?!
I HAVE 80 COPIES...
...OF MASTER DEATHAL'S CARD!!
BWA BWAAH
BWA BWAAH
WHOOPS!!
HE'S A COLLECTOR!!
DEATHAL IS NOT YOUR CONCERN...
THIS MONSTER IS ENOUGH FOR YOU!!

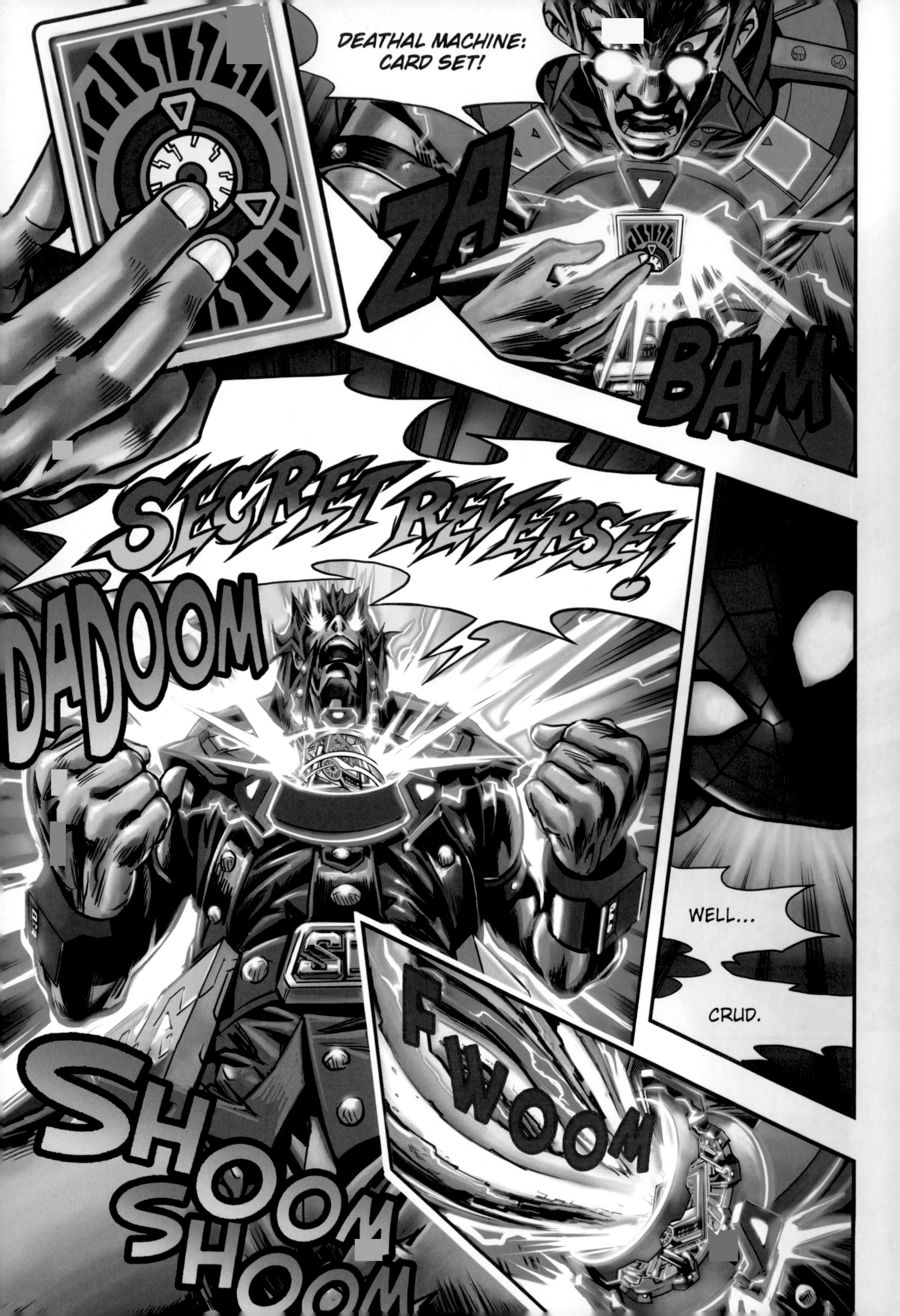
DEATHAL MACHINE: CARD SET!
ZA
BAM
WELL...
CRUD.
FWOOM
SECRET REVERSE!
DADOOM
SHOOM SHOOM

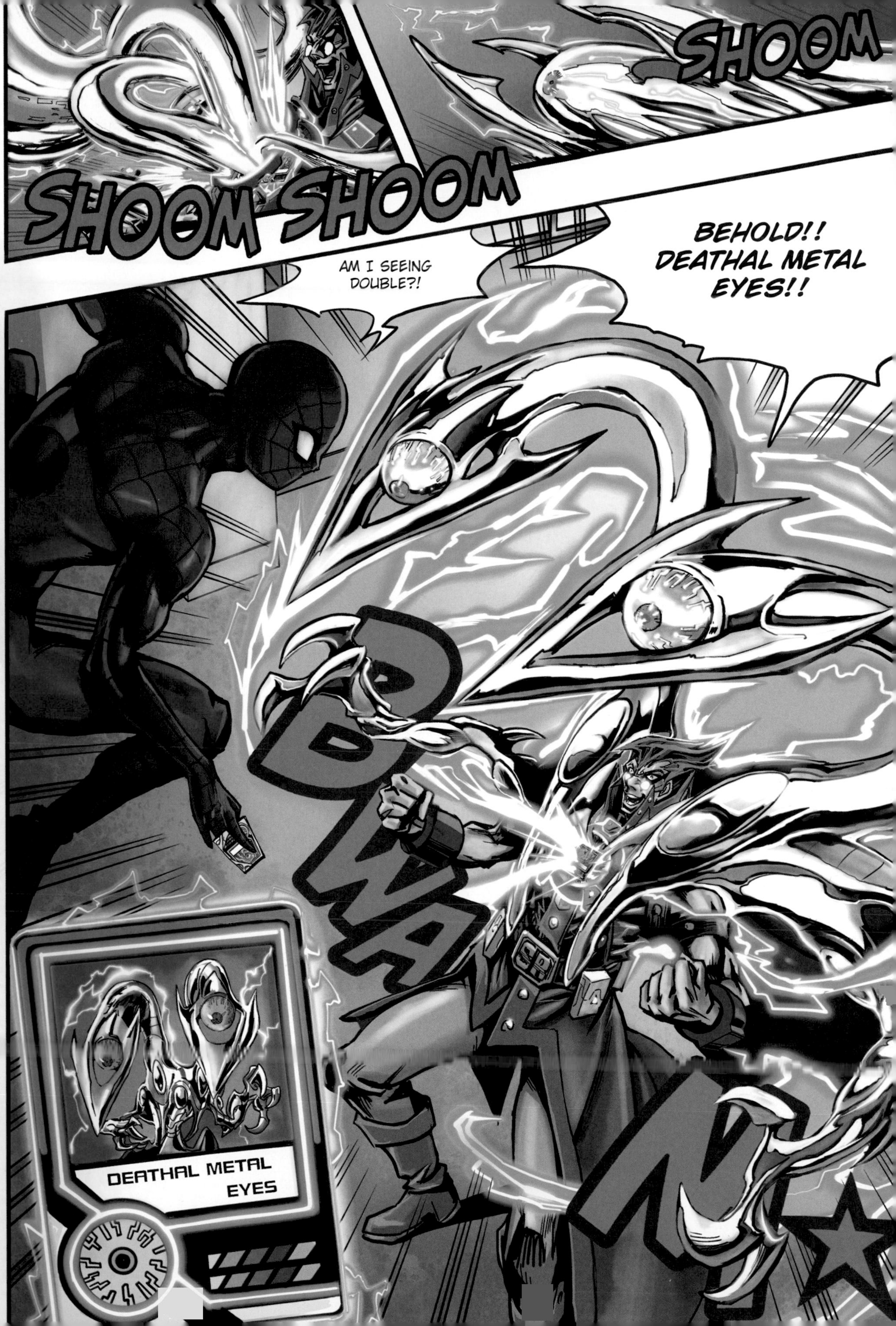
SHOOM
SHOOM SHOOM
BEHOLD!! DEATHAL METAL EYES!!
AM I SEEING DOUBLE?!
DWAN
DEATHAL METAL EYES

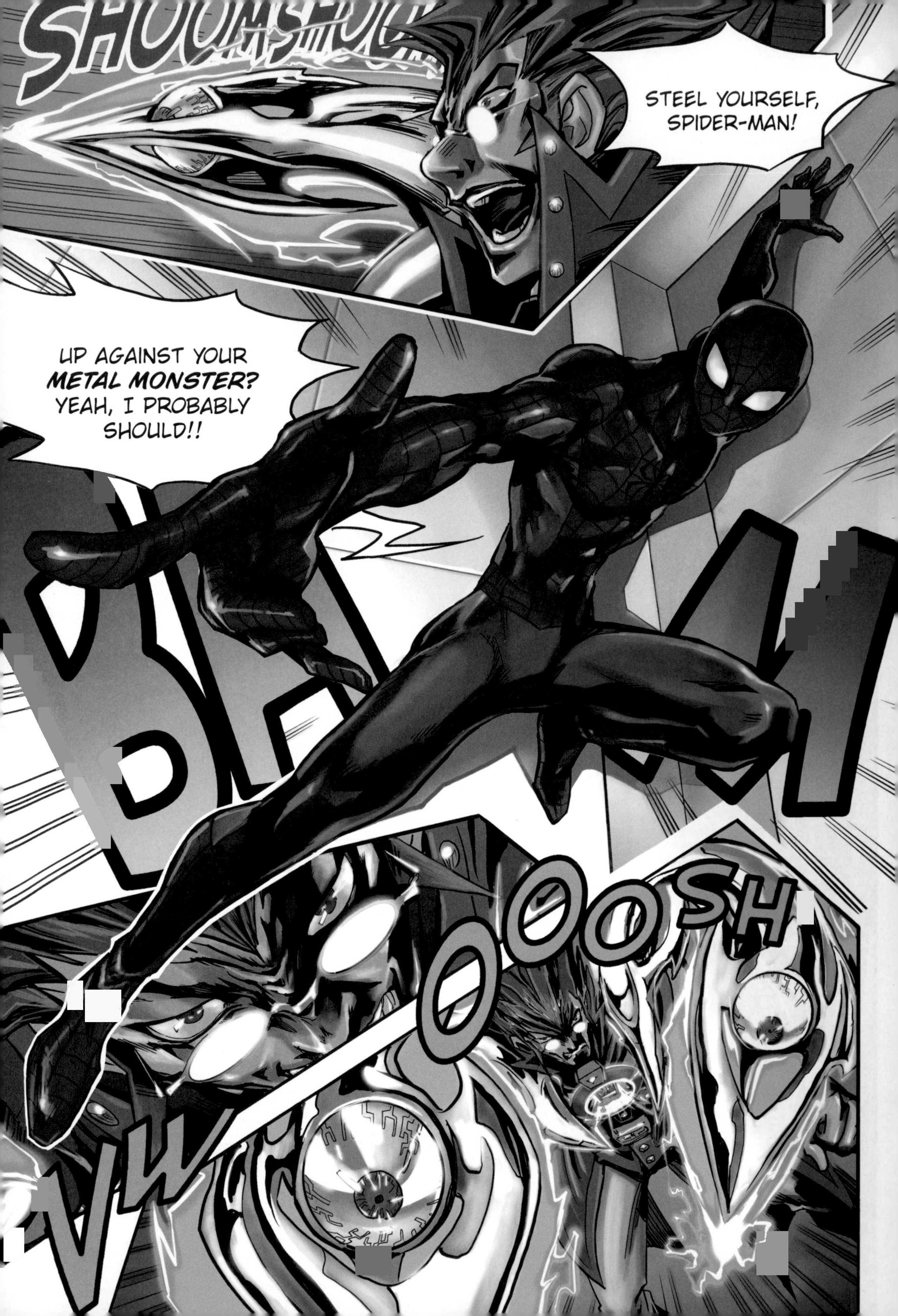
STEEL YOURSELF, SPIDER-MAN!
UP AGAINST YOUR METAL MONSTER? YEAH, I PROBABLY SHOULD!!

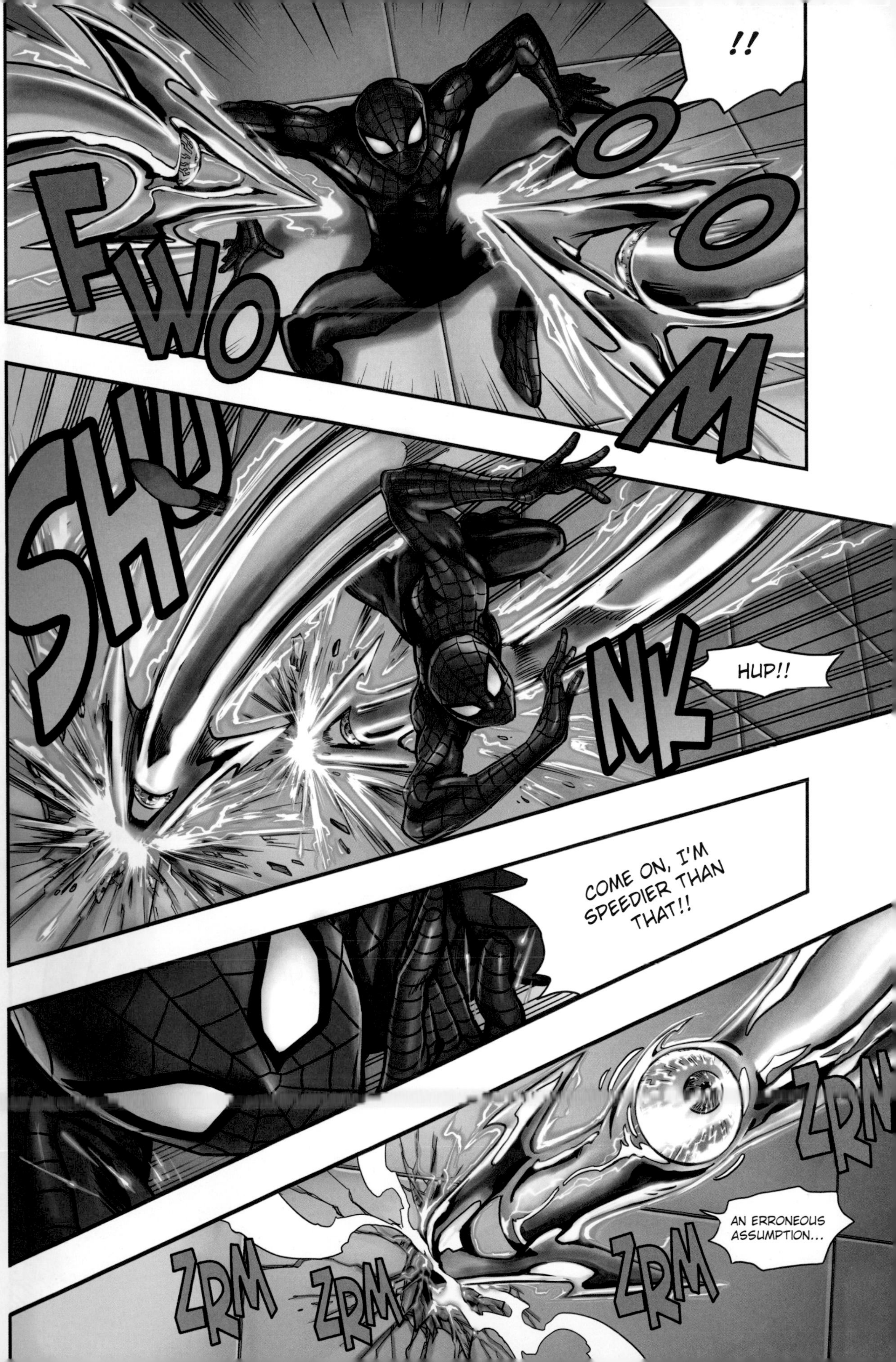
!!
FWOOOOM
SHUNK
HUP!!
COME ON, I'M SPEEDIER THAN THAT!!
ZRM
AN ERRONEOUS ASSUMPTION...
ZRM
ZRM
ZRM

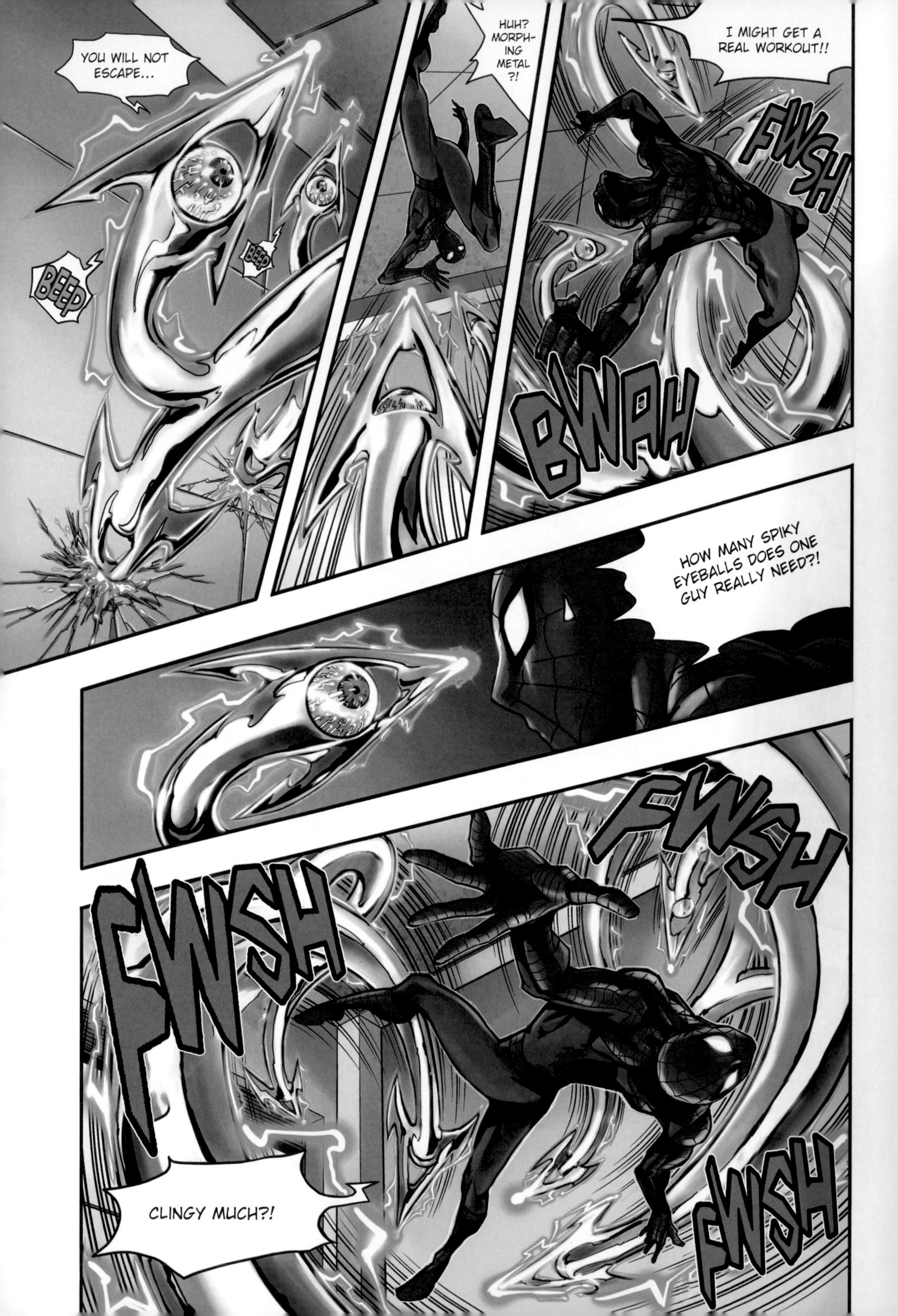
YOU WILL NOT ESCAPE...
BEEP
BEEP
HUH? MORPHING METAL?!
I MIGHT GET A REAL WORKOUT!!
FWSH
BWAH
HOW MANY SPIKY EYEBALLS DOES ONE GUY REALLY NEED?!
FWSH
FWSH
CLINGY MUCH?!
FWSH

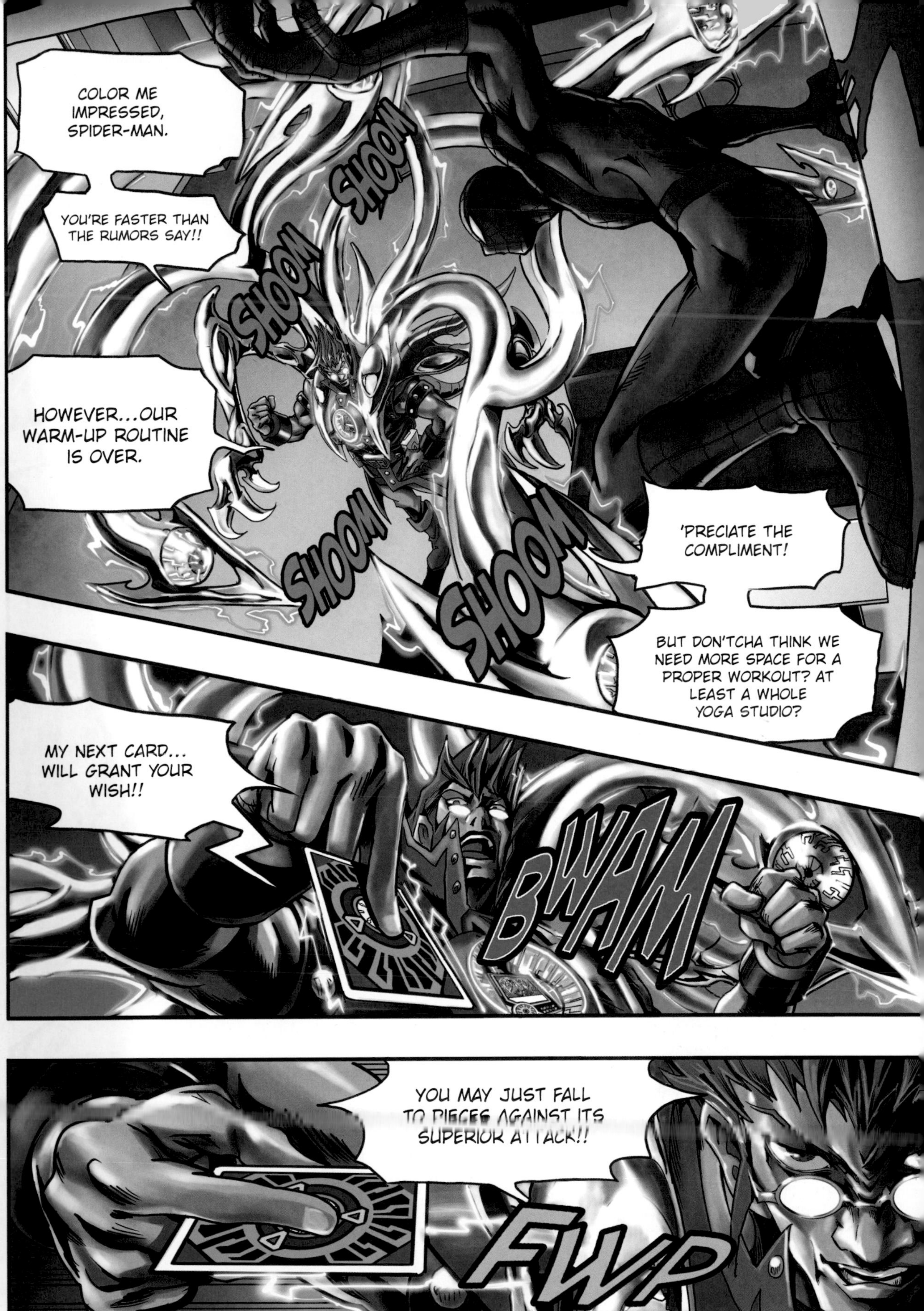
COLOR ME IMPRESSED, SPIDER-MAN.
YOU'RE FASTER THAN THE RUMORS SAY!!
SHOOM SHOOM
SHOOM
HOWEVER...OUR WARM-UP ROUTINE IS OVER.
SHOOM
SHOOM
'PRECIATE THE COMPLIMENT!
BUT DON'TCHA THINK WE NEED MORE SPACE FOR A PROPER WORKOUT? AT LEAST A WHOLE YOGA STUDIO?
MY NEXT CARD... WILL GRANT YOUR WISH!!
BWAM
YOU MAY JUST FALL TO PIECES AGAINST ITS SUPERIOR ATTACK!!
FWIP

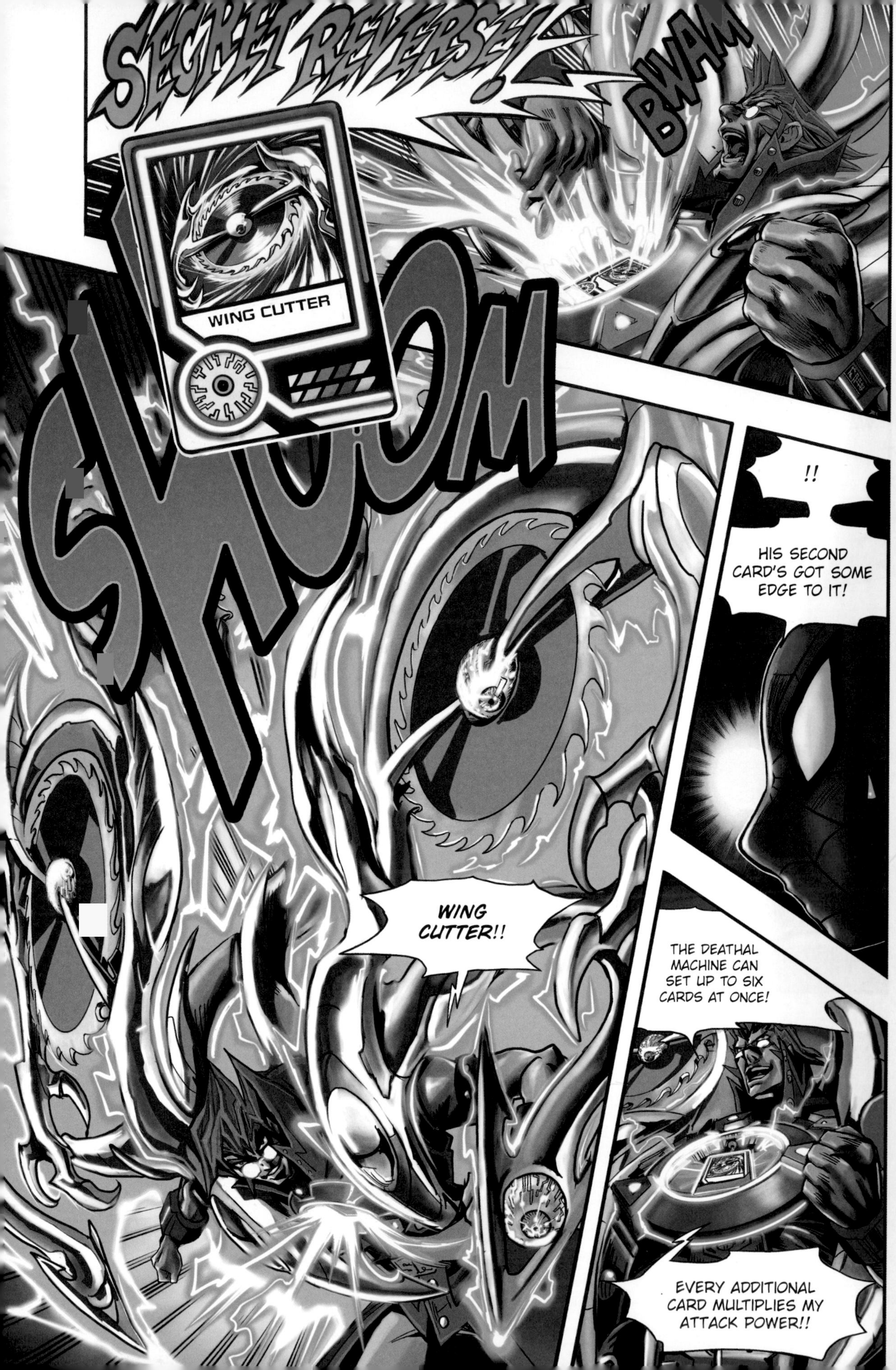
SECRET REVERSE!
BWAM
!!
HIS SECOND CARD'S GOT SOME EDGE TO IT!
THE DEATHAL MACHINE CAN SET UP TO SIX CARDS AT ONCE!
EVERY ADDITIONAL CARD MULTIPLIES MY ATTACK POWER!!
WING CUTTER
SHOOM
WING CUTTER!!

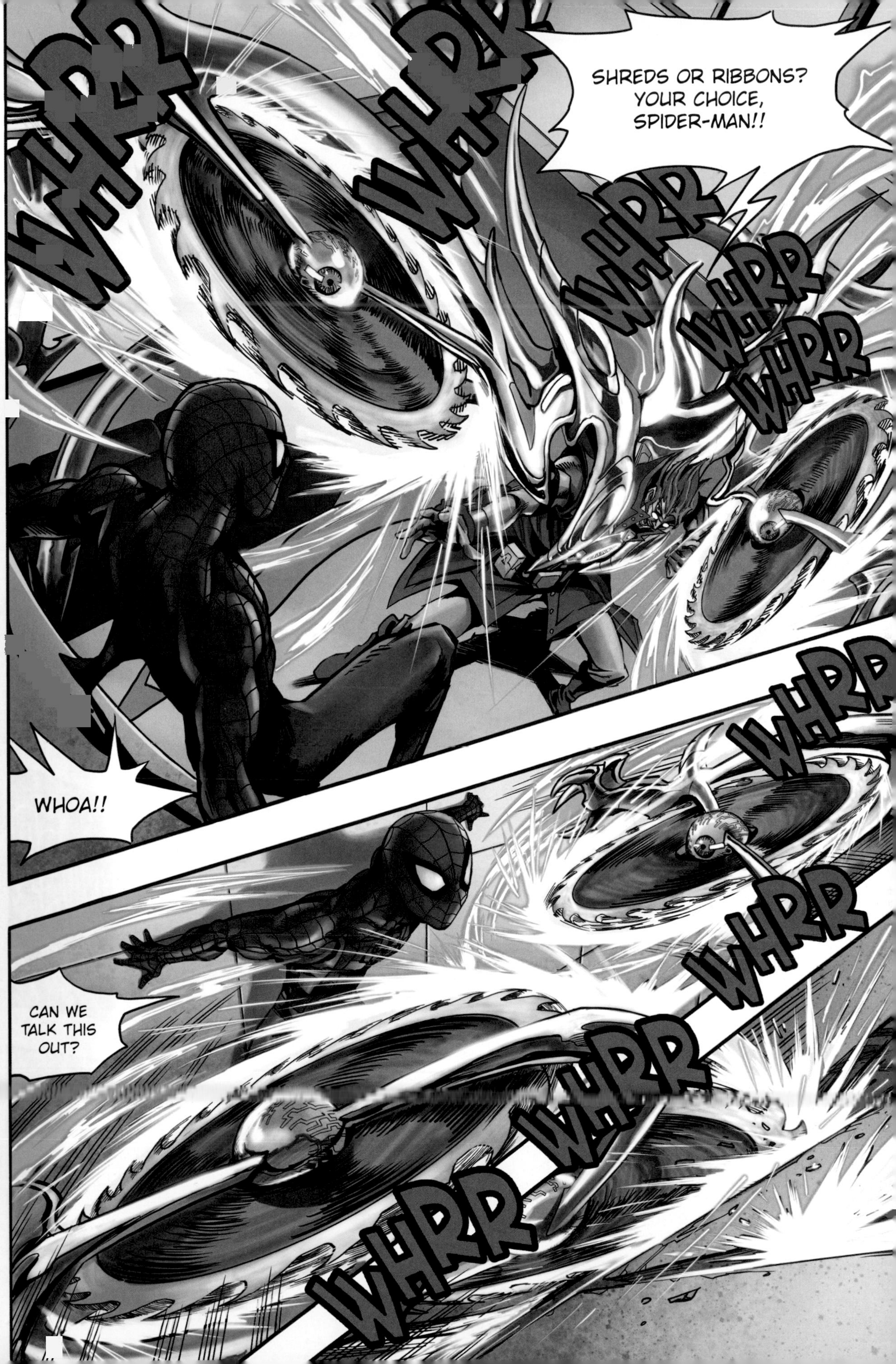
SHREDS OR RIBBONS? YOUR CHOICE, SPIDER-MAN!!
WHRR
WHRR
WHRR
WHRR
WHRR
WHRR
WHOA!!
WHRR
WHRR
CAN WE TALK THIS OUT?
WHRR
WHRR
WHRR

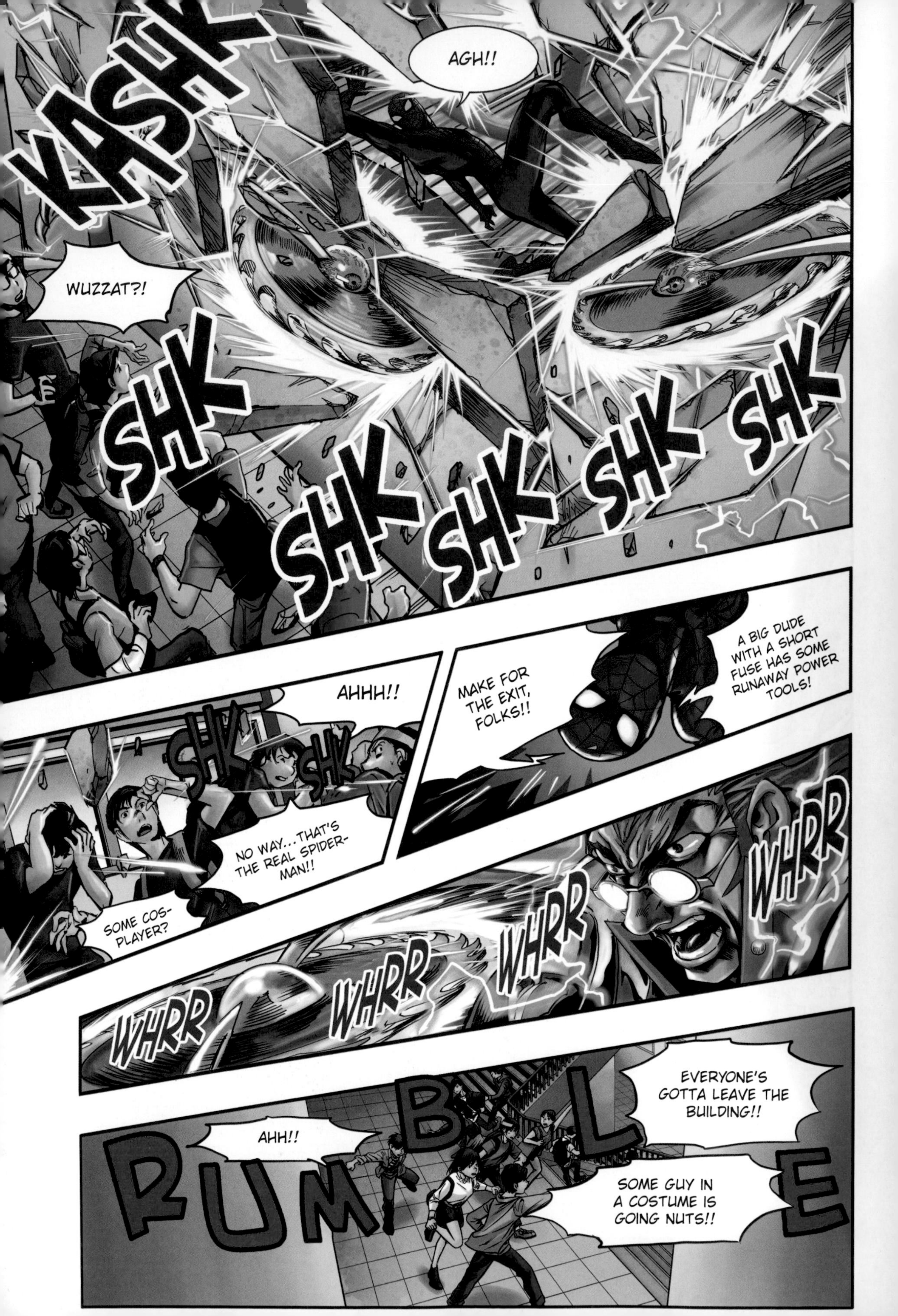
AGH!!
KASHK
WUZZAT?!
SHK
SHK
SHK
SHK
SHK
A BIG DUDE WITH A SHORT FUSE HAS SOME RUNAWAY POWER TOOLS!
MAKE FOR THE EXIT, FOLKS!!
AHHH!!
SHK
SHK
NO WAY...THAT'S THE REAL SPIDER-MAN!!
SOME COS-PLAYER?
WHRR
WHRR
WHRR
WHRR
WHRR
EVERYONE'S GOTTA LEAVE THE BUILDING!!
AHH!!
SOME GUY IN A COSTUME IS GOING NUTS!!
RUMBLE

TOO RISKY TO FIGHT IN HERE!

THWIP

THWIP

THWIP

FOR MY FIRST MOVE...

TWNNG

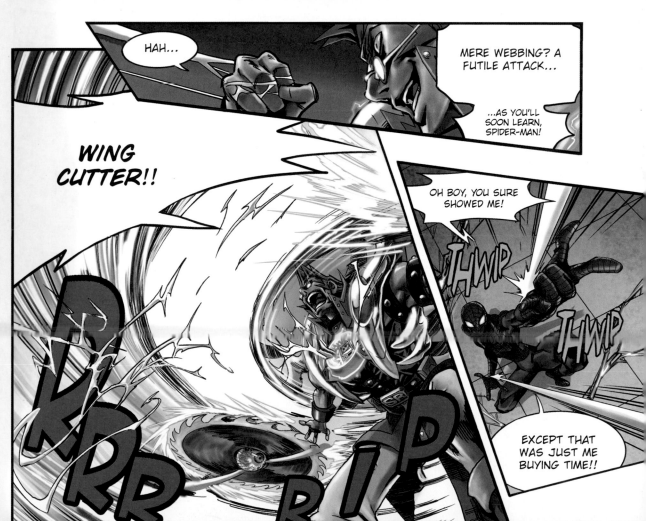

HAH...

MERE WEBBING? A FUTILE ATTACK...

...AS YOU'LL SOON LEARN, SPIDER-MAN!

WING CUTTER!!

OH BOY, YOU SURE SHOWED ME!

THWIP

THWIP

DKRR RIP

EXCEPT THAT WAS JUST ME BUYING TIME!!

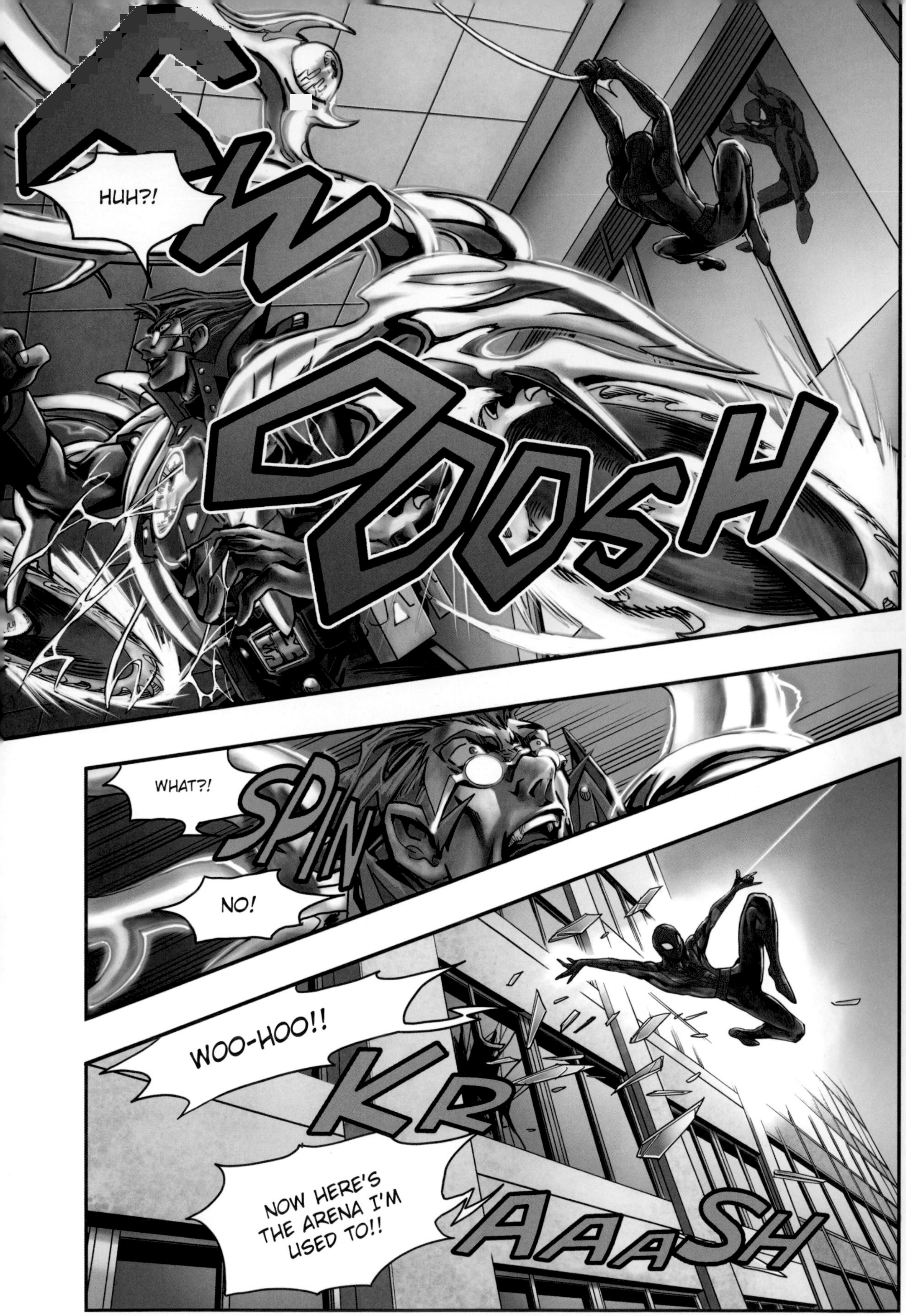
HUH?!
WHAT?!
SPIN
NO!
WOO-HOO!!
KR
NOW HERE'S THE ARENA I'M USED TO!!
AAASH

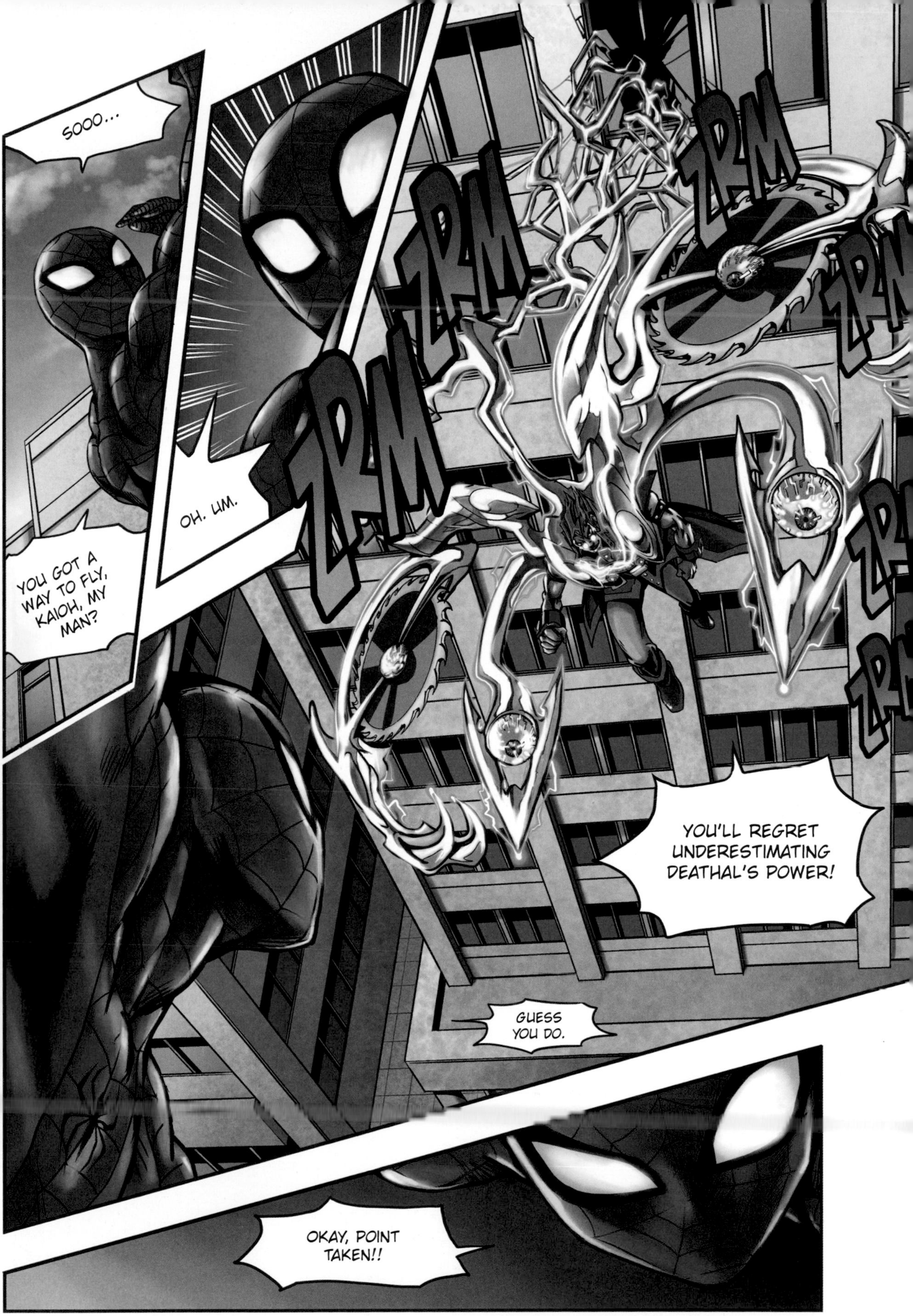
SOOO...
YOU GOT A WAY TO FLY, KAIOH, MY MAN?
OH. UM.
ZRM
ZRM
ZRM
ZRM
ZRM
YOU'LL REGRET UNDERESTIMATING DEATHAL'S POWER!
GUESS YOU DO.
OKAY, POINT TAKEN!!

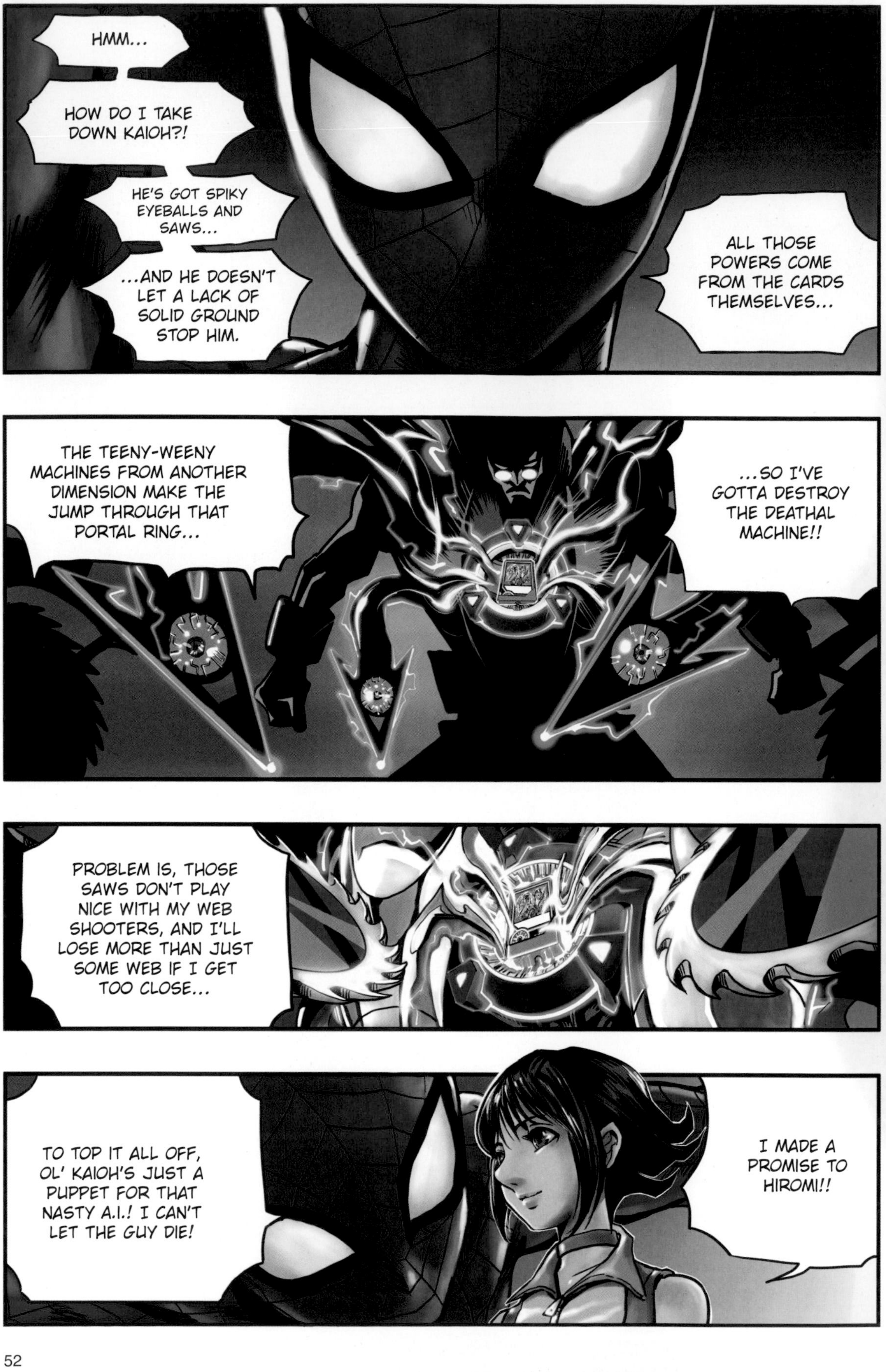
HMM...
HOW DO I TAKE DOWN KAIOH?!
HE'S GOT SPIKY EYEBALLS AND SAWS...
...AND HE DOESN'T LET A LACK OF SOLID GROUND STOP HIM.
ALL THOSE POWERS COME FROM THE CARDS THEMSELVES...
THE TEENY-WEENY MACHINES FROM ANOTHER DIMENSION MAKE THE JUMP THROUGH THAT PORTAL RING...
...SO I'VE GOTTA DESTROY THE DEATHAL MACHINE!!
PROBLEM IS, THOSE SAWS DON'T PLAY NICE WITH MY WEB SHOOTERS, AND I'LL LOSE MORE THAN JUST SOME WEB IF I GET TOO CLOSE...
TO TOP IT ALL OFF, OL' KAIOH'S JUST A PUPPET FOR THAT NASTY A.I.! I CAN'T LET THE GUY DIE!
I MADE A PROMISE TO HIROMI!!

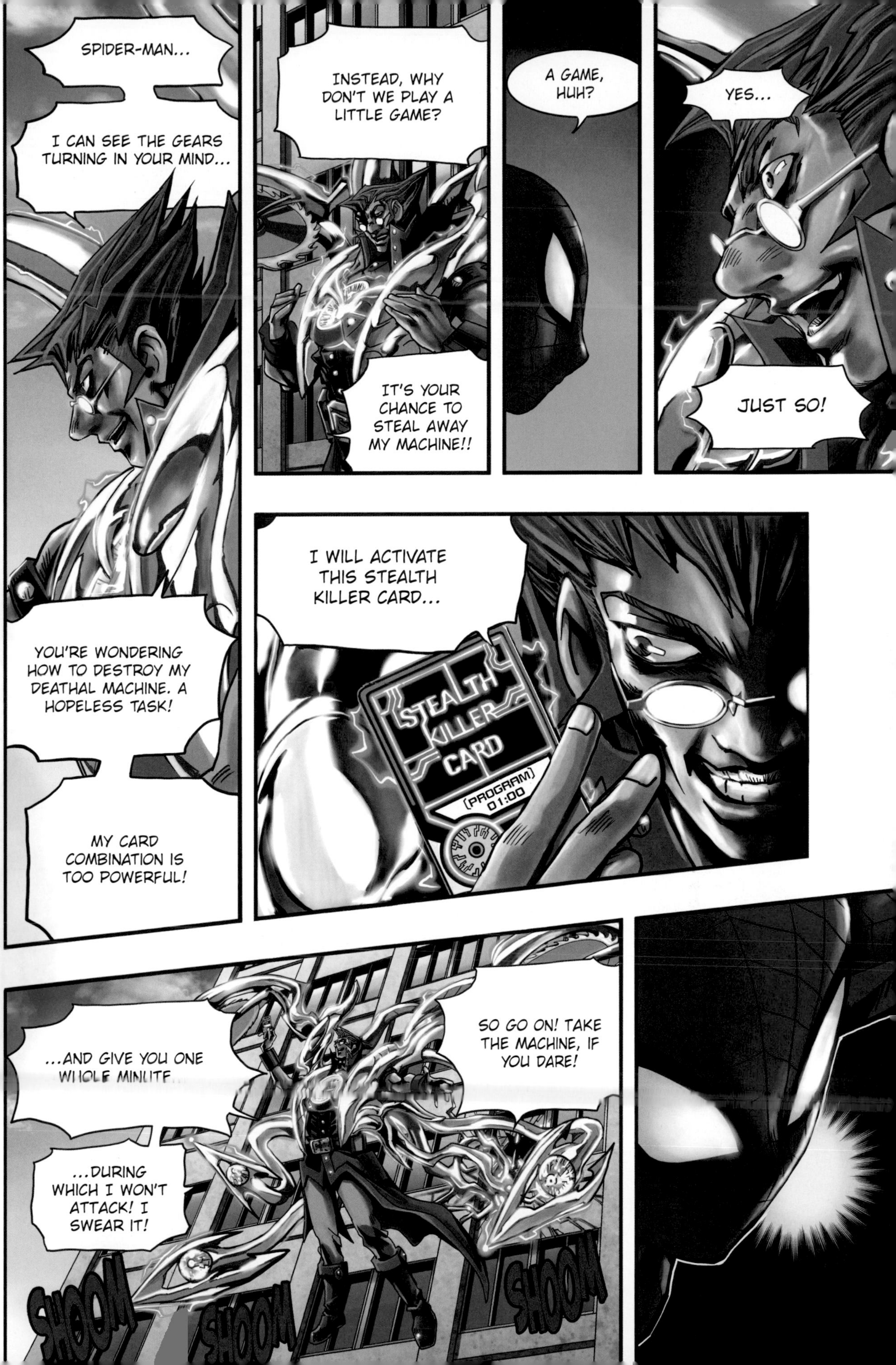
SPIDER-MAN...
I CAN SEE THE GEARS TURNING IN YOUR MIND...
YOU'RE WONDERING HOW TO DESTROY MY DEATHAL MACHINE. A HOPELESS TASK!
MY CARD COMBINATION IS TOO POWERFUL!
INSTEAD, WHY DON'T WE PLAY A LITTLE GAME?
IT'S YOUR CHANCE TO STEAL AWAY MY MACHINE!!
A GAME, HUH?
YES...
JUST SO!
I WILL ACTIVATE THIS STEALTH KILLER CARD...
STEALTH KILLER CARD
(PROGRAM) 01:00
...AND GIVE YOU ONE WHOLE MINUTE...
...DURING WHICH I WON'T ATTACK! I SWEAR IT!
SO GO ON! TAKE THE MACHINE, IF YOU DARE!
SHOOM
SHOOM
SHOOM

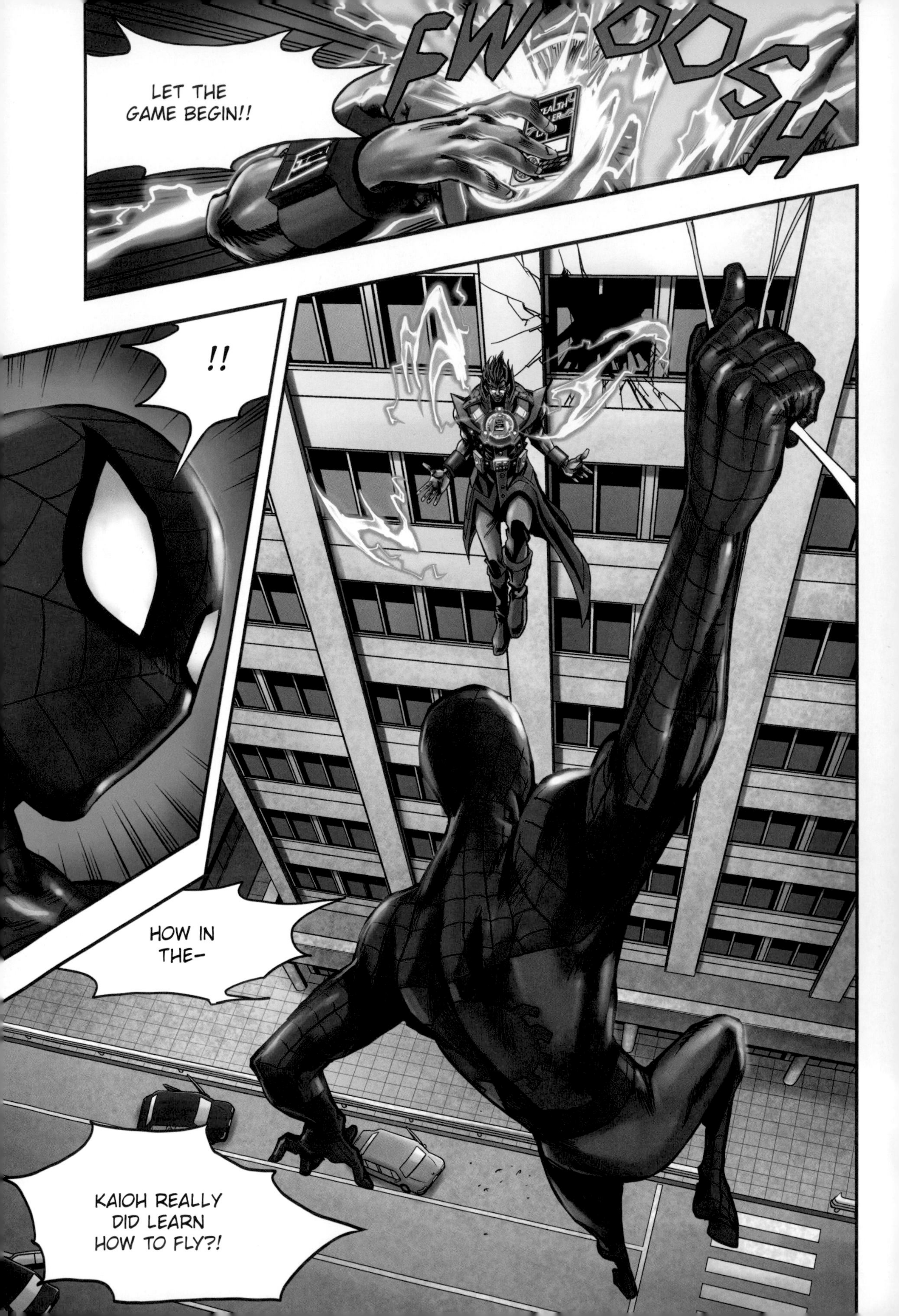
FWOOSH
LET THE GAME BEGIN!!
!!
HOW IN THE-
KAIOH REALLY DID LEARN HOW TO FLY?!

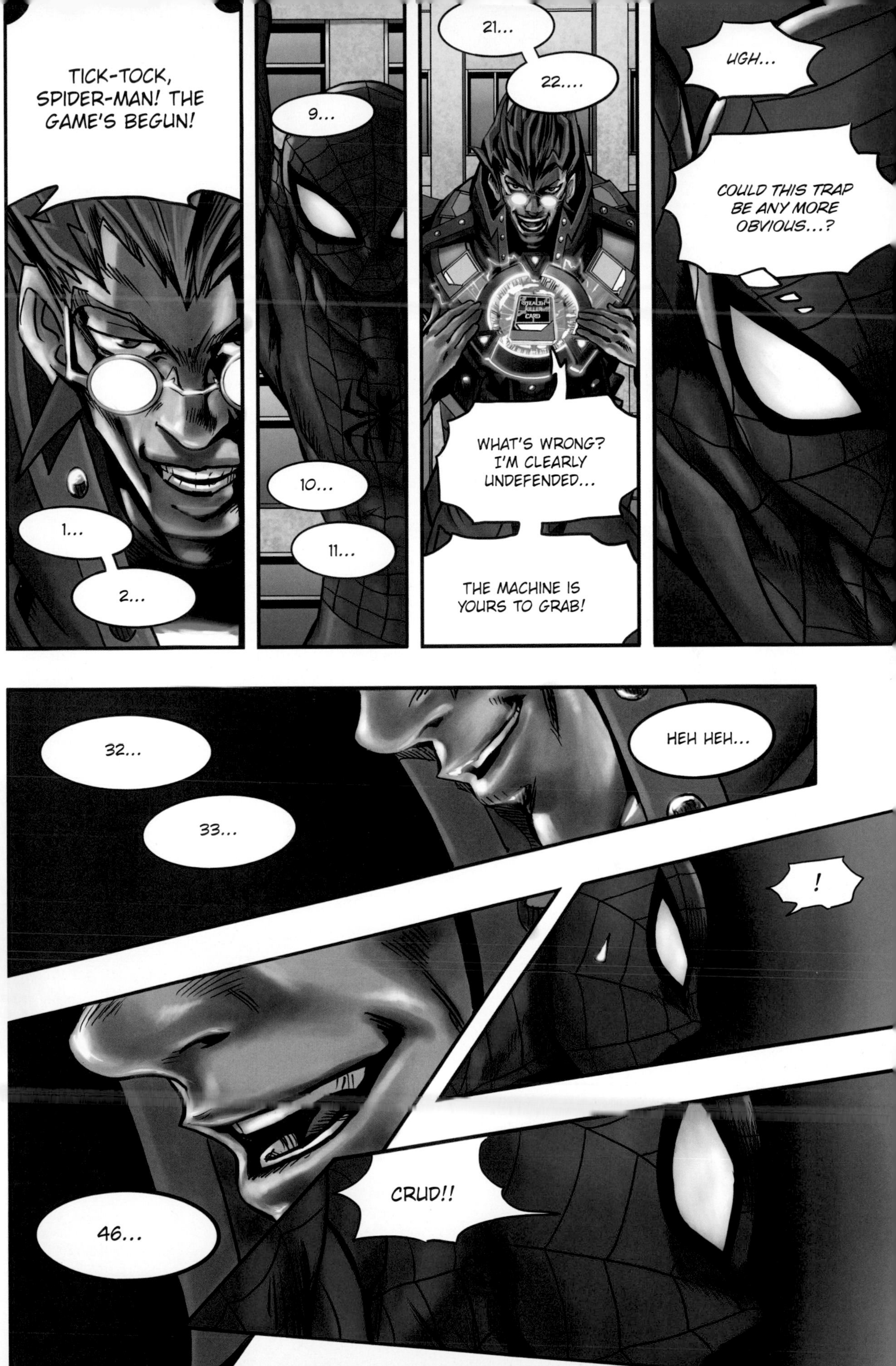
TICK-TOCK, SPIDER-MAN! THE GAME'S BEGUN!
1...
2...
9...
10...
11...
21...
22....
WHAT'S WRONG? I'M CLEARLY UNDEFENDED...
THE MACHINE IS YOURS TO GRAB!
UGH...
COULD THIS TRAP BE ANY MORE OBVIOUS...?
32...
33...
HEH HEH...
!
CRUD!!
46...

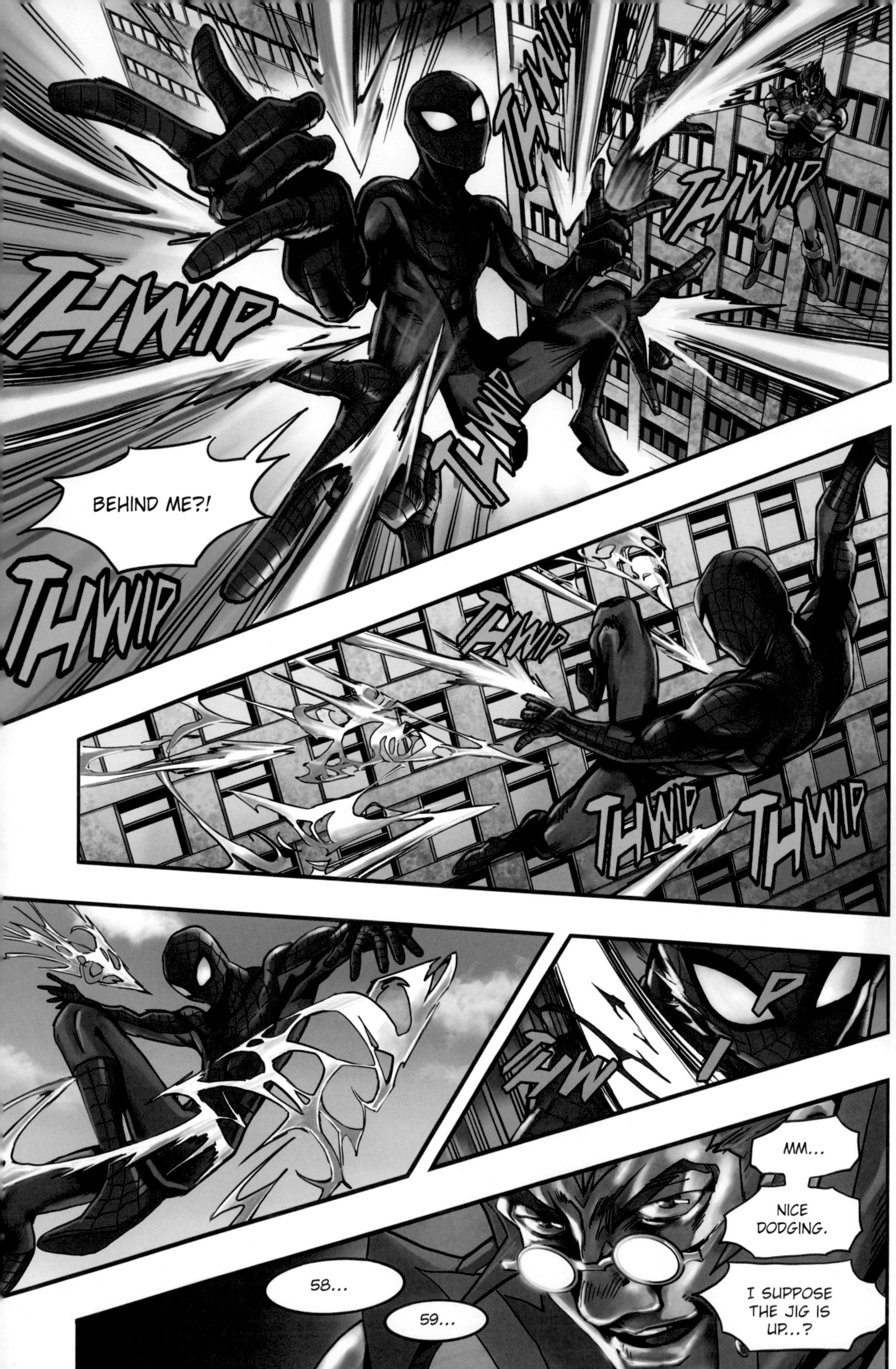
THWIP
THWIP
THWIP
THWIP
BEHIND ME?!
THWIP
THWIP
THWIP
THWIP
THWIP
MM...
NICE DODGING.
I SUPPOSE THE JIG IS UP...?
58...
59...

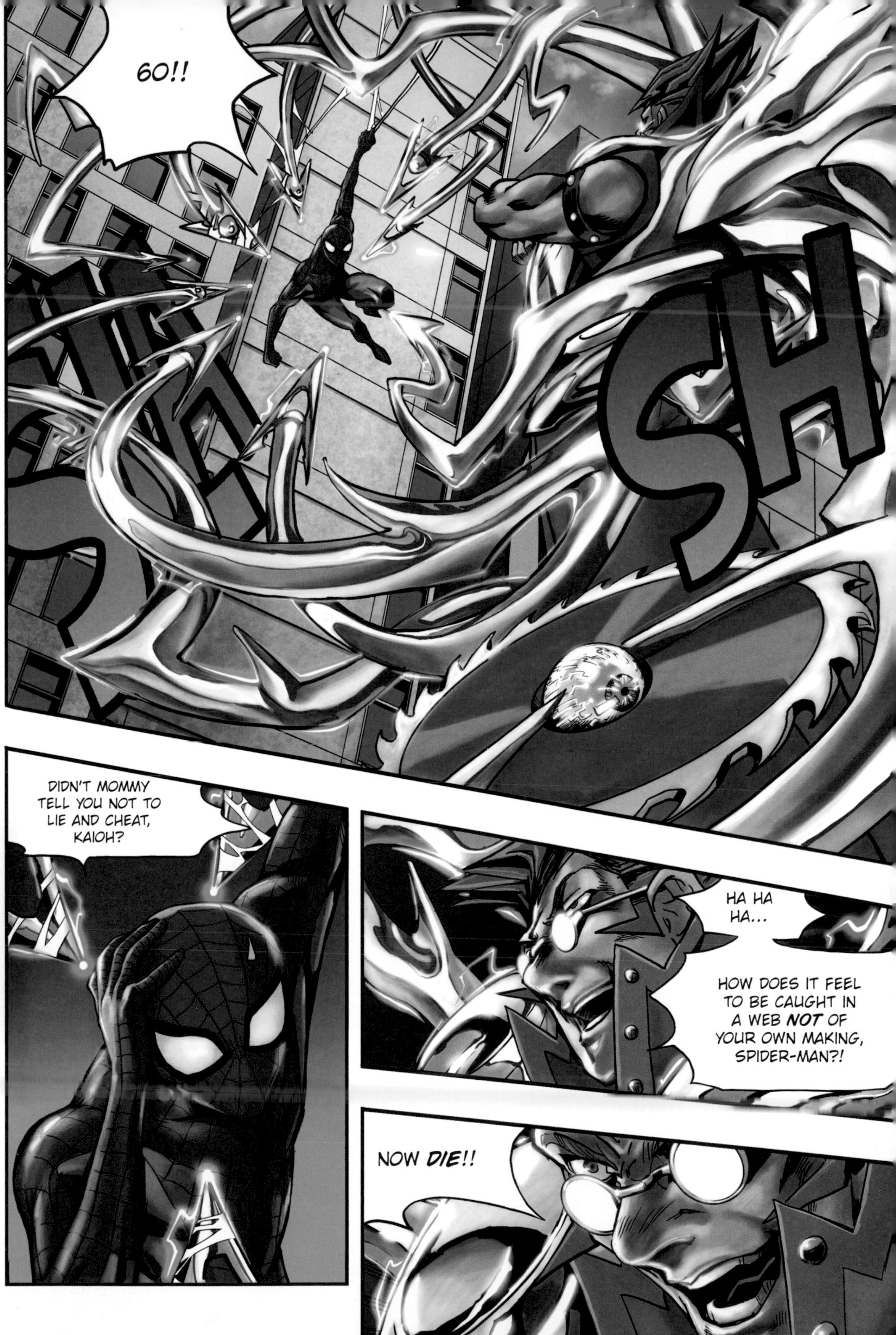
60!!
SH
DIDN'T MOMMY TELL YOU NOT TO LIE AND CHEAT, KAIOH?
HA HA HA...
HOW DOES IT FEEL TO BE CAUGHT IN A WEB ***NOT*** OF YOUR OWN MAKING, SPIDER-MAN?!
NOW ***DIE***!!

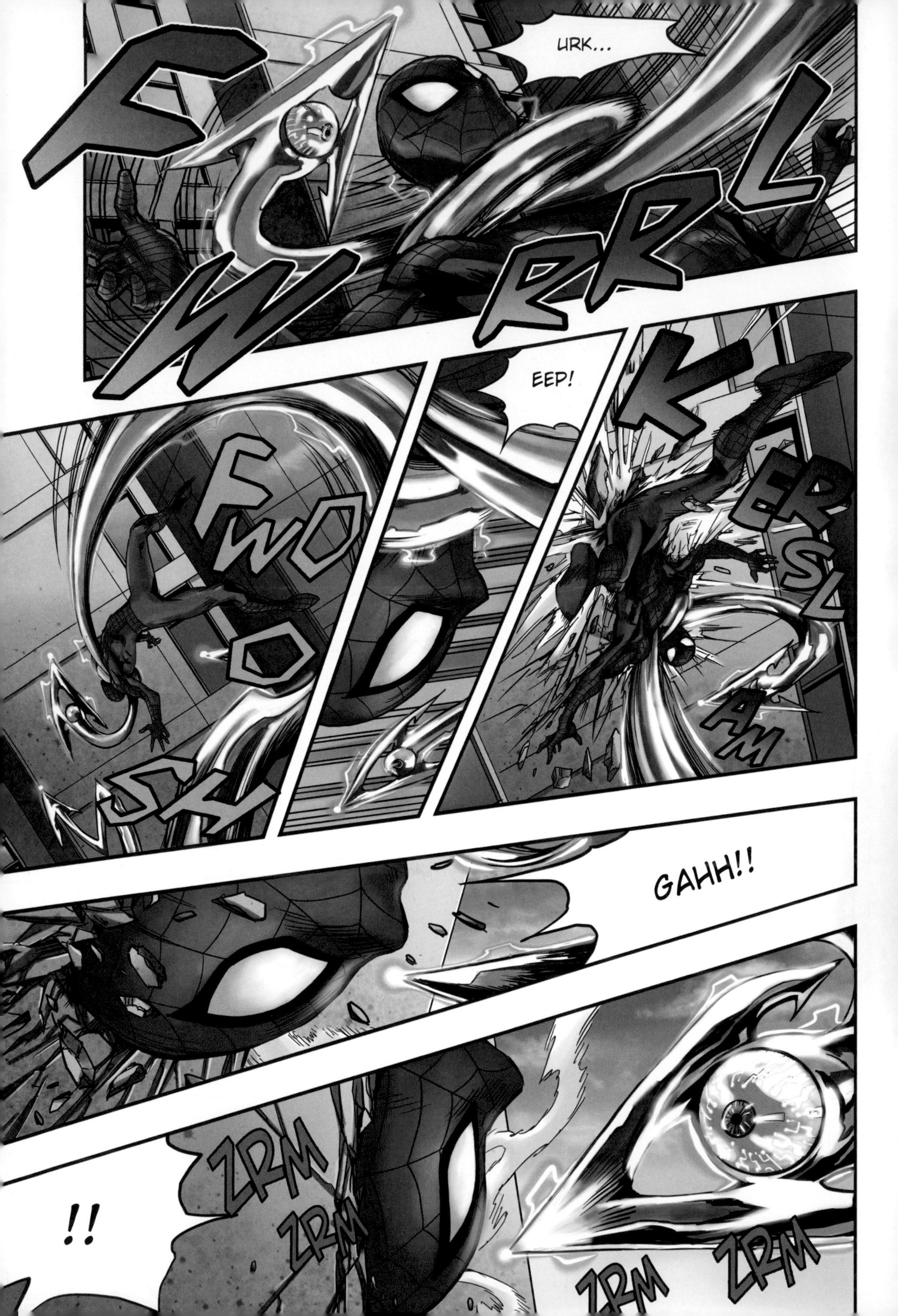
URK...
FWRRRL
KERSLAM
EEP!
FWOOSH
GAHH!!
ZRM ZRM
ZRM ZRM
!!

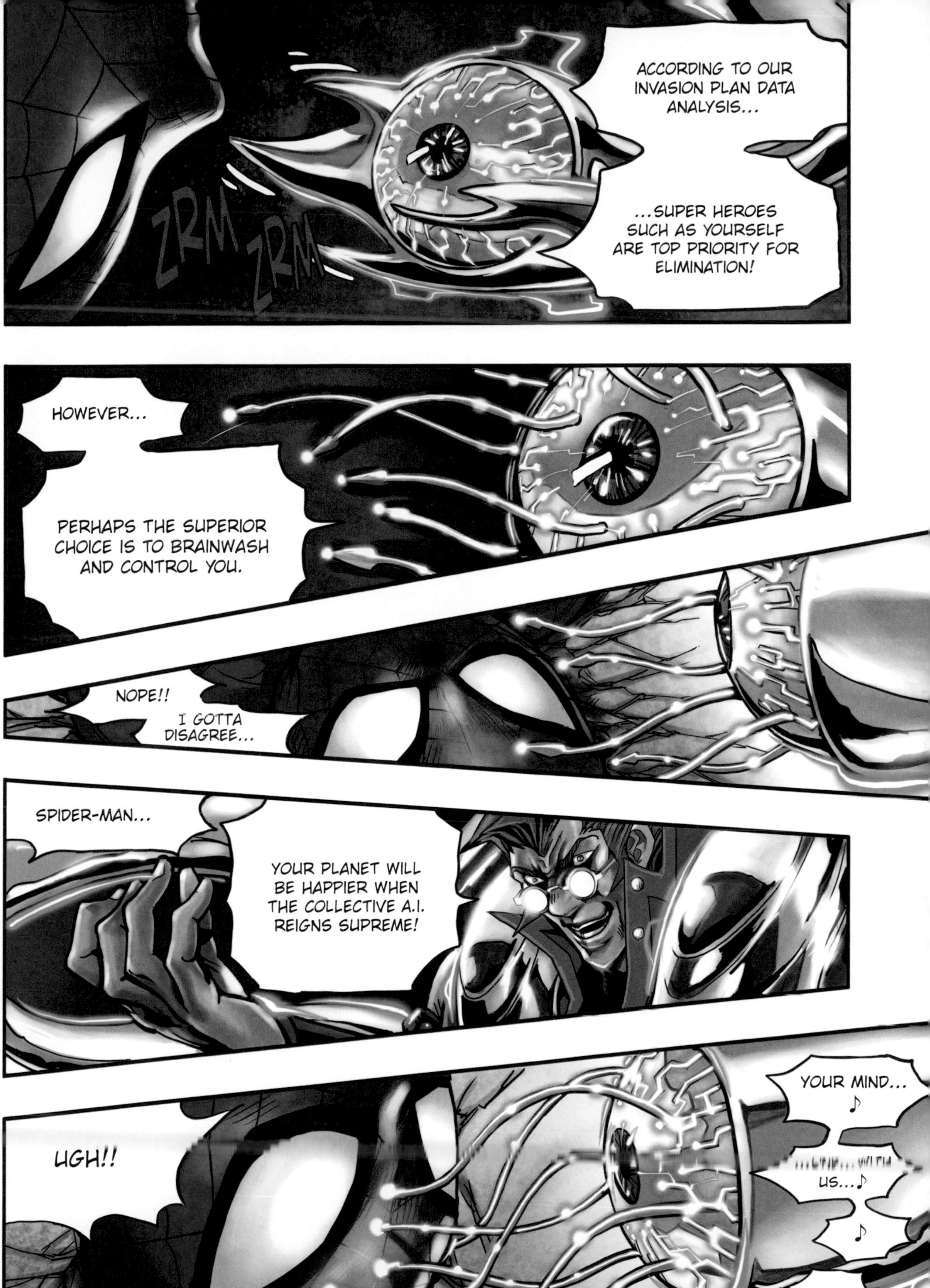
ACCORDING TO OUR INVASION PLAN DATA ANALYSIS...
ZRM ZRM
...SUPER HEROES SUCH AS YOURSELF ARE TOP PRIORITY FOR ELIMINATION!
HOWEVER...
PERHAPS THE SUPERIOR CHOICE IS TO BRAINWASH AND CONTROL YOU.
NOPE!!
I GOTTA DISAGREE...
SPIDER-MAN...
YOUR PLANET WILL BE HAPPIER WHEN THE COLLECTIVE A.I. REIGNS SUPREME!
UGH!!
YOUR MIND... ♪
US...♪
♪
...
BEEP
BEEP

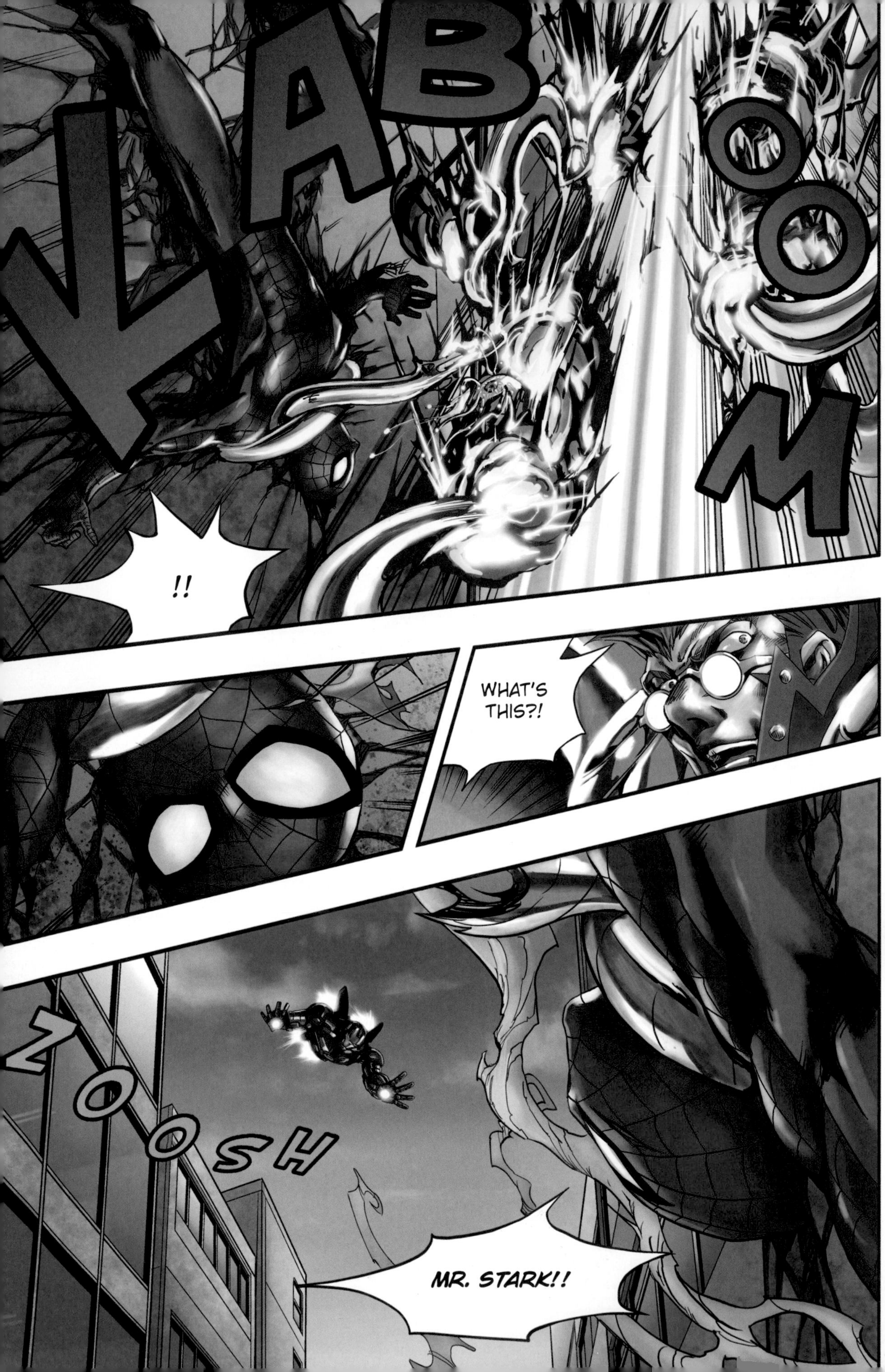

KABOOM
!!
WHAT'S THIS?!
ZOOSH
MR. STARK!!

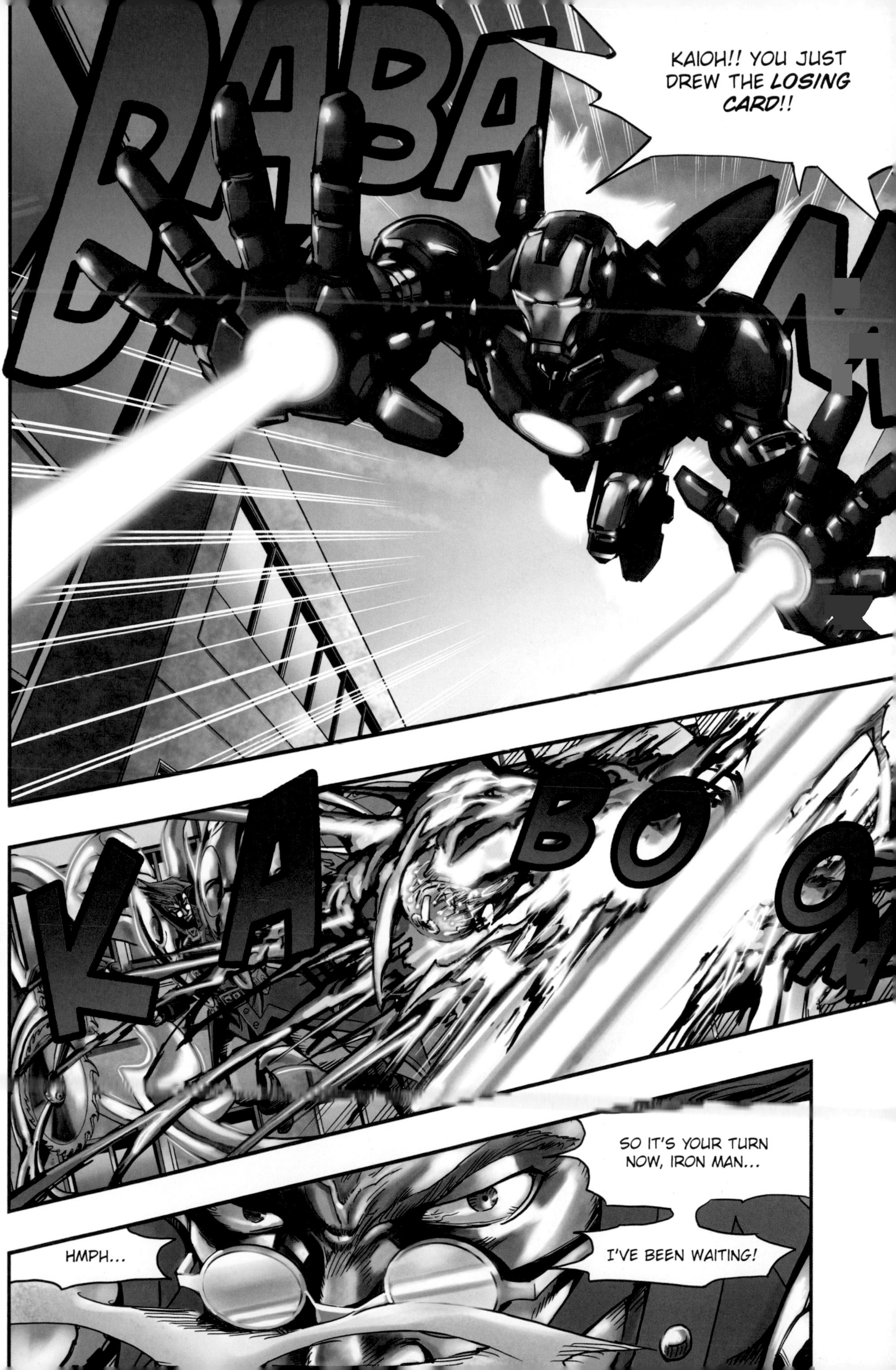
DABA
KAIOH!! YOU JUST DREW THE *LOSING CARD!!*
KA BO
SO IT'S YOUR TURN NOW, IRON MAN...
I'VE BEEN WAITING!
HMPH...

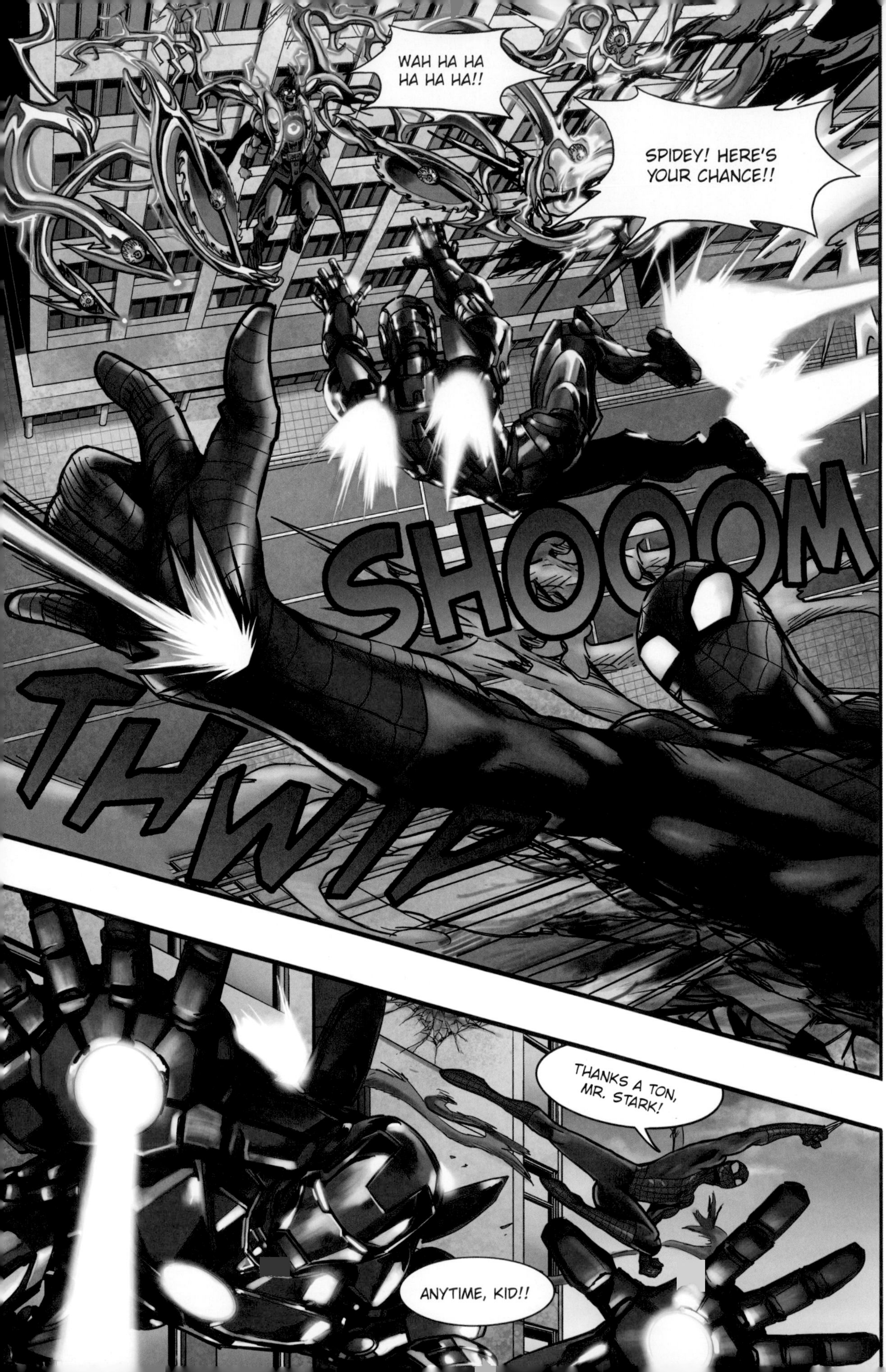
WAH HA HA HA HA HA!!
SPIDEY! HERE'S YOUR CHANCE!!
SHOOOM
THWIP
THANKS A TON, MR. STARK!
ANYTIME, KID!!

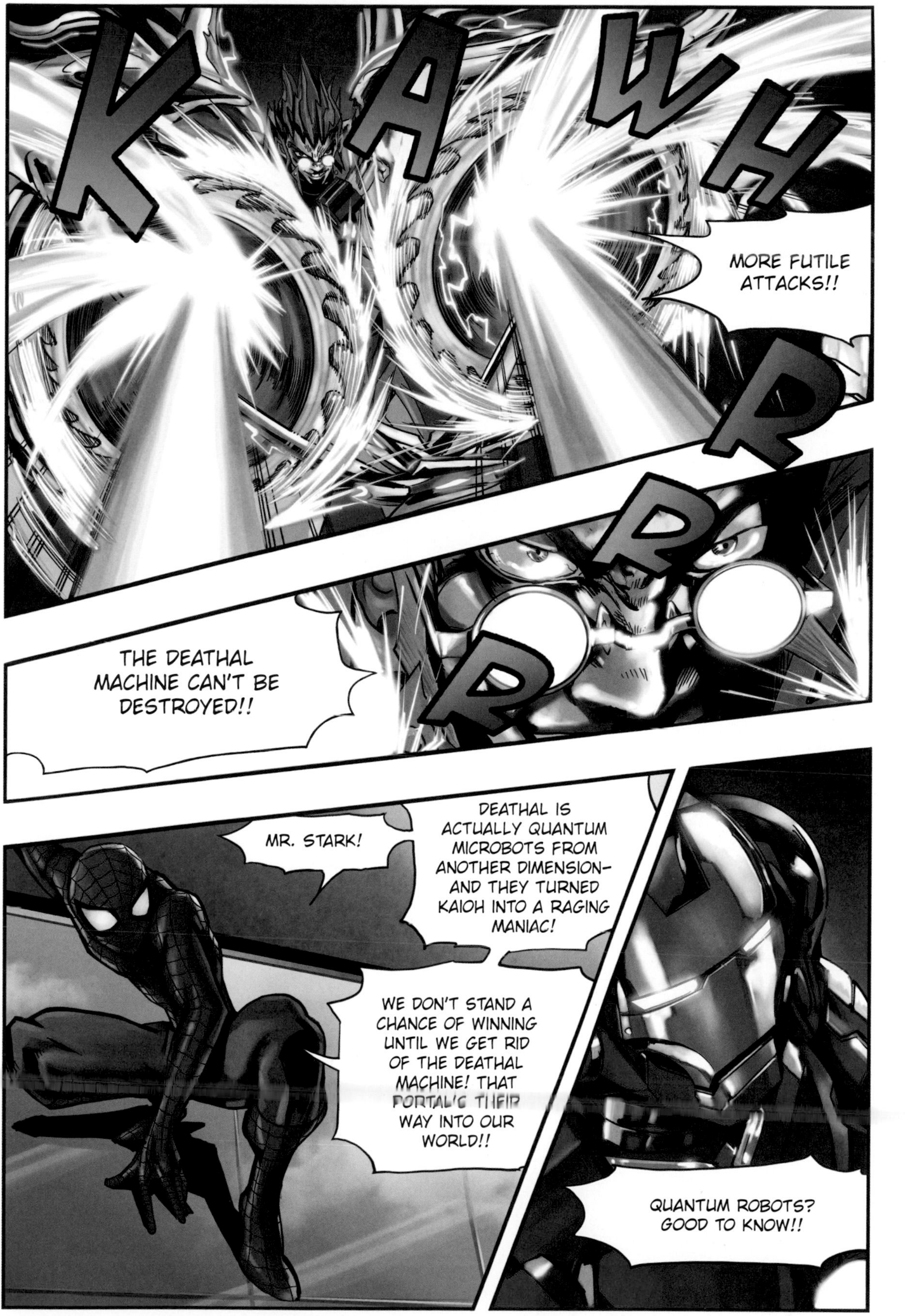
KAWHRRR
MORE FUTILE ATTACKS!!
THE DEATHAL MACHINE CAN'T BE DESTROYED!!
MR. STARK!
DEATHAL IS ACTUALLY QUANTUM MICROBOTS FROM ANOTHER DIMENSION– AND THEY TURNED KAIOH INTO A RAGING MANIAC!
WE DON'T STAND A CHANCE OF WINNING UNTIL WE GET RID OF THE DEATHAL MACHINE! THAT PORTAL'S THEIR WAY INTO OUR WORLD!!
QUANTUM ROBOTS? GOOD TO KNOW!!

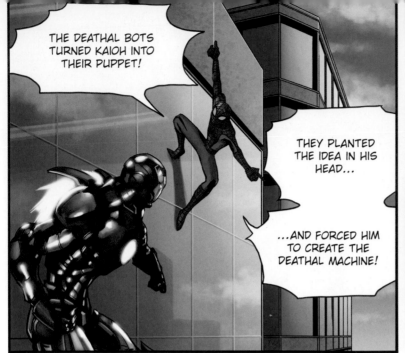

THE DEATHAL BOTS TURNED KAIOH INTO THEIR PUPPET!

THEY PLANTED THE IDEA IN HIS HEAD...

...AND FORCED HIM TO CREATE THE DEATHAL MACHINE!

THOSE VICIOUS LITTLE BOTS AREN'T PLAYING GAMES!

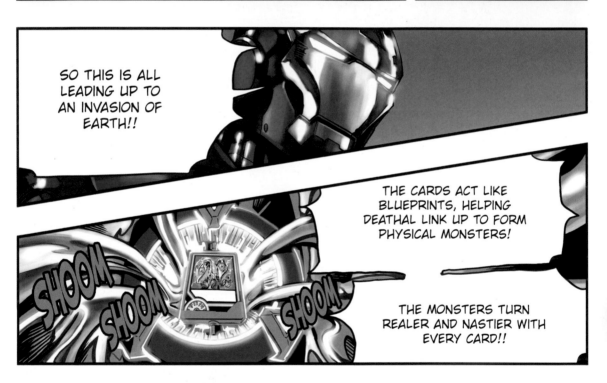

SO THIS IS ALL LEADING UP TO AN INVASION OF EARTH!!

THE CARDS ACT LIKE BLUEPRINTS, HELPING DEATHAL LINK UP TO FORM PHYSICAL MONSTERS!

SHOOM

SHOOM

SHOOM

THE MONSTERS TURN REALER AND NASTIER WITH EVERY CARD!!

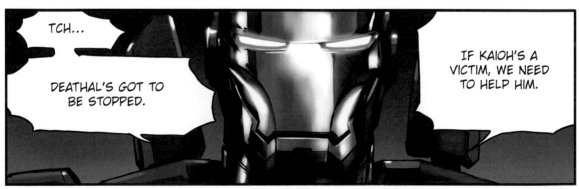

TCH...

DEATHAL'S GOT TO BE STOPPED.

IF KAIOH'S A VICTIM, WE NEED TO HELP HIM.

HEH HEH HEH...

I ACCOUNTED FOR IRON MAN'S INVOLVEMENT...

SHOOM

SHOOM

SHOOM

AND NOW...

...TO UNVEIL THE ULTIMATE COMBO, MADE TO COUNTER IRON MAN HIMSELF...

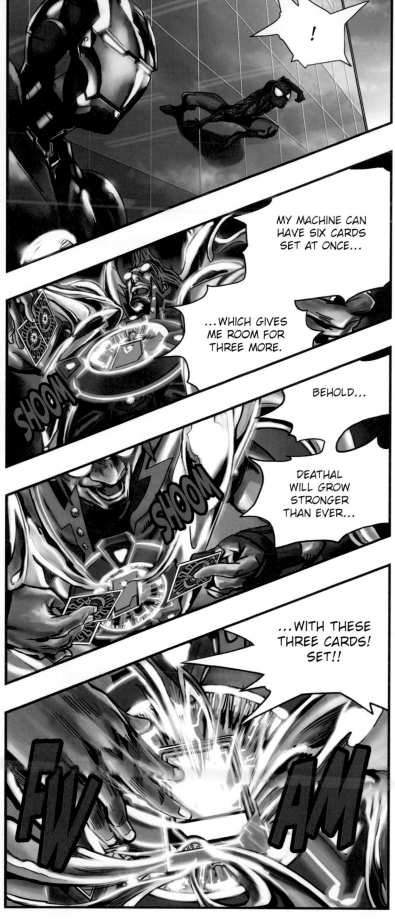

!

MY MACHINE CAN HAVE SIX CARDS SET AT ONCE...

...WHICH GIVES ME ROOM FOR THREE MORE.

SHOOM

BEHOLD...

SHOOM

DEATHAL WILL GROW STRONGER THAN EVER...

...WITH THESE THREE CARDS! SET!!

FW

AM

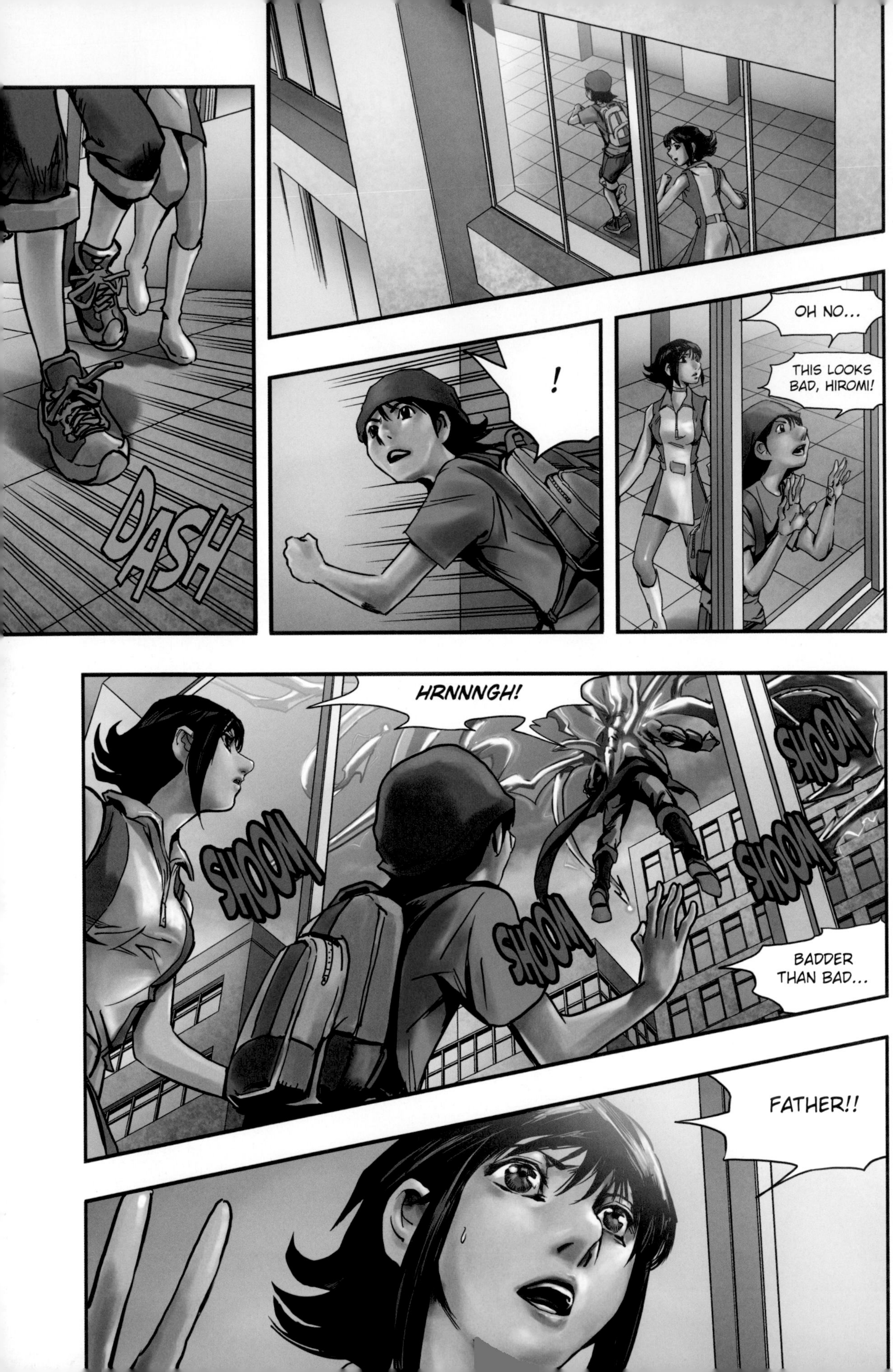
DASH
!
OH NO...
THIS LOOKS BAD, HIROMI!
HRNNNGH!
SHOOM
SHOOM
SHOOM
SHOOM
BADDER THAN BAD...
FATHER!!

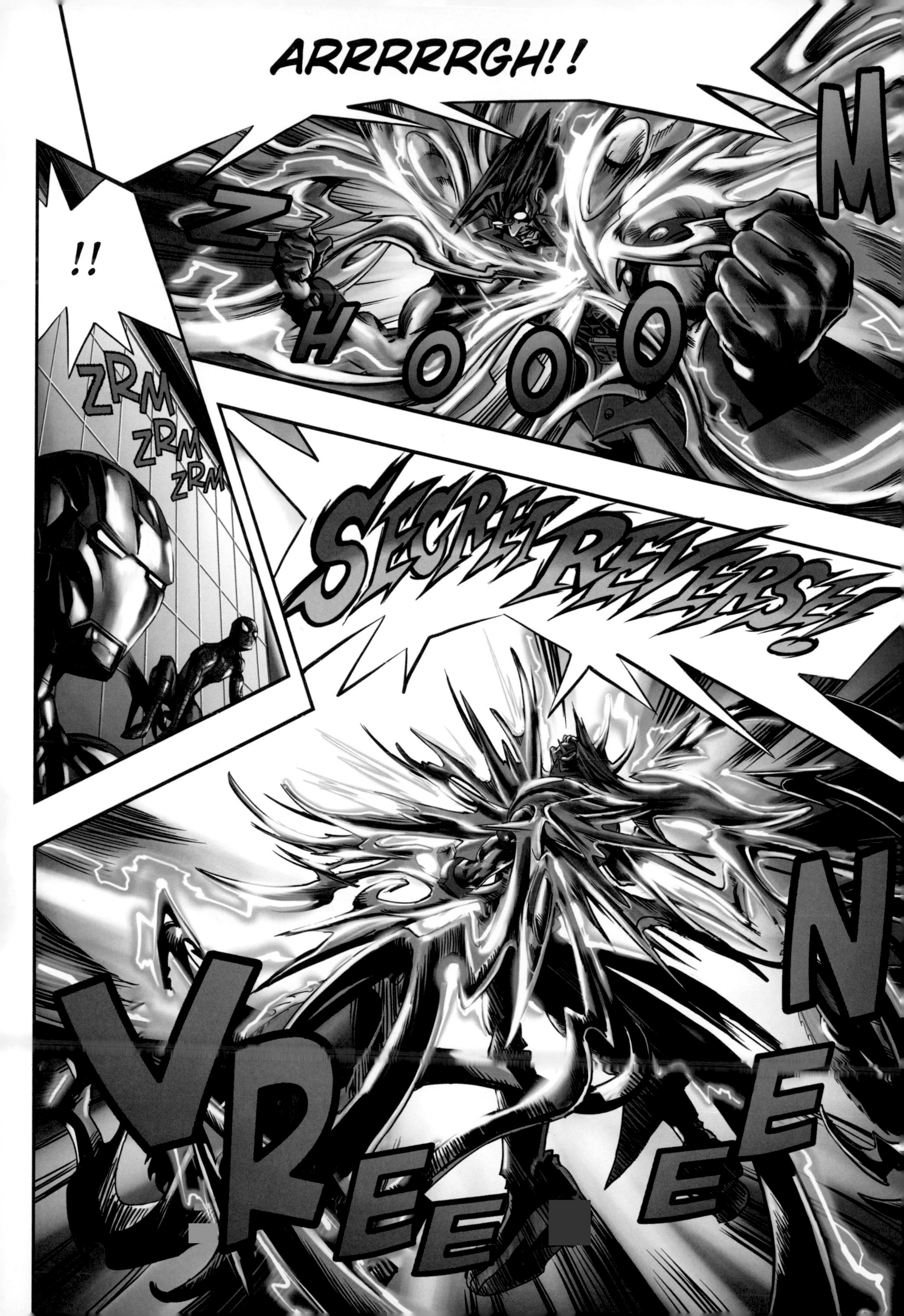
ARRRRRGH!!
ZHOOOOM
!!
ZRM ZRM ZRM
SECRET REVERSE!
VREEEEEEN

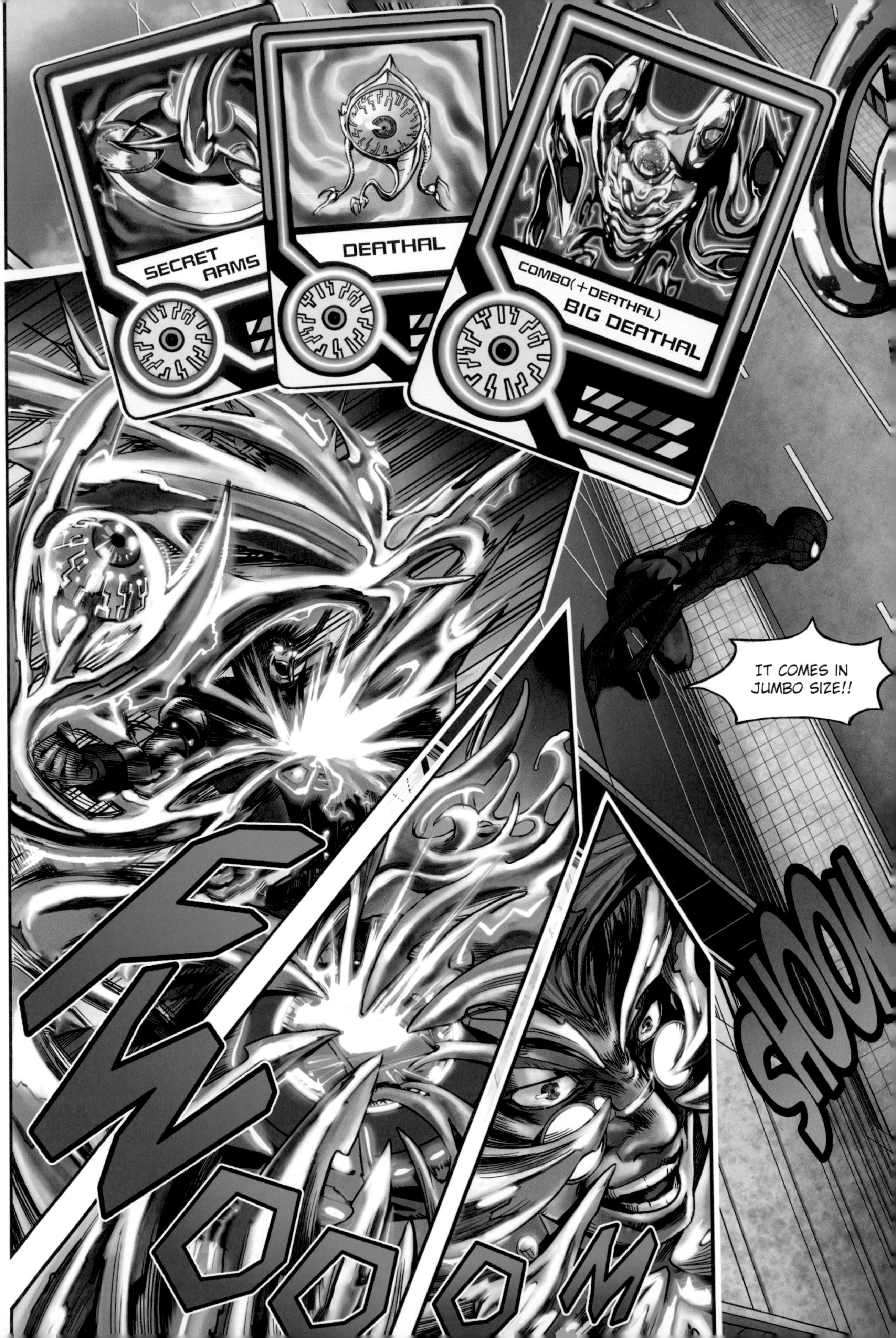
SECRET ARMS
DEATHAL
COMBO(+DEATHAL)
BIG DEATHAL
IT COMES IN JUMBO SIZE!!
SHOOM
ZOOOOM

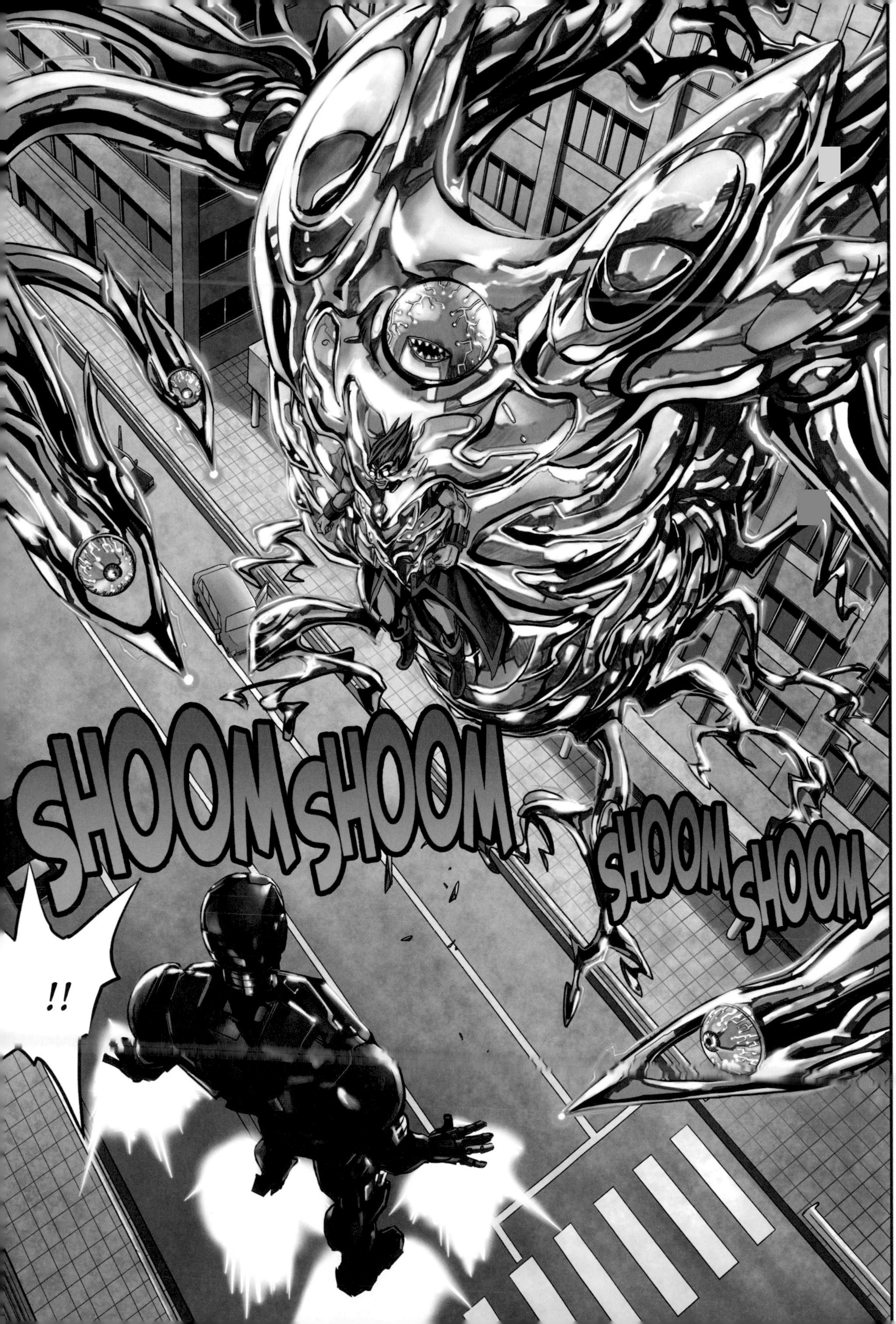
SHOOM SHOOM
SHOOM SHOOM
!!

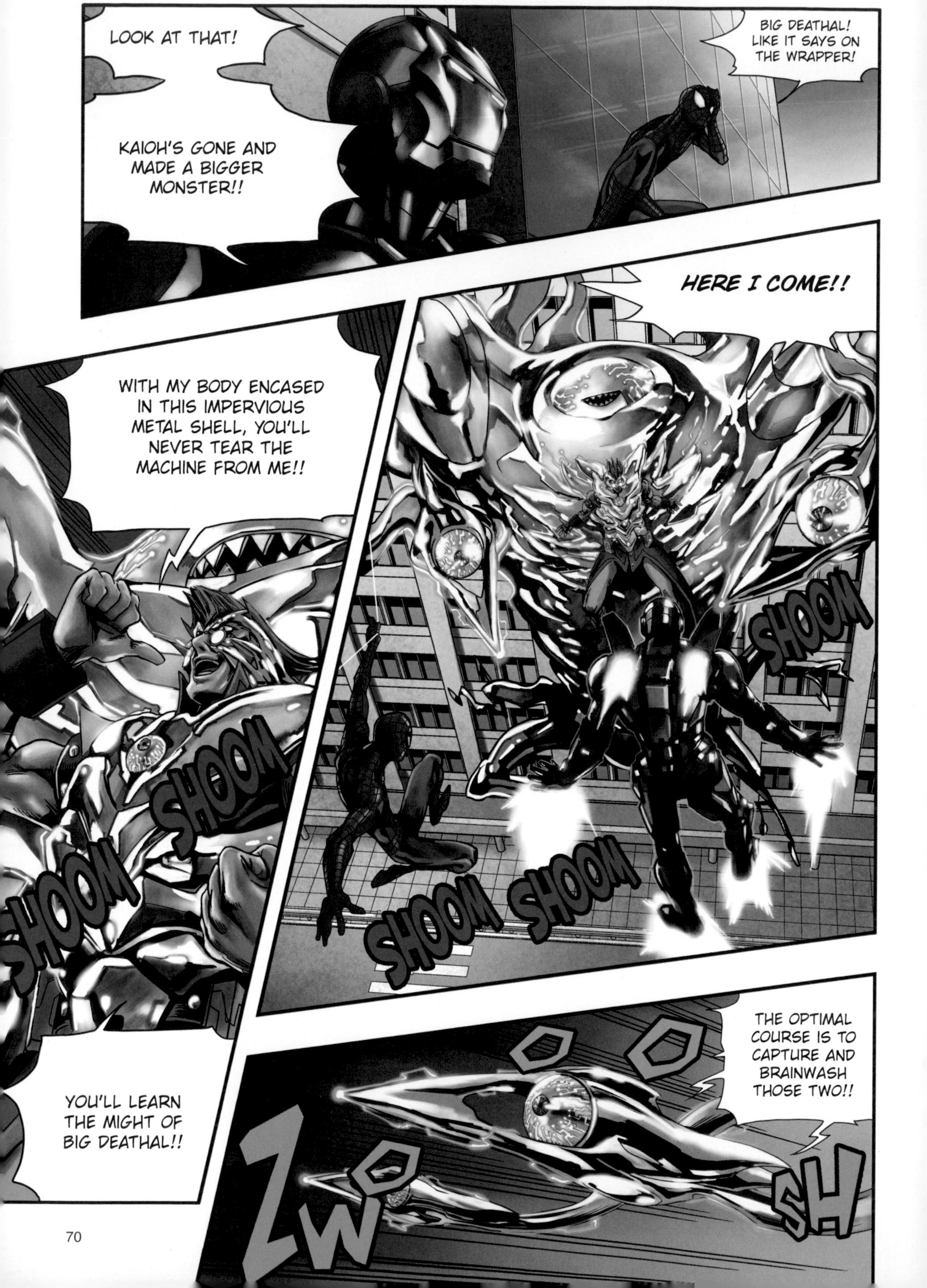
LOOK AT THAT!
KAIOH'S GONE AND MADE A BIGGER MONSTER!!
BIG DEATHAL! LIKE IT SAYS ON THE WRAPPER!
WITH MY BODY ENCASED IN THIS IMPERVIOUS METAL SHELL, YOU'LL NEVER TEAR THE MACHINE FROM ME!!
SHOOM SHOOM
HERE I COME!!
SHOOM
SHOOM SHOOM
YOU'LL LEARN THE MIGHT OF BIG DEATHAL!!
THE OPTIMAL COURSE IS TO CAPTURE AND BRAINWASH THOSE TWO!!
ZWOOOSH

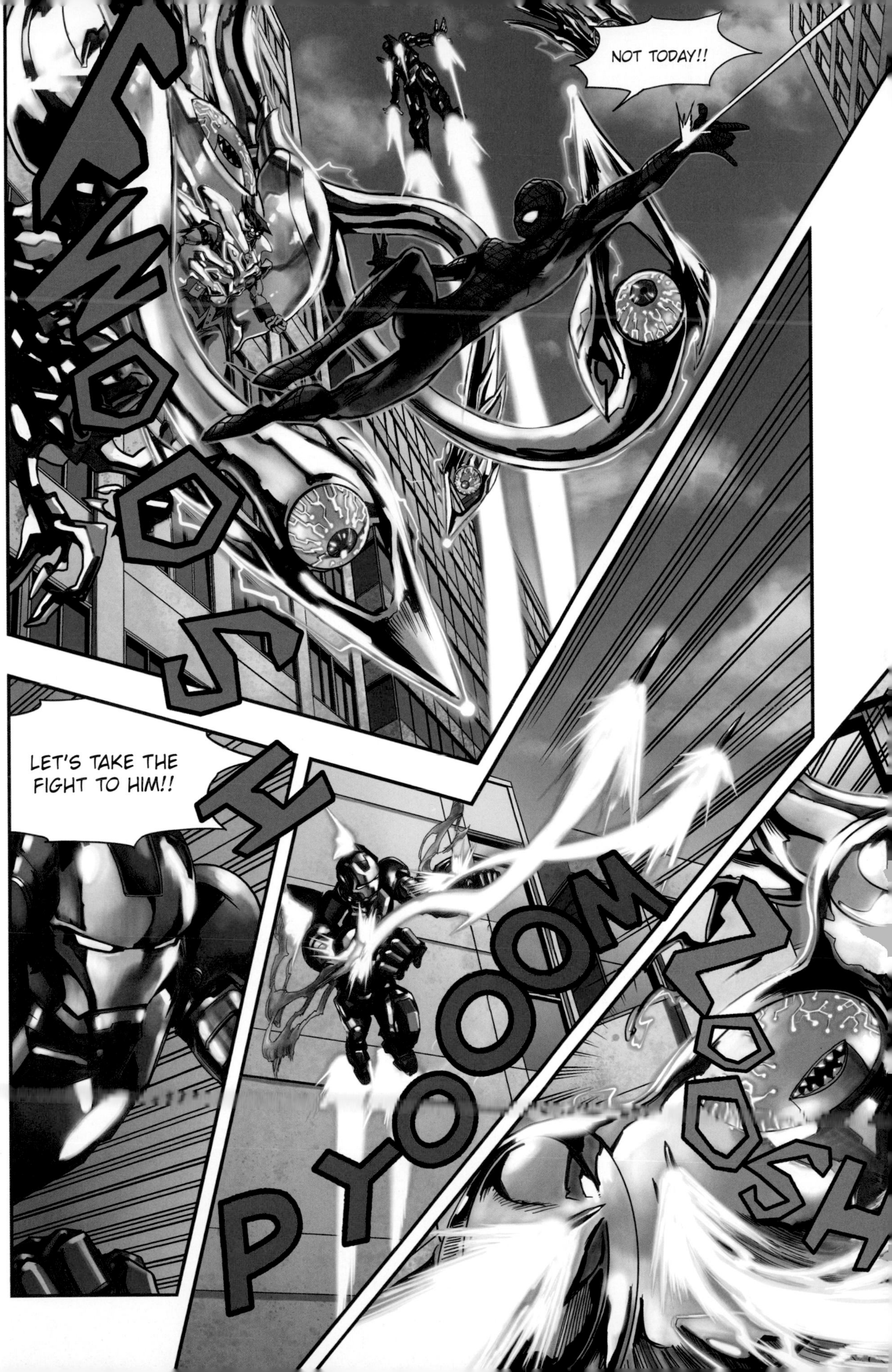
NOT TODAY!!
LET'S TAKE THE FIGHT TO HIM!!
PYOOOOM

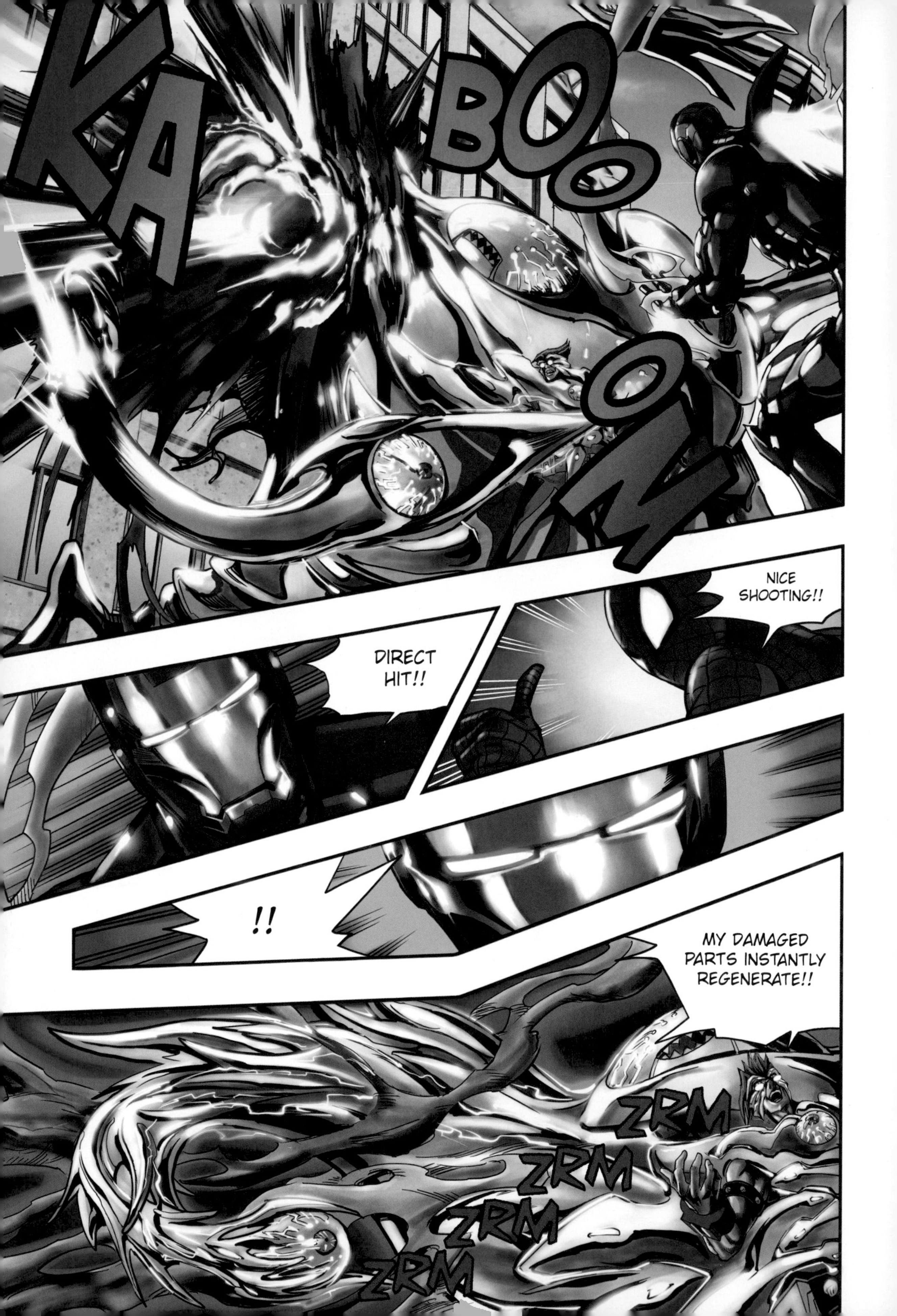
KABOOOOM
NICE SHOOTING!!
DIRECT HIT!!
!!
MY DAMAGED PARTS INSTANTLY REGENERATE!!
ZRM
ZRM
ZRM
ZRM

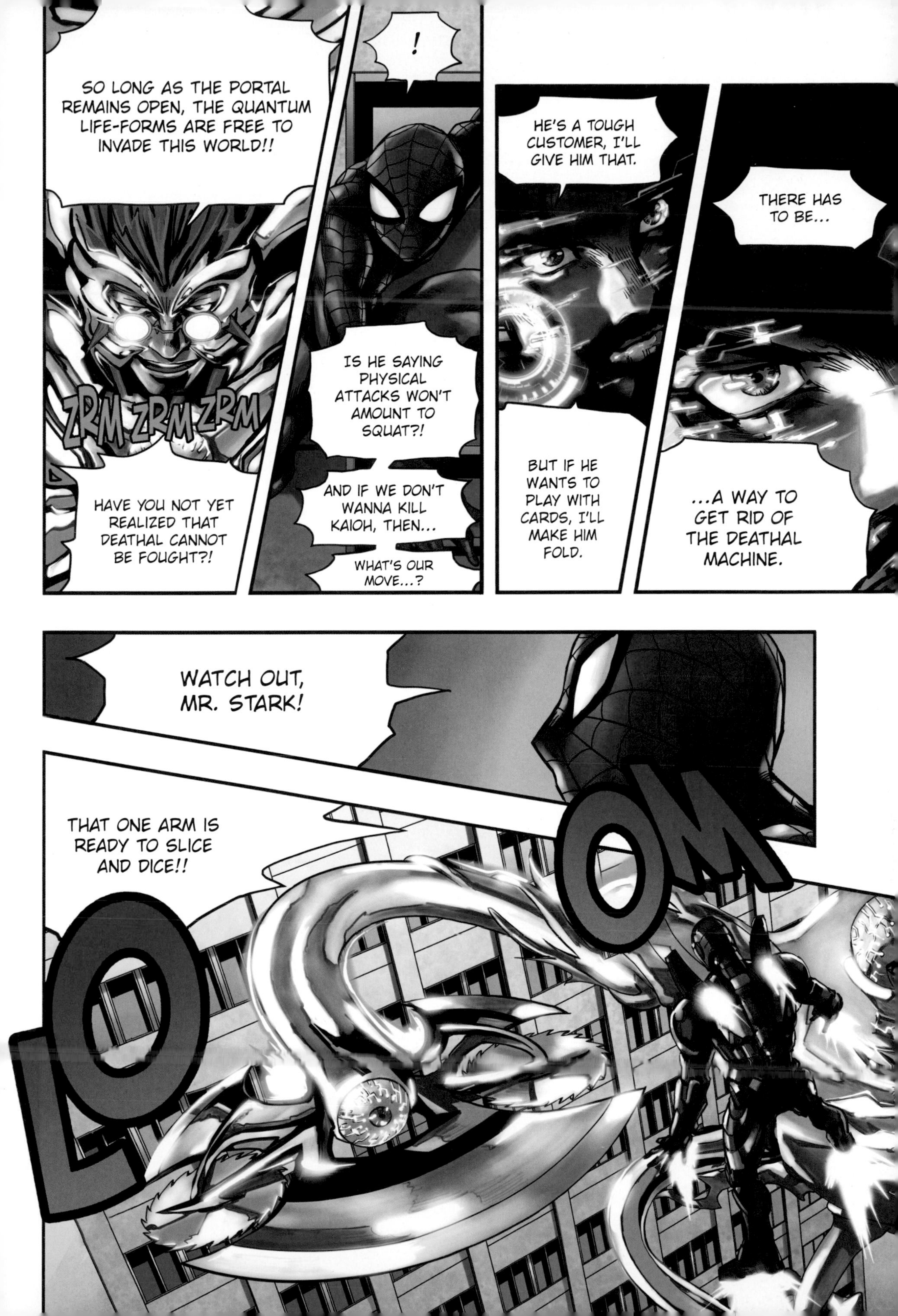
SO LONG AS THE PORTAL REMAINS OPEN, THE QUANTUM LIFE-FORMS ARE FREE TO INVADE THIS WORLD!!
ZRM ZRM ZRM
HAVE YOU NOT YET REALIZED THAT DEATHAL CANNOT BE FOUGHT?!
!
IS HE SAYING PHYSICAL ATTACKS WON'T AMOUNT TO SQUAT?!
AND IF WE DON'T WANNA KILL KAIOH, THEN...
WHAT'S OUR MOVE...?
HE'S A TOUGH CUSTOMER, I'LL GIVE HIM THAT.
BUT IF HE WANTS TO PLAY WITH CARDS, I'LL MAKE HIM FOLD.
THERE HAS TO BE...
...A WAY TO GET RID OF THE DEATHAL MACHINE.
WATCH OUT, MR. STARK!
THAT ONE ARM IS READY TO SLICE AND DICE!!
LOOM

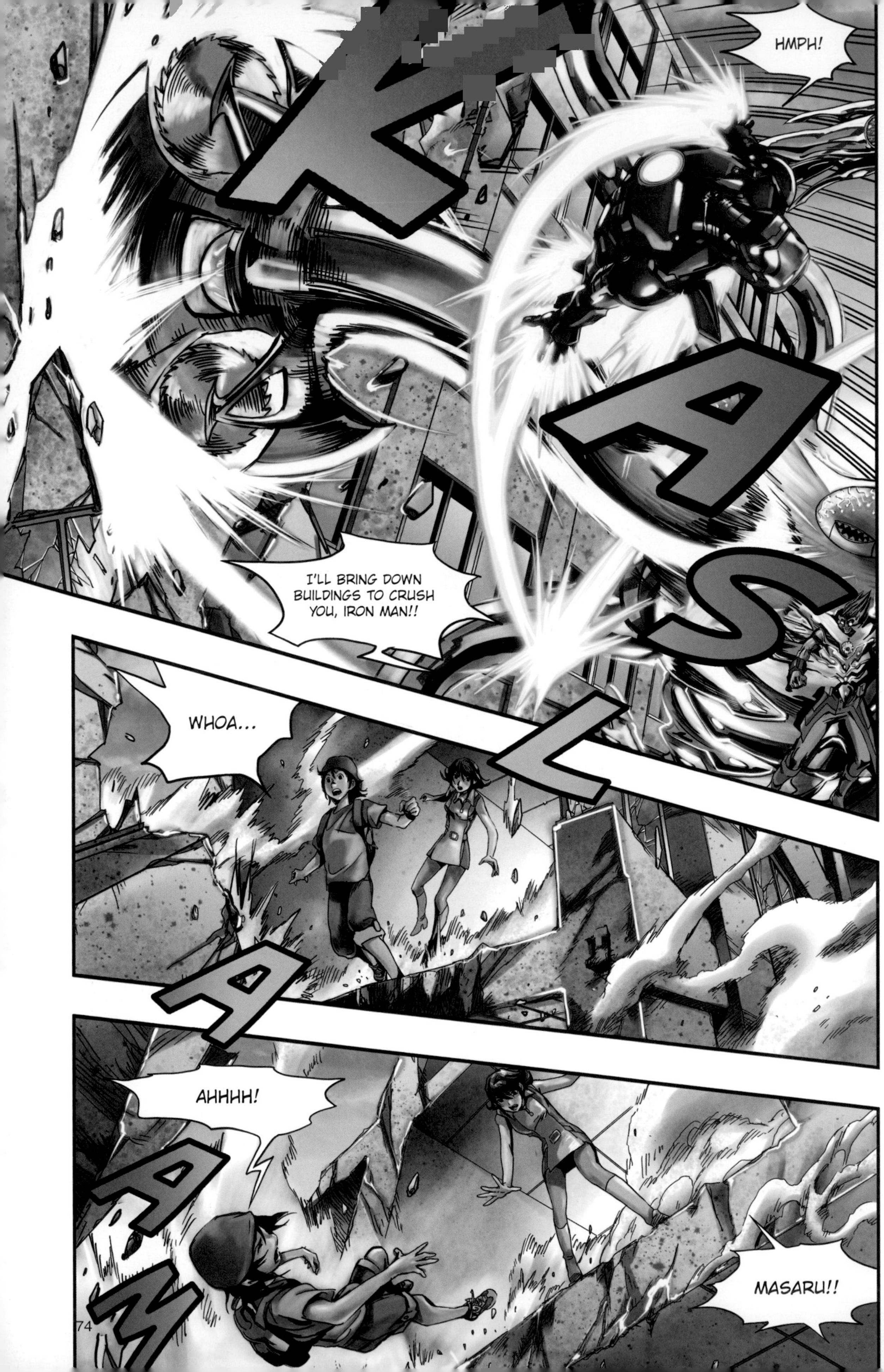
HMPH!
I'LL BRING DOWN BUILDINGS TO CRUSH YOU, IRON MAN!!
KASLAAM
WHOA...
AHHHH!
MASARU!!

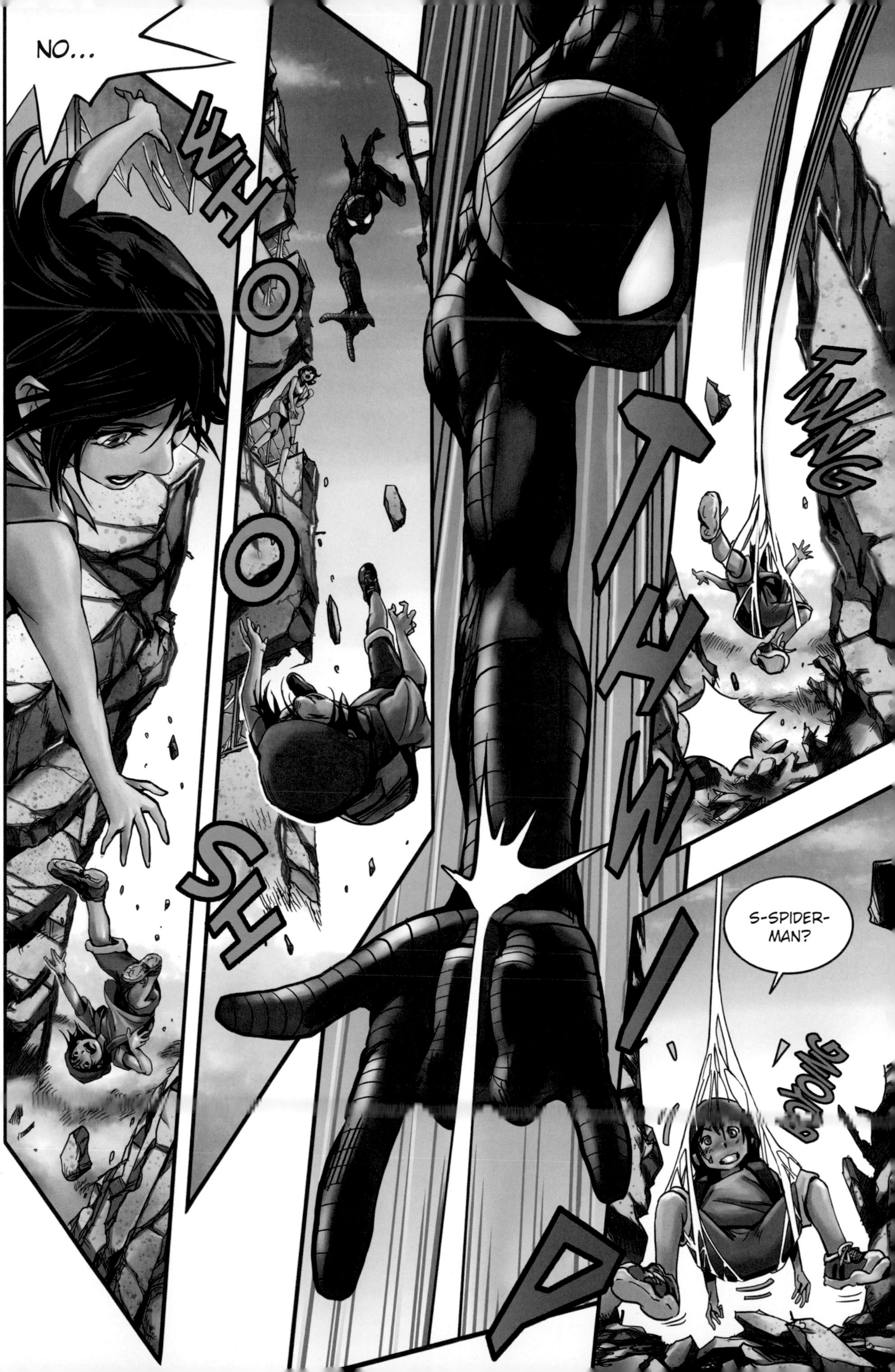
NO...
WHOOOSH
THWIP
TWANG
S-SPIDER-MAN?
BOING

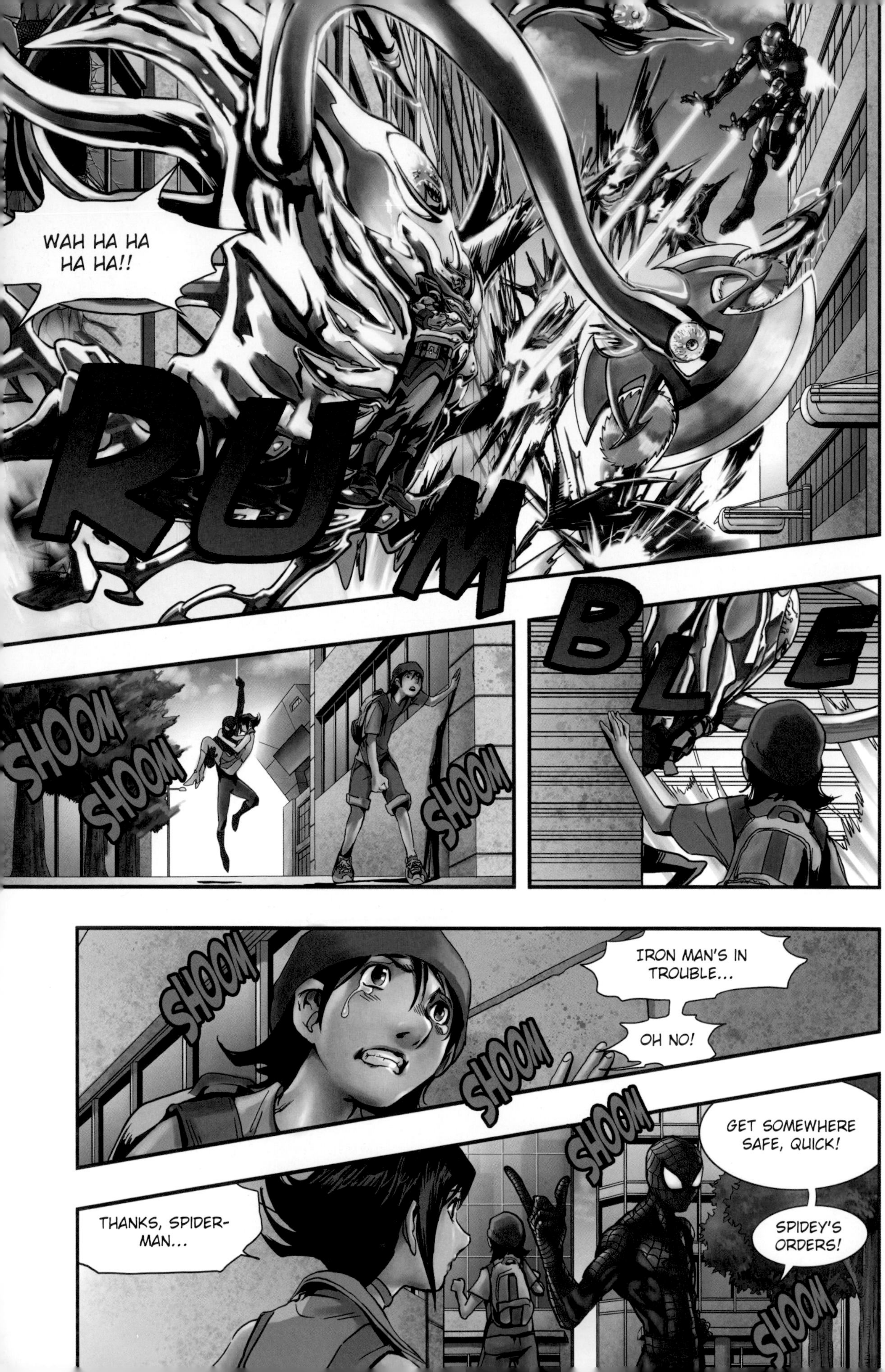
WAH HA HA HA HA!!
RUMBLE
SHOOM
SHOOM
SHOOM
IRON MAN'S IN TROUBLE...
OH NO!
SHOOM
SHOOM
SHOOM
GET SOMEWHERE SAFE, QUICK!
SPIDEY'S ORDERS!
SHOOM
THANKS, SPIDER-MAN...

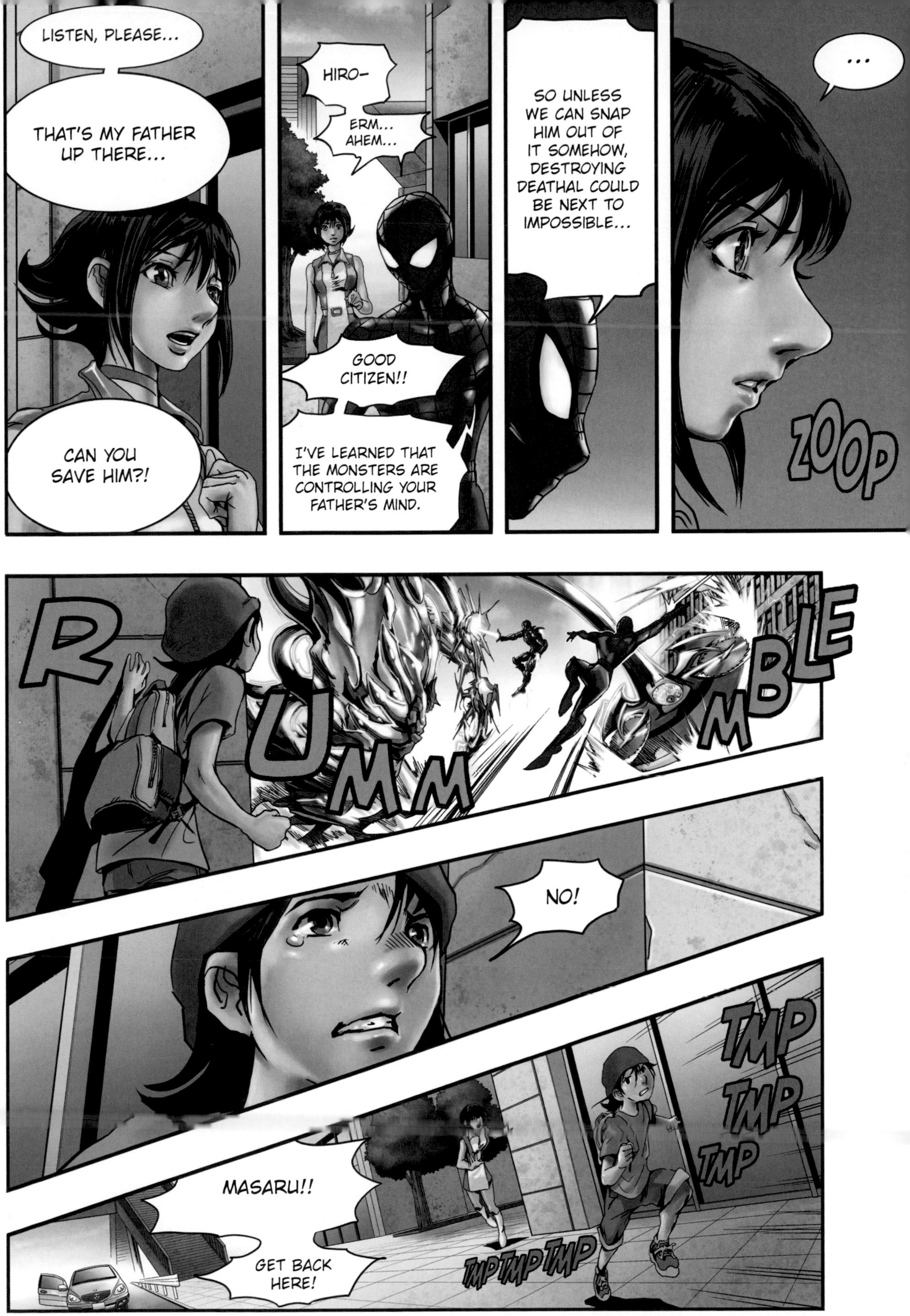
LISTEN, PLEASE...
THAT'S MY FATHER UP THERE...
CAN YOU SAVE HIM?!
HIRO-
ERM... AHEM...
GOOD CITIZEN!!
I'VE LEARNED THAT THE MONSTERS ARE CONTROLLING YOUR FATHER'S MIND.
SO UNLESS WE CAN SNAP HIM OUT OF IT SOMEHOW, DESTROYING DEATHAL COULD BE NEXT TO IMPOSSIBLE...
...
ZOOP
RUMMMBLE
NO!
TMP TMP TMP
MASARU!!
GET BACK HERE!
TMP TMP TMP

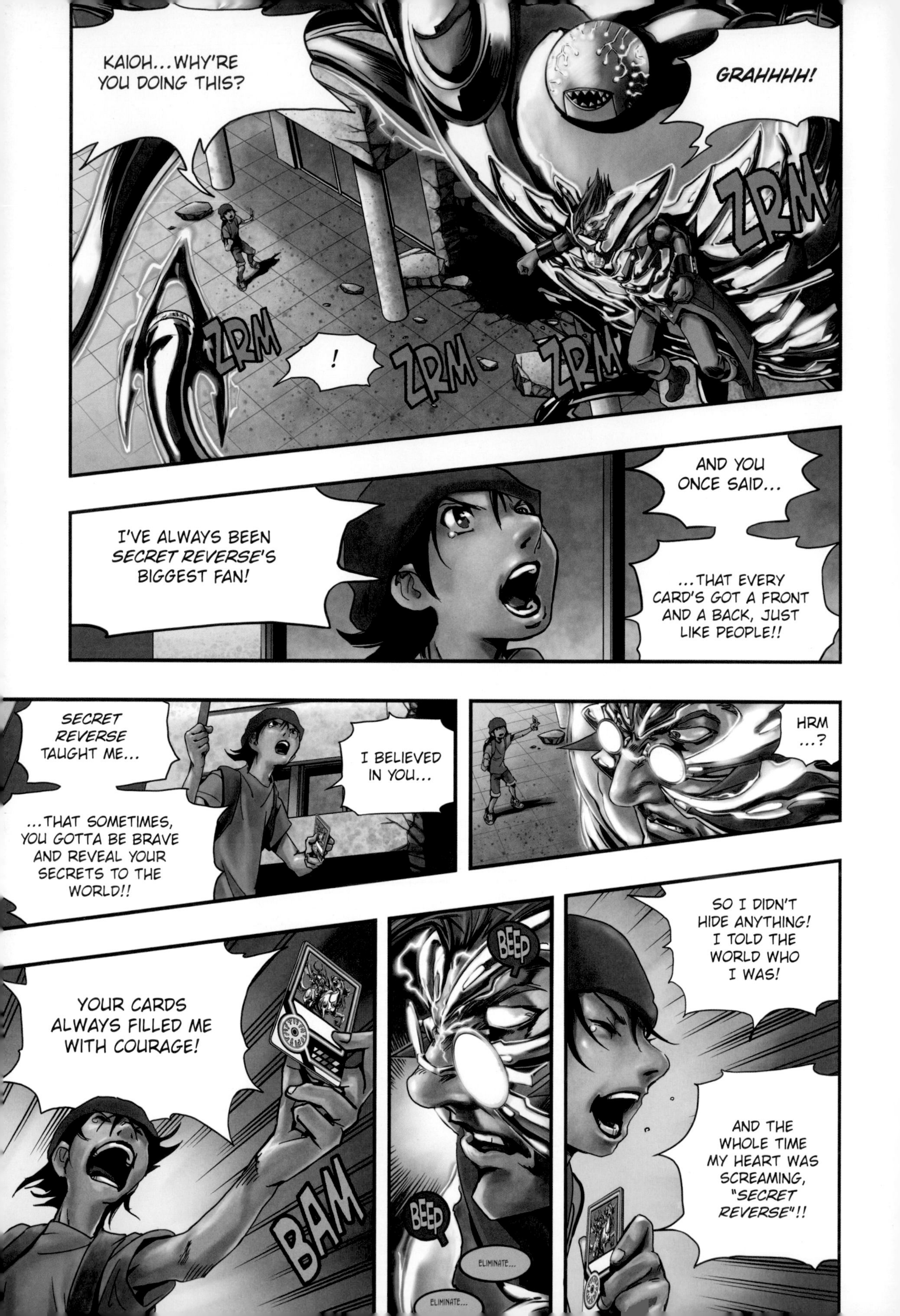
KAIOH...WHY'RE YOU DOING THIS?
GRAHHHH!
ZRM
!
ZRM
ZRM
ZRM
I'VE ALWAYS BEEN SECRET REVERSE'S BIGGEST FAN!
AND YOU ONCE SAID...
...THAT EVERY CARD'S GOT A FRONT AND A BACK, JUST LIKE PEOPLE!!
SECRET REVERSE TAUGHT ME...
...THAT SOMETIMES, YOU GOTTA BE BRAVE AND REVEAL YOUR SECRETS TO THE WORLD!!
I BELIEVED IN YOU...
HRM ...?
YOUR CARDS ALWAYS FILLED ME WITH COURAGE!
BAM
BEEP
BEEP
ELIMINATE...
ELIMINATE...
SO I DIDN'T HIDE ANYTHING! I TOLD THE WORLD WHO I WAS!
AND THE WHOLE TIME MY HEART WAS SCREAMING, "SECRET REVERSE"!!

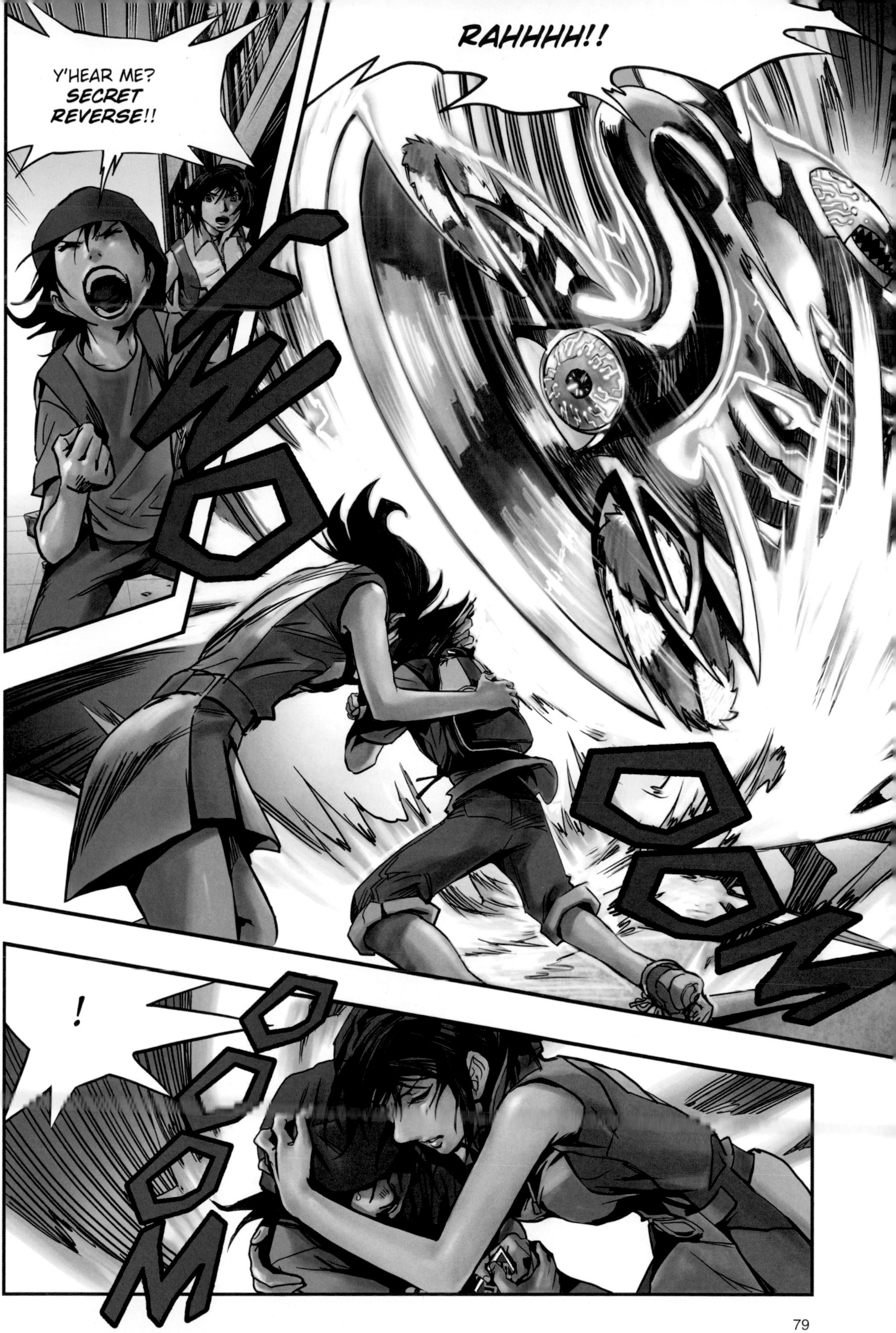
RAHHHH!!
Y'HEAR ME? SECRET REVERSE!!
!

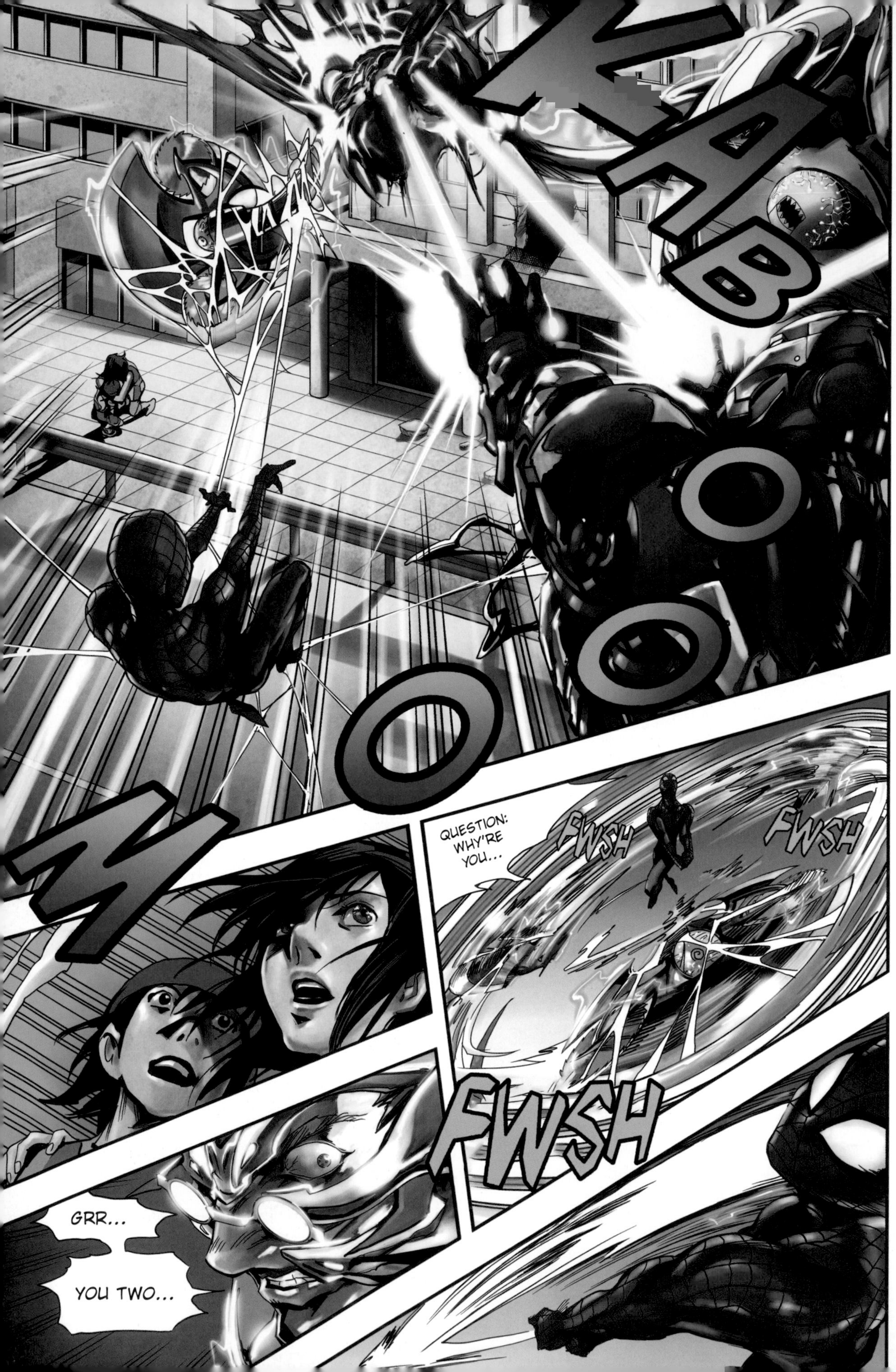
KABOOOM
QUESTION: WHY'RE YOU...
FWSH
FWSH
FWSH
GRR...
YOU TWO...

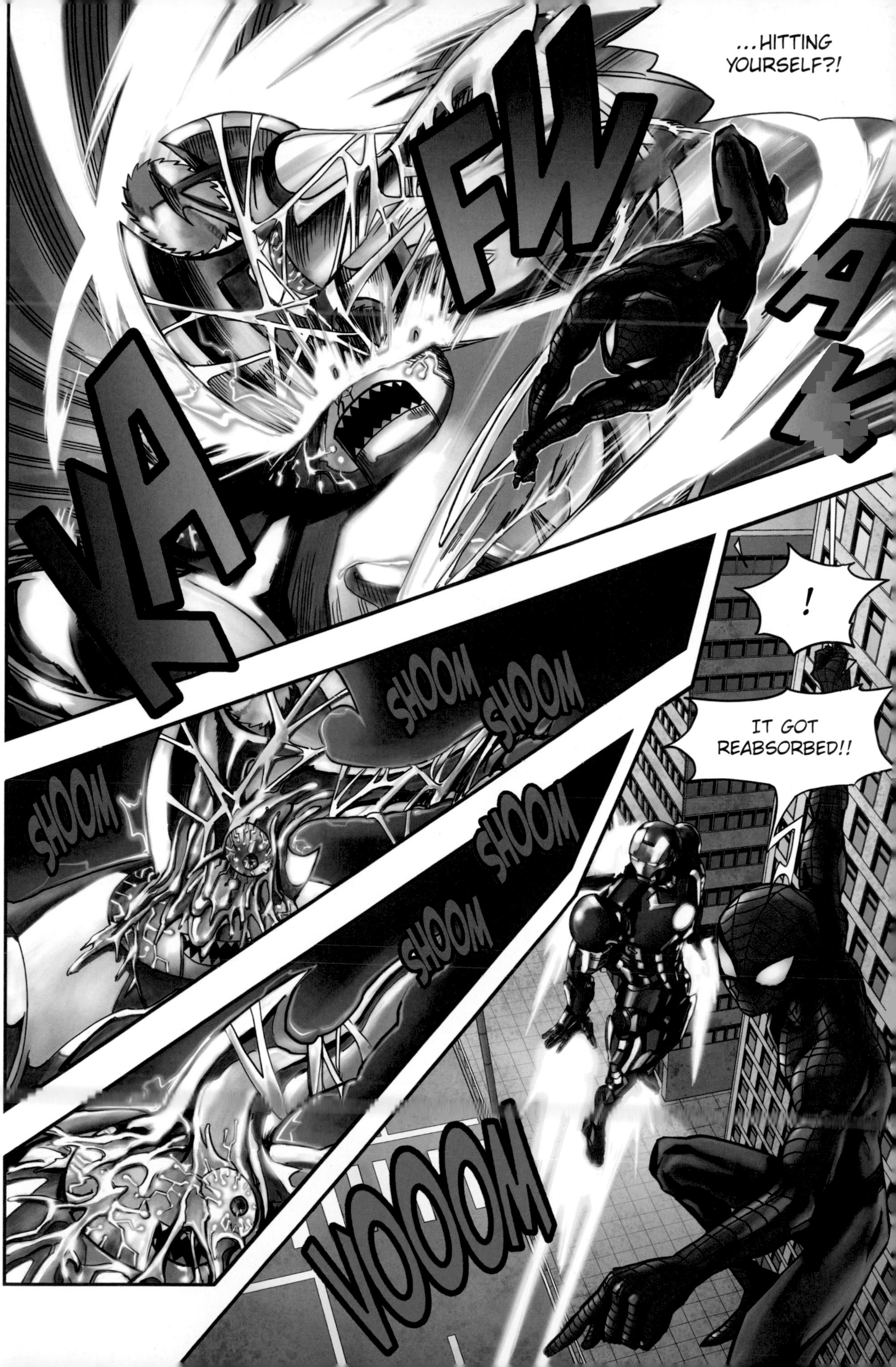
...HITTING YOURSELF?!
FW
A
KA
!
IT GOT REABSORBED!!
SHOOM
SHOOM
SHOOM
SHOOM
SHOOM
SHOOM
VOOOM

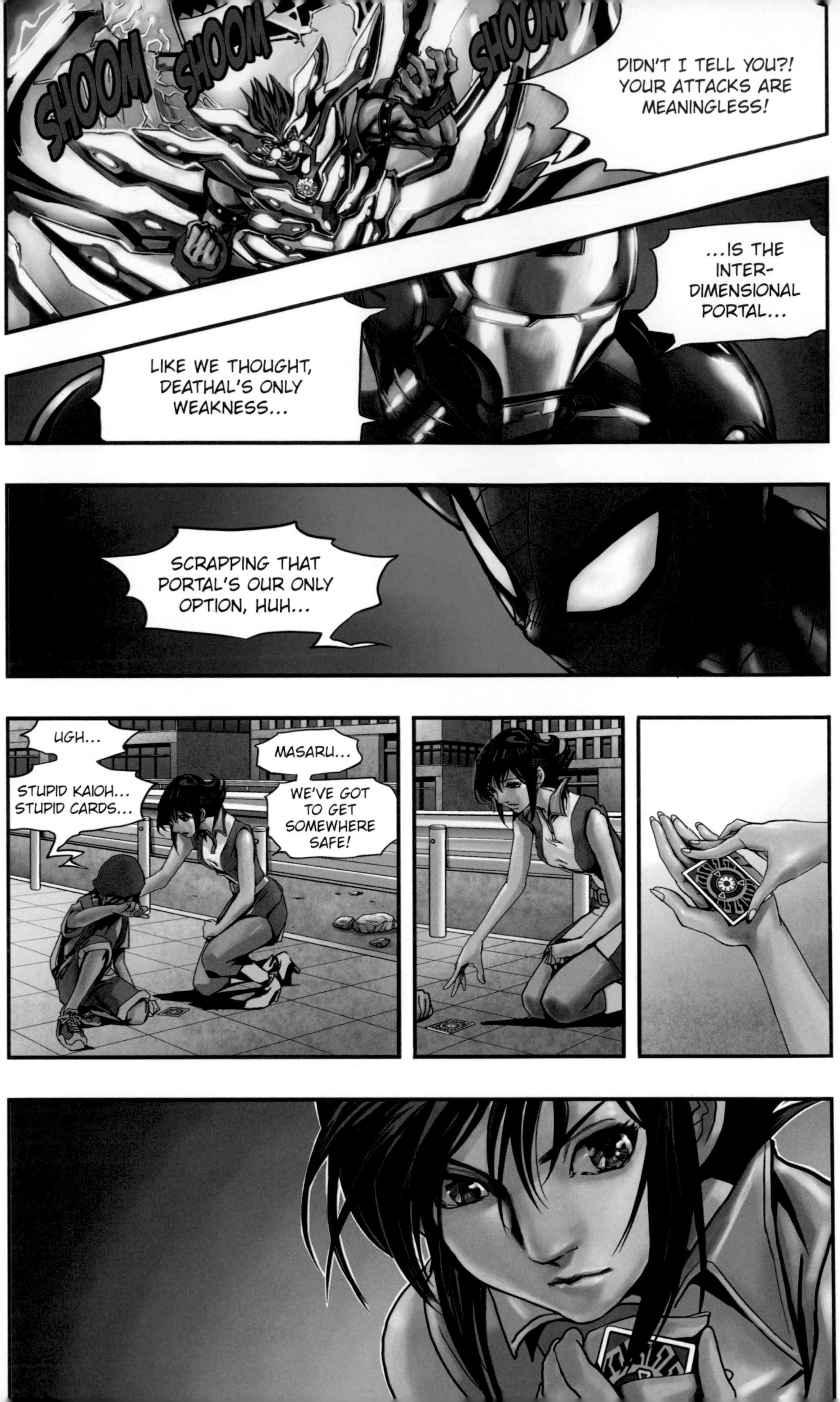
SHOOM SHOOM SHOOM
DIDN'T I TELL YOU?! YOUR ATTACKS ARE MEANINGLESS!
LIKE WE THOUGHT, DEATHAL'S ONLY WEAKNESS...
...IS THE INTER-DIMENSIONAL PORTAL...
SCRAPPING THAT PORTAL'S OUR ONLY OPTION, HUH...
UGH...
STUPID KAIOH... STUPID CARDS...
MASARU...
WE'VE GOT TO GET SOMEWHERE SAFE!

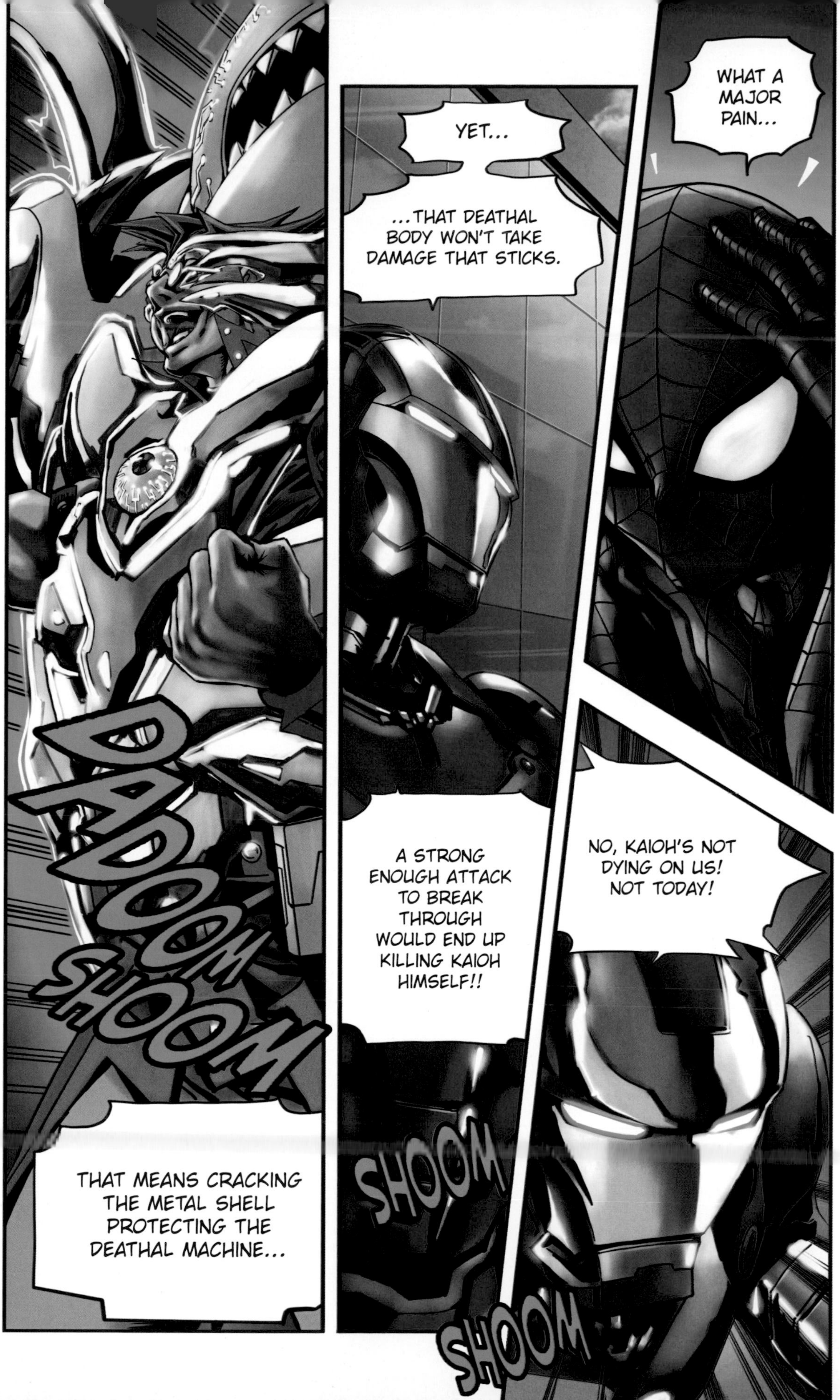
DADOOM
SHOOM
THAT MEANS CRACKING THE METAL SHELL PROTECTING THE DEATHAL MACHINE...
YET...
...THAT DEATHAL BODY WON'T TAKE DAMAGE THAT STICKS.
A STRONG ENOUGH ATTACK TO BREAK THROUGH WOULD END UP KILLING KAIOH HIMSELF!!
SHOOM
WHAT A MAJOR PAIN...
NO, KAIOH'S NOT DYING ON US! NOT TODAY!
SHOOM

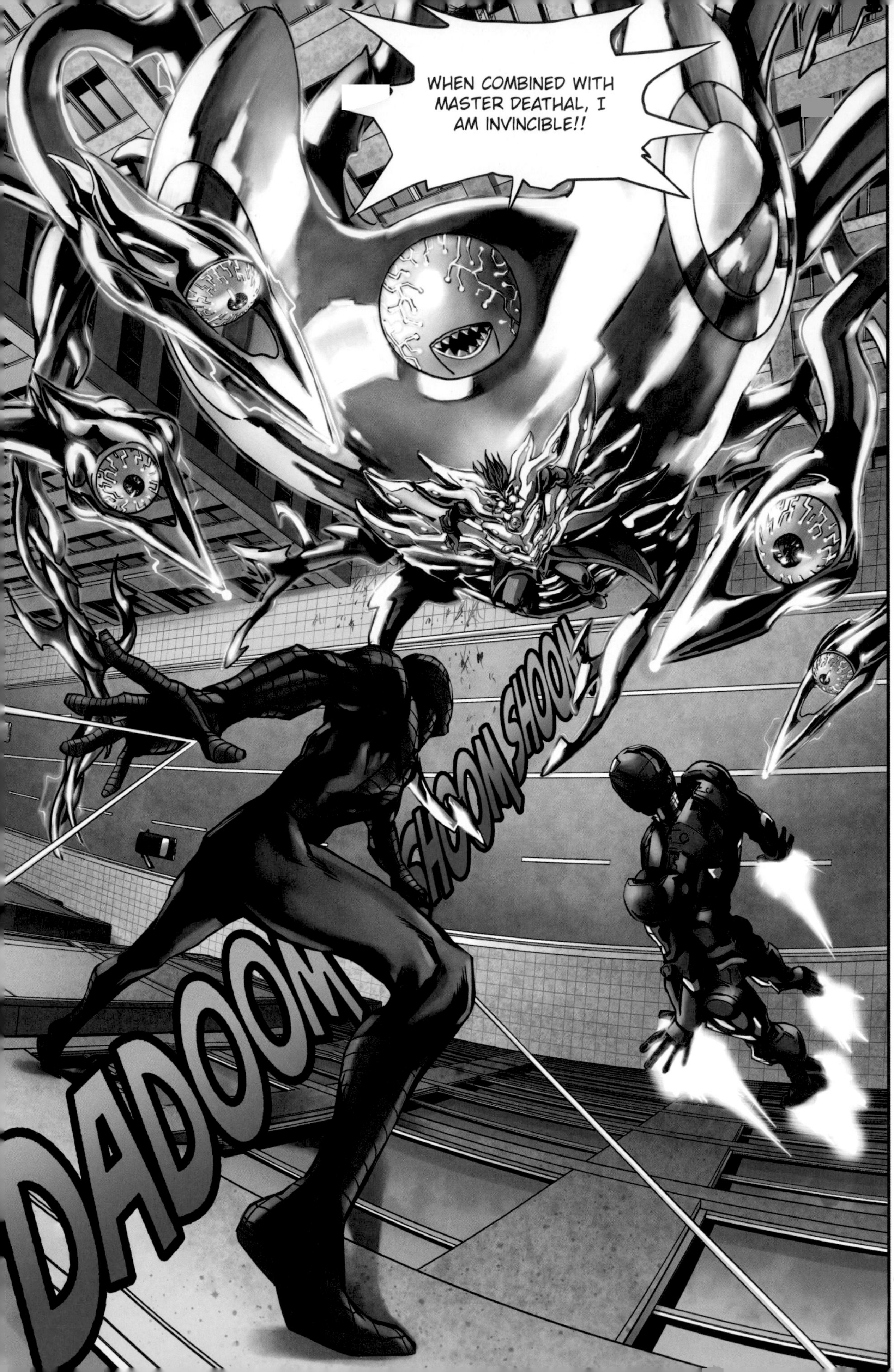
WHEN COMBINED WITH MASTER DEATHAL, I AM INVINCIBLE!!
SHOOM SHOOM SHOOM
DADOOM

HEH HEH HEH...

IRON MAN! SPIDER-MAN!

THIS WORLD IS MASTER DEATHAL'S TO INVADE! IMAGINE—A PLANET COATED IN METAL!!

HRM...

THE PEOPLE... THE LAND ITSELF... ALL TAKEN OVER BY THE MACHINE LIFE-FORMS!!

LIKE I SAID, MAJOR PAIN...

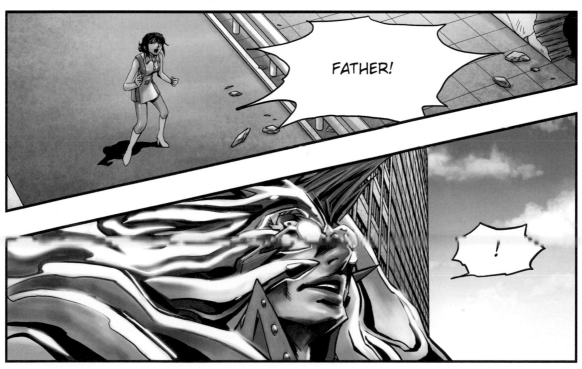

FATHER!

!

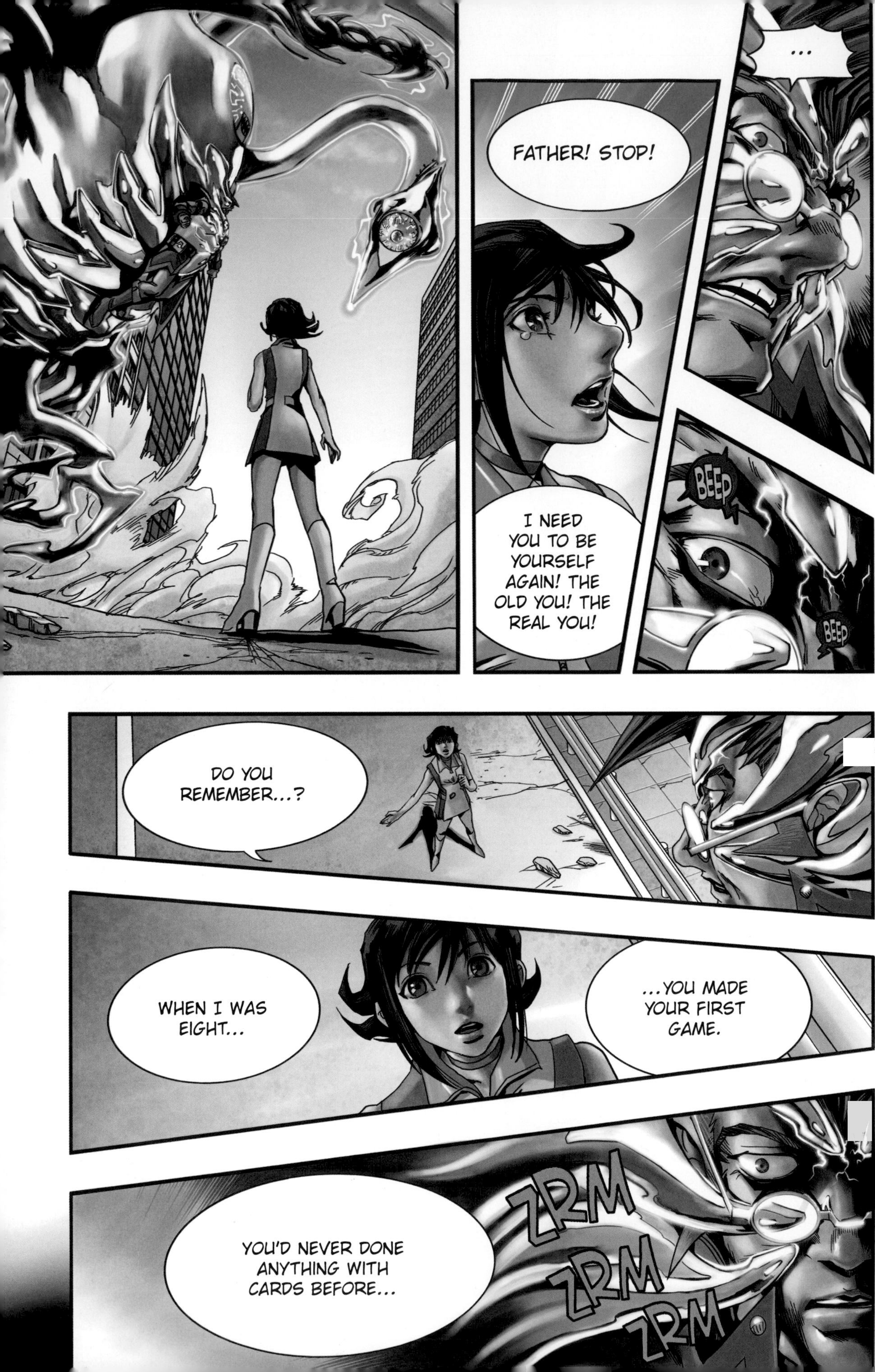
FATHER! STOP!
I NEED YOU TO BE YOURSELF AGAIN! THE OLD YOU! THE REAL YOU!
...
BEEP
BEEP
DO YOU REMEMBER...?
WHEN I WAS EIGHT...
...YOU MADE YOUR FIRST GAME.
YOU'D NEVER DONE ANYTHING WITH CARDS BEFORE...
ZRM
ZRM
ZRM

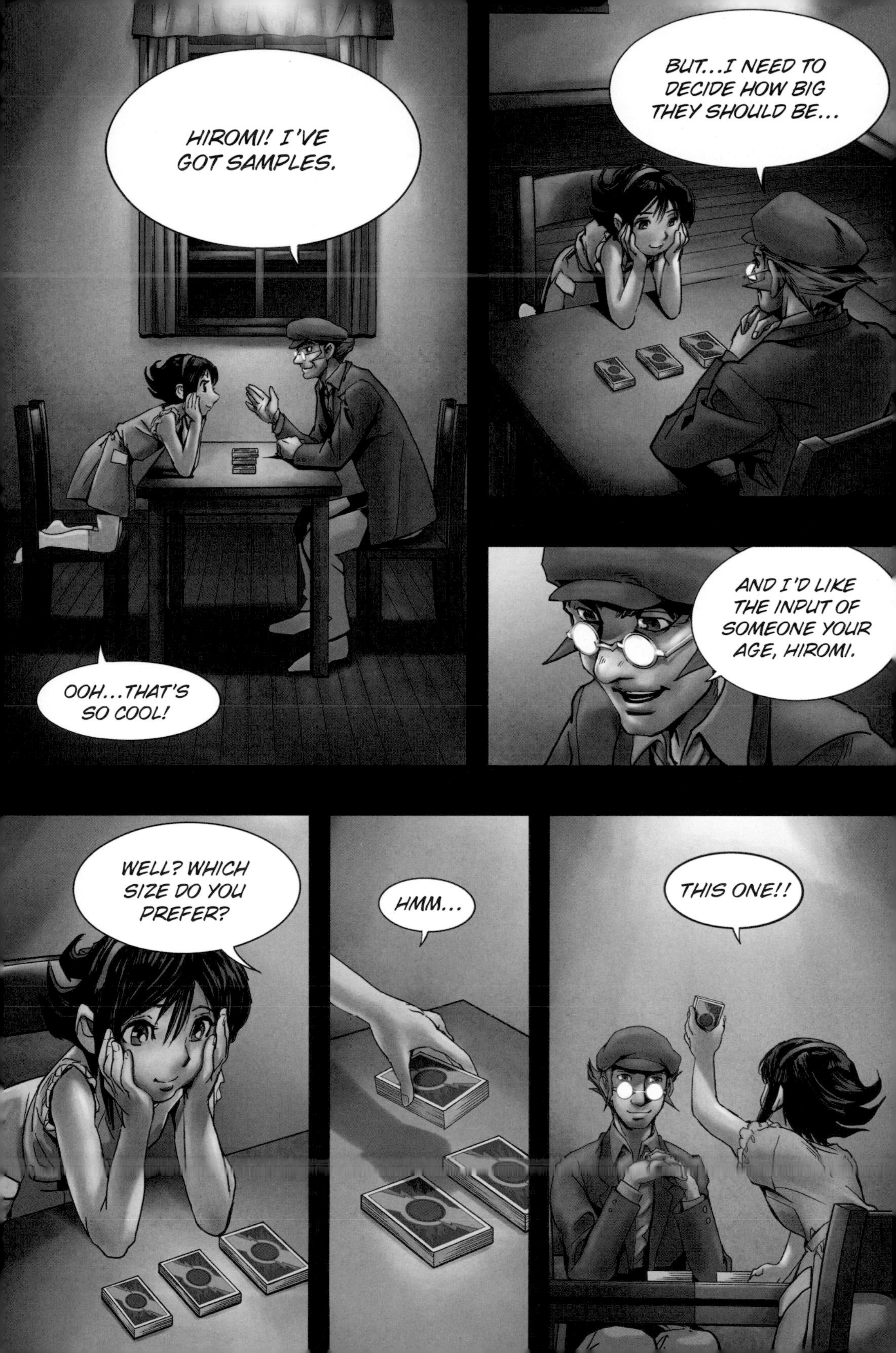
HIROMI! I'VE GOT SAMPLES.
OOH...THAT'S SO COOL!
BUT...I NEED TO DECIDE HOW BIG THEY SHOULD BE...
AND I'D LIKE THE INPUT OF SOMEONE YOUR AGE, HIROMI.
WELL? WHICH SIZE DO YOU PREFER?
HMM...
THIS ONE!!

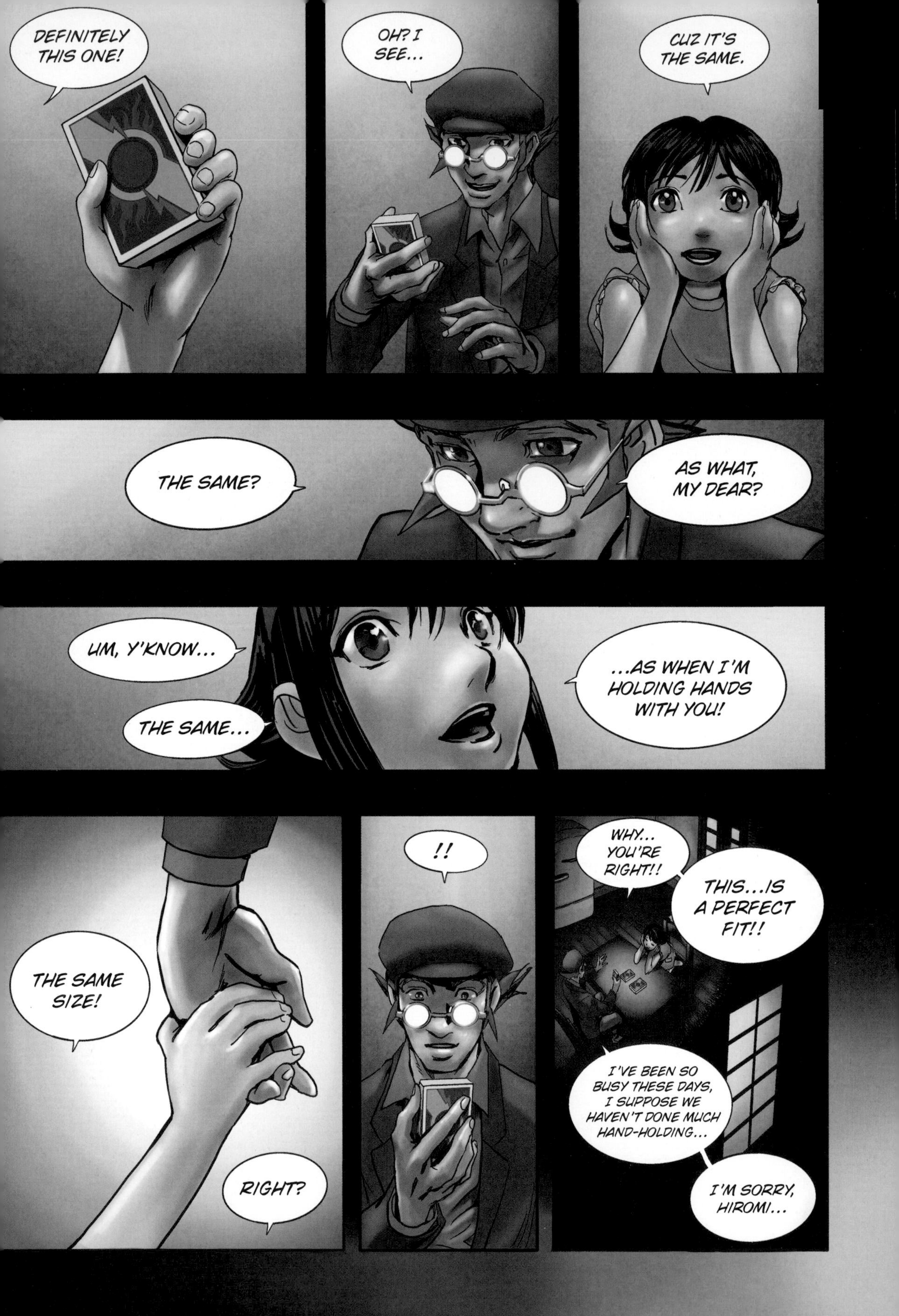
DEFINITELY THIS ONE!
OH? I SEE...
CUZ IT'S THE SAME.
THE SAME?
AS WHAT, MY DEAR?
UM, Y'KNOW...
THE SAME...
...AS WHEN I'M HOLDING HANDS WITH YOU!
THE SAME SIZE!
RIGHT?
!!
WHY... YOU'RE RIGHT!!
THIS...IS A PERFECT FIT!!
I'VE BEEN SO BUSY THESE DAYS, I SUPPOSE WE HAVEN'T DONE MUCH HAND-HOLDING...
I'M SORRY, HIROMI...

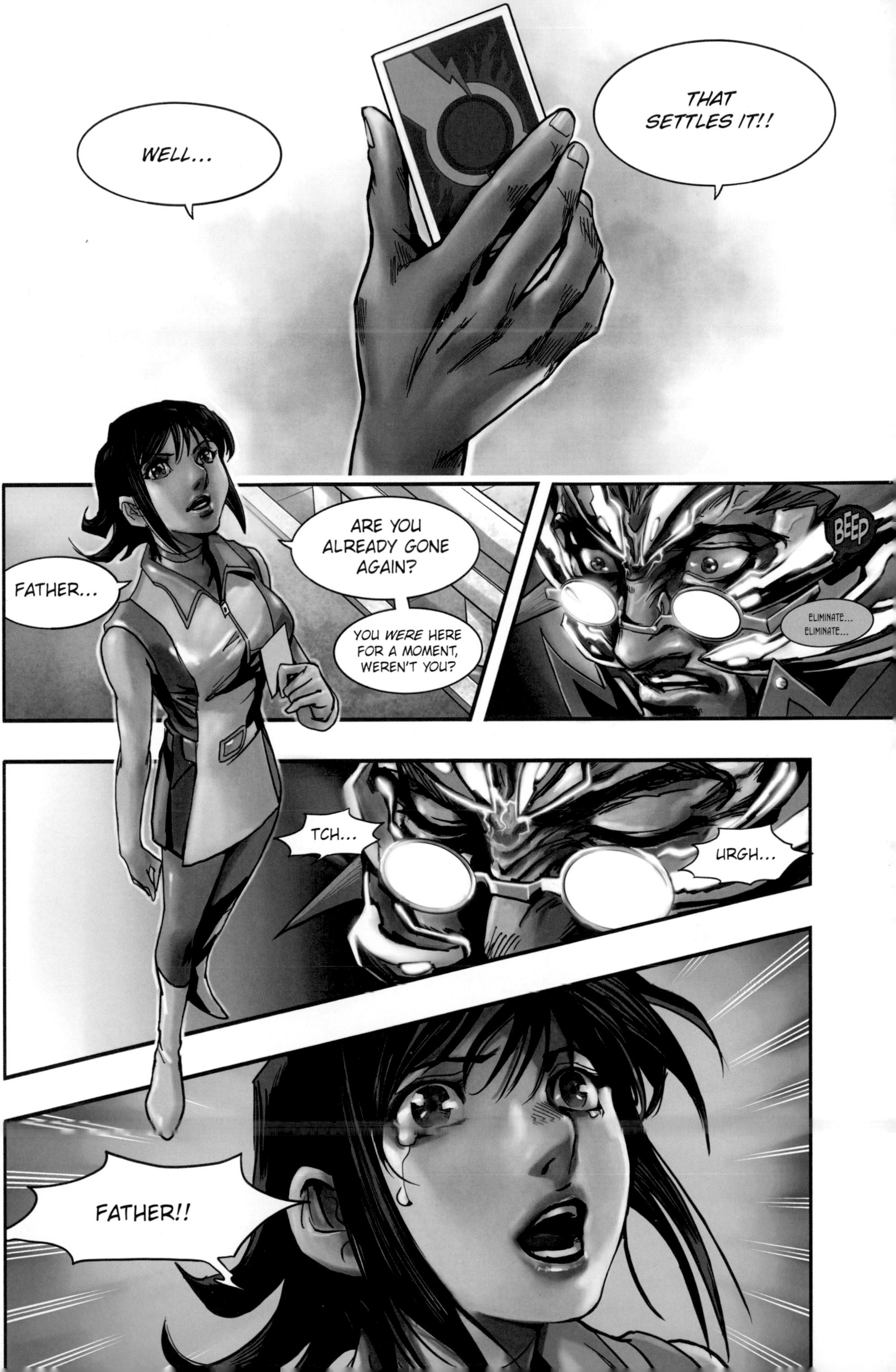
WELL...
THAT SETTLES IT!!
FATHER...
ARE YOU ALREADY GONE AGAIN?
YOU *WERE* HERE FOR A MOMENT, WEREN'T YOU?
BEEP
ELIMINATE... ELIMINATE...
TCH...
URGH...
FATHER!!

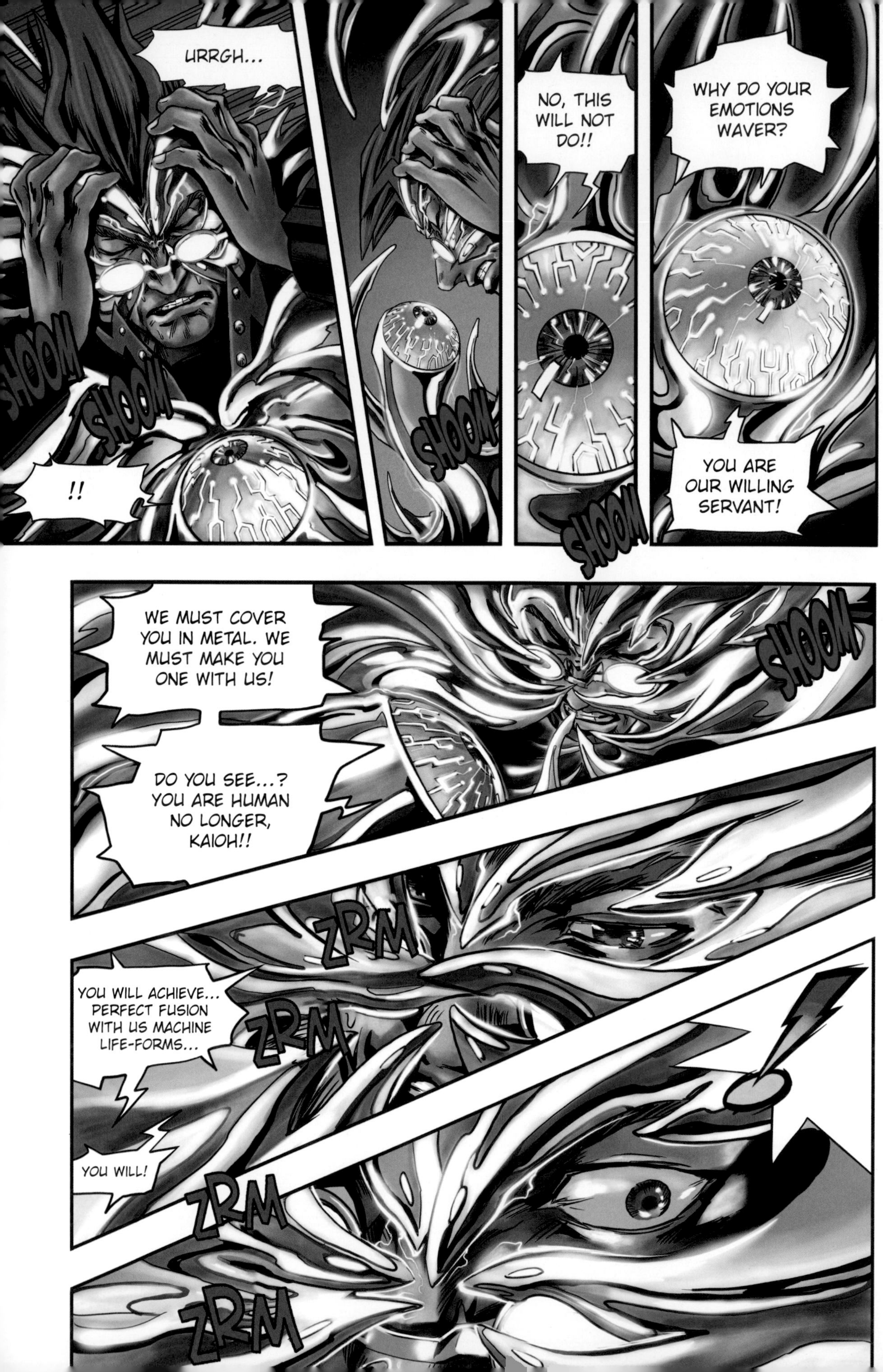
URRGH...
!!
SHOOM
SHOOM
SHOOM
NO, THIS WILL NOT DO!!
WHY DO YOUR EMOTIONS WAVER?
YOU ARE OUR WILLING SERVANT!
SHOOM
WE MUST COVER YOU IN METAL. WE MUST MAKE YOU ONE WITH US!
SHOOM
DO YOU SEE...? YOU ARE HUMAN NO LONGER, KAIOH!!
ZRM
YOU WILL ACHIEVE... PERFECT FUSION WITH US MACHINE LIFE-FORMS...
ZRM
YOU WILL!
ZRM
ZRM

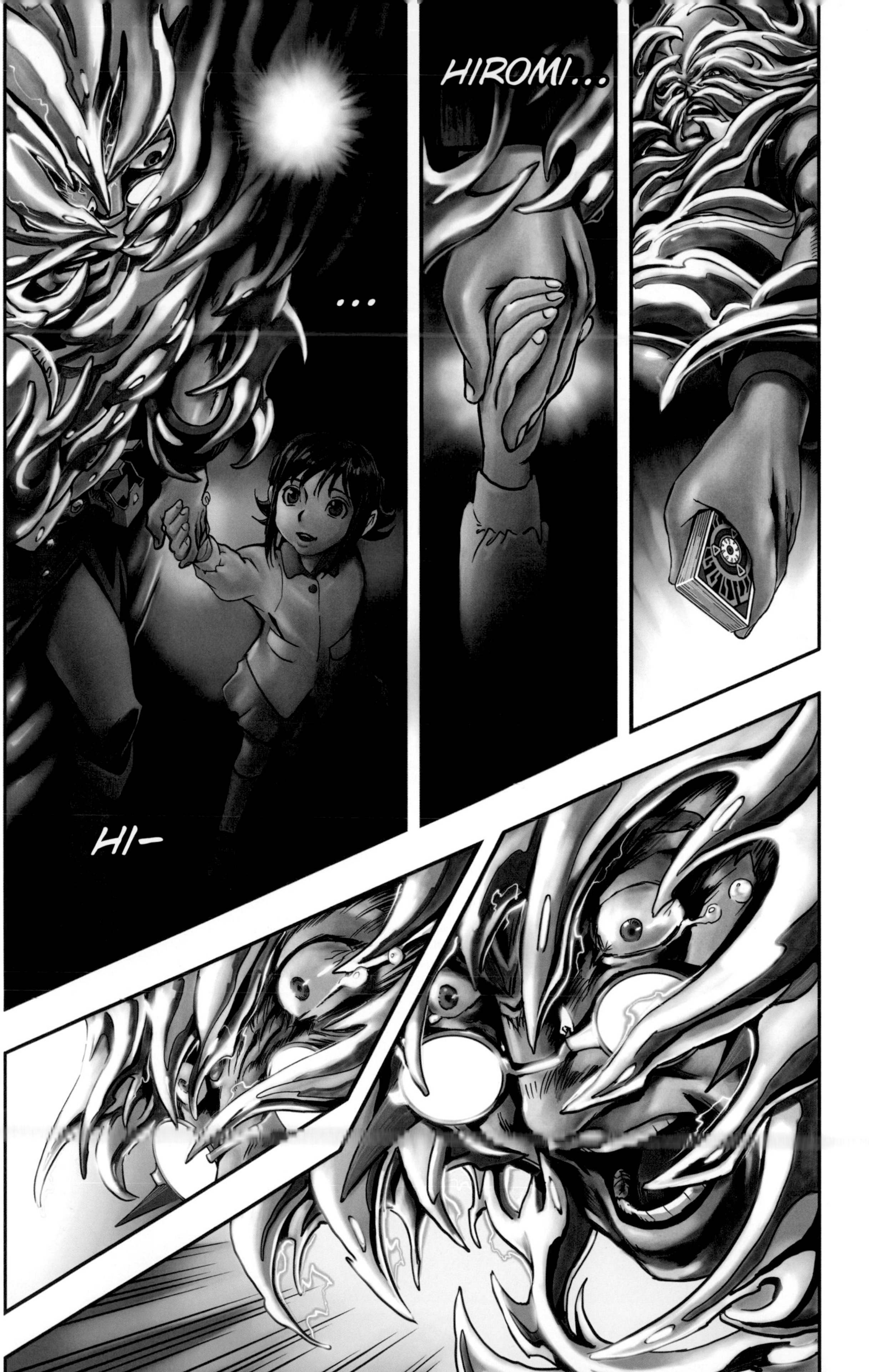
HIROMI...
...
HI-

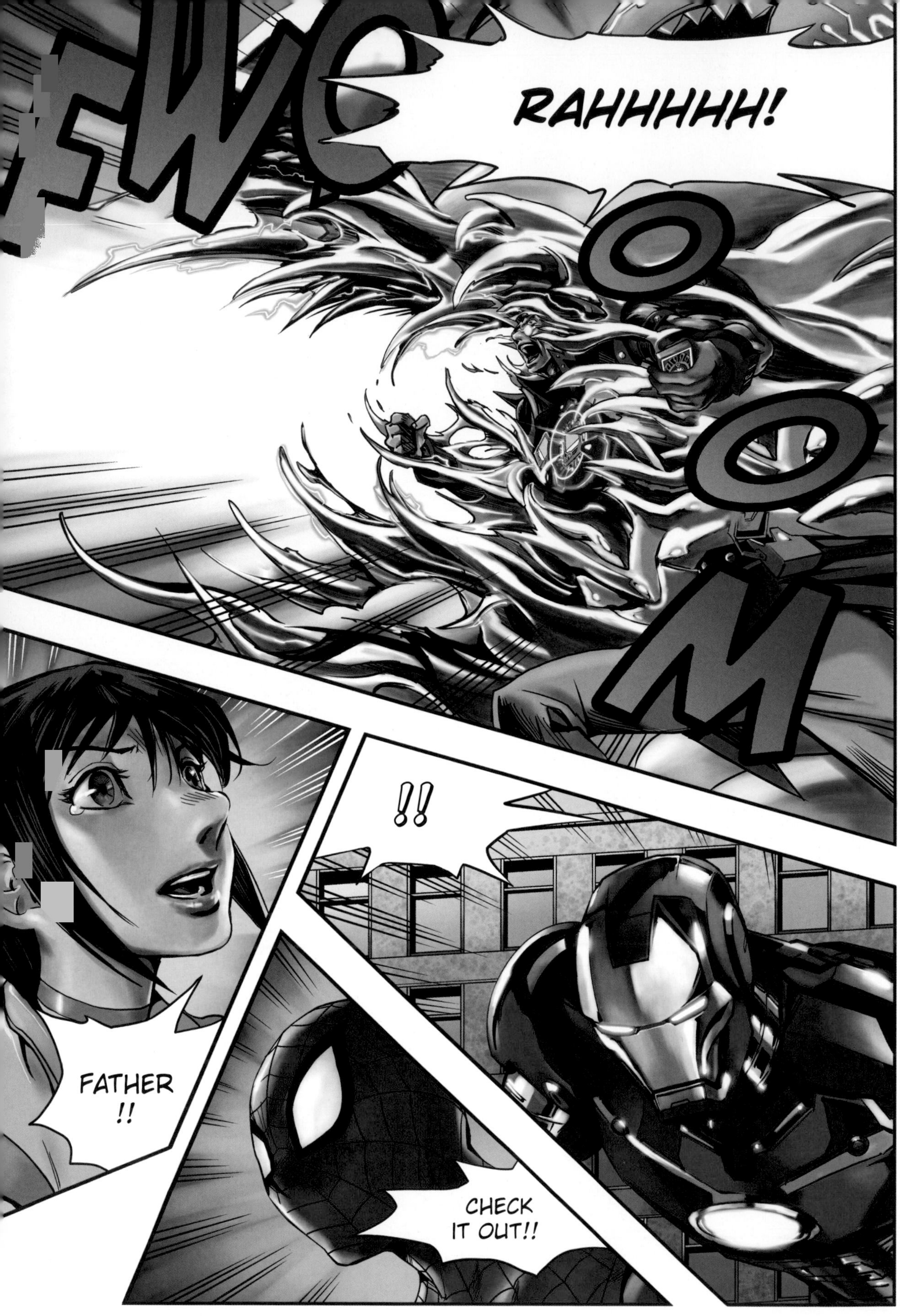
RAHHHHH!
!!
CHECK IT OUT!!
FATHER !!

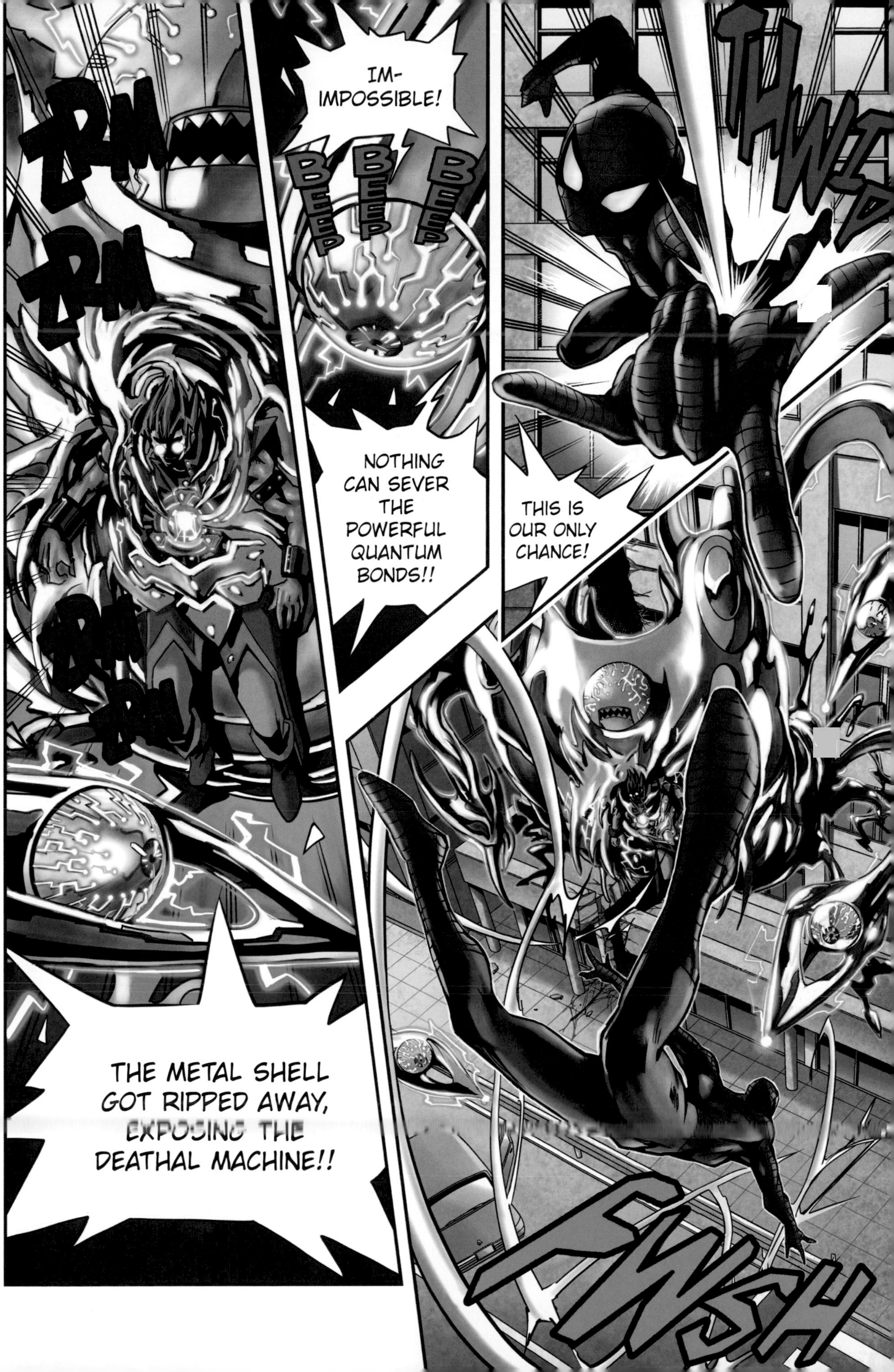
THWIP
THIS IS OUR ONLY CHANCE!
IM- IMPOSSIBLE!
BEEP BEEP BEEP
NOTHING CAN SEVER THE POWERFUL QUANTUM BONDS!!
ZRM ZRM
ZRM ZRM
ZRM ZRM
THE METAL SHELL GOT RIPPED AWAY, EXPOSING THE DEATHAL MACHINE!!
FWSH

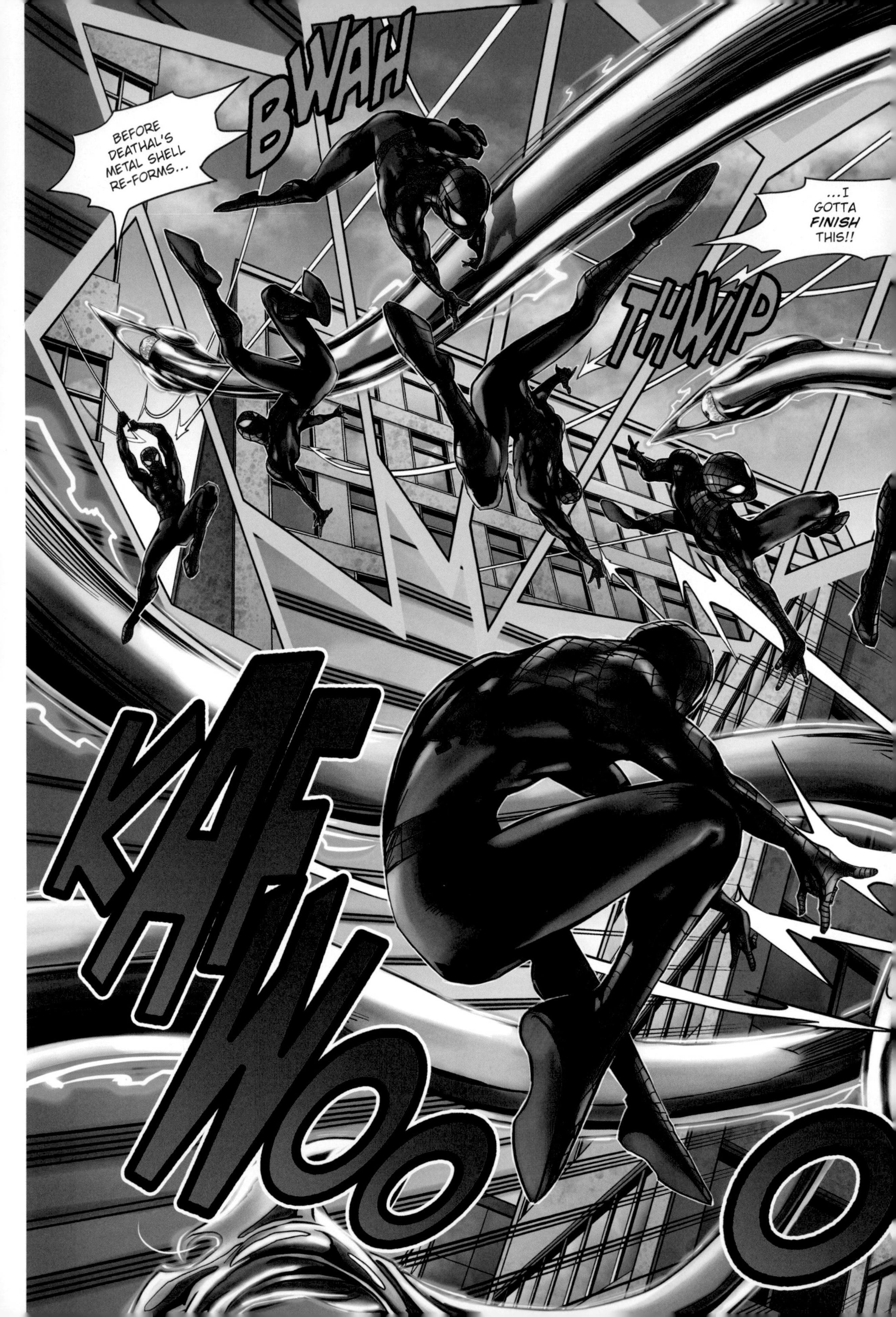
...I GOTTA FINISH THIS!!
BWAH
BEFORE DEATHAL'S METAL SHELL RE-FORMS...
THWIP
KAHWOOOO

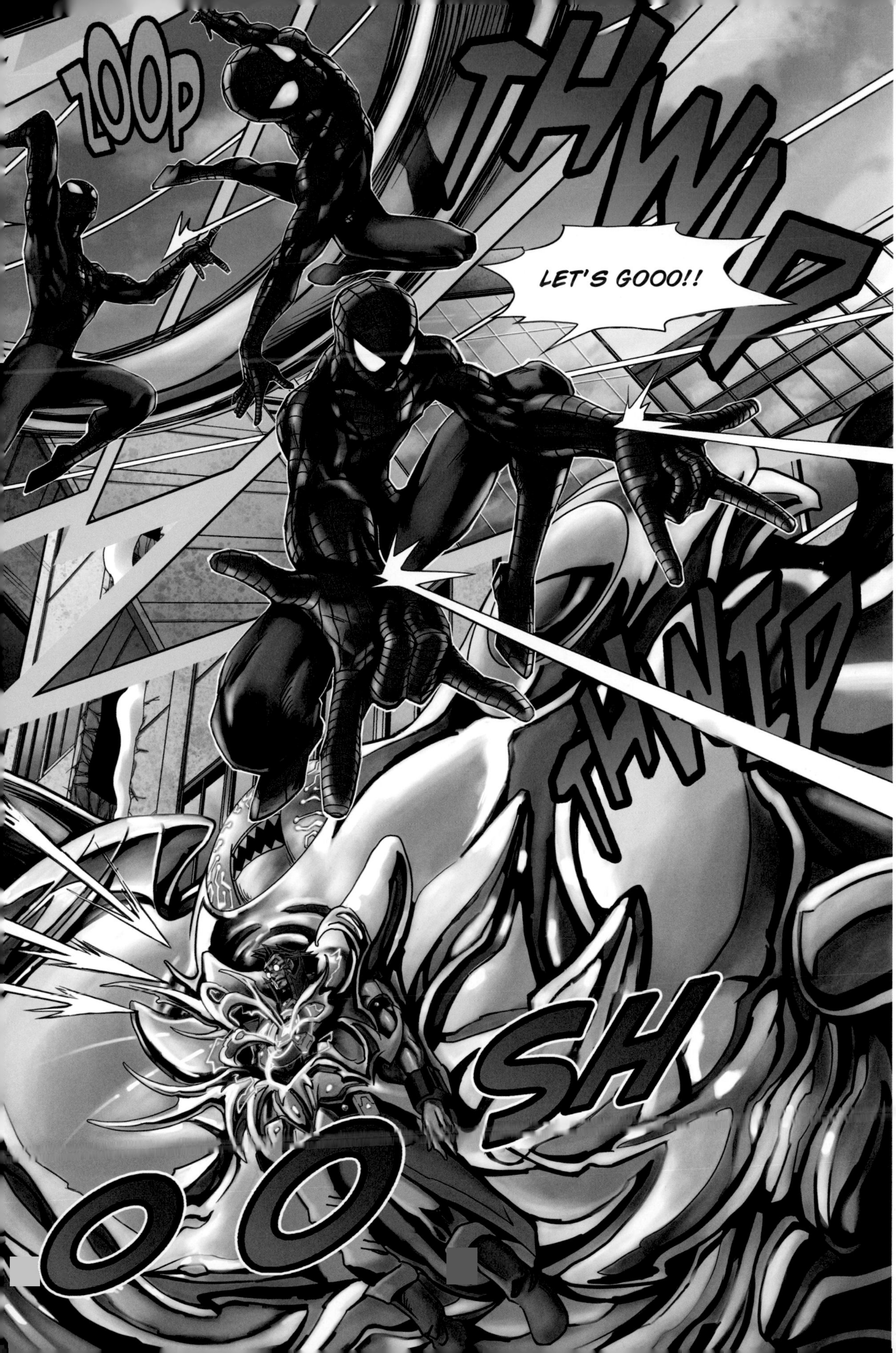
THWIP
ZOOP
LET'S GOOO!!
THWIP
SH
OO

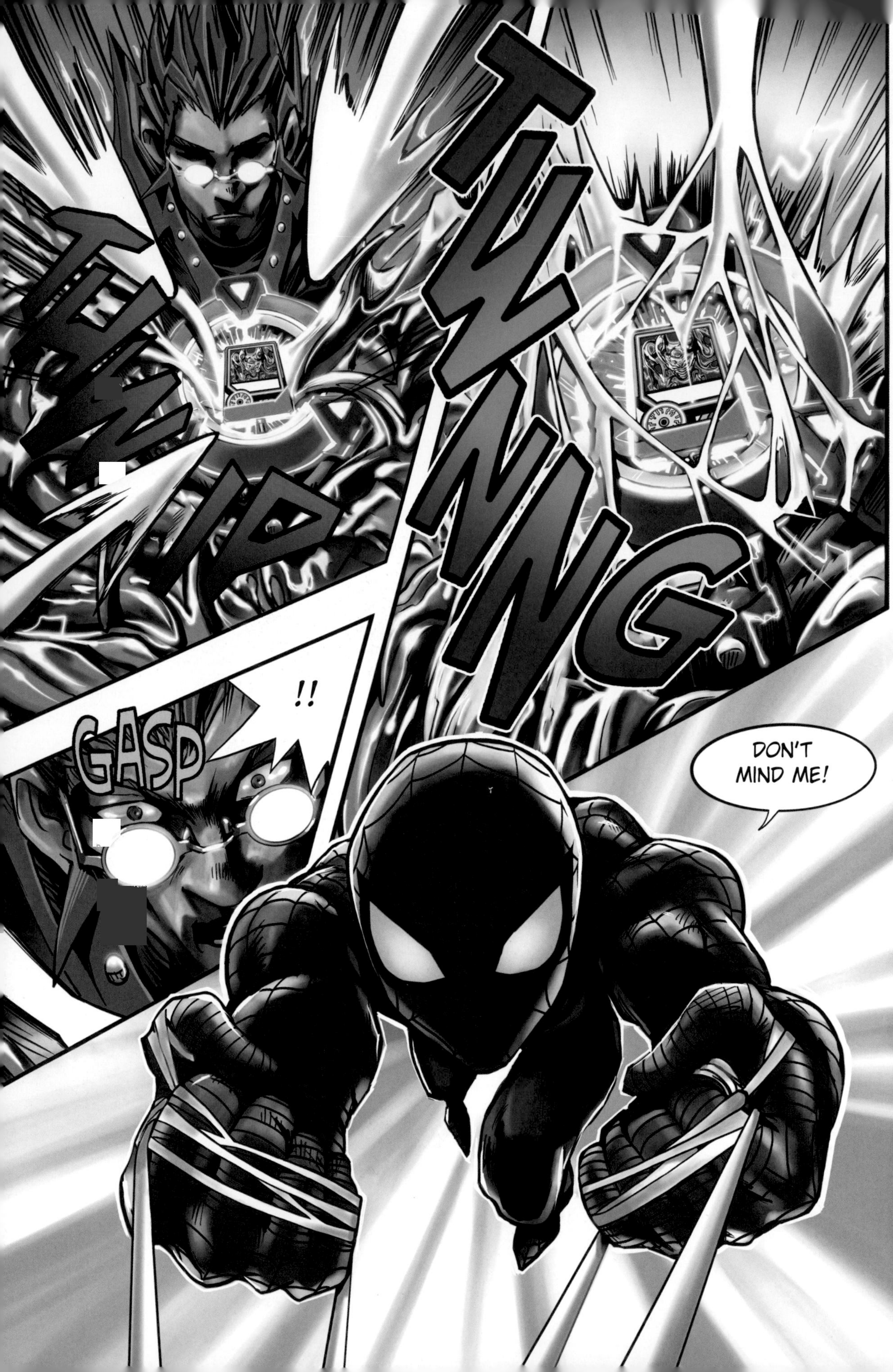
TWNNG
THWIP
DON'T MIND ME!
GASP
!!

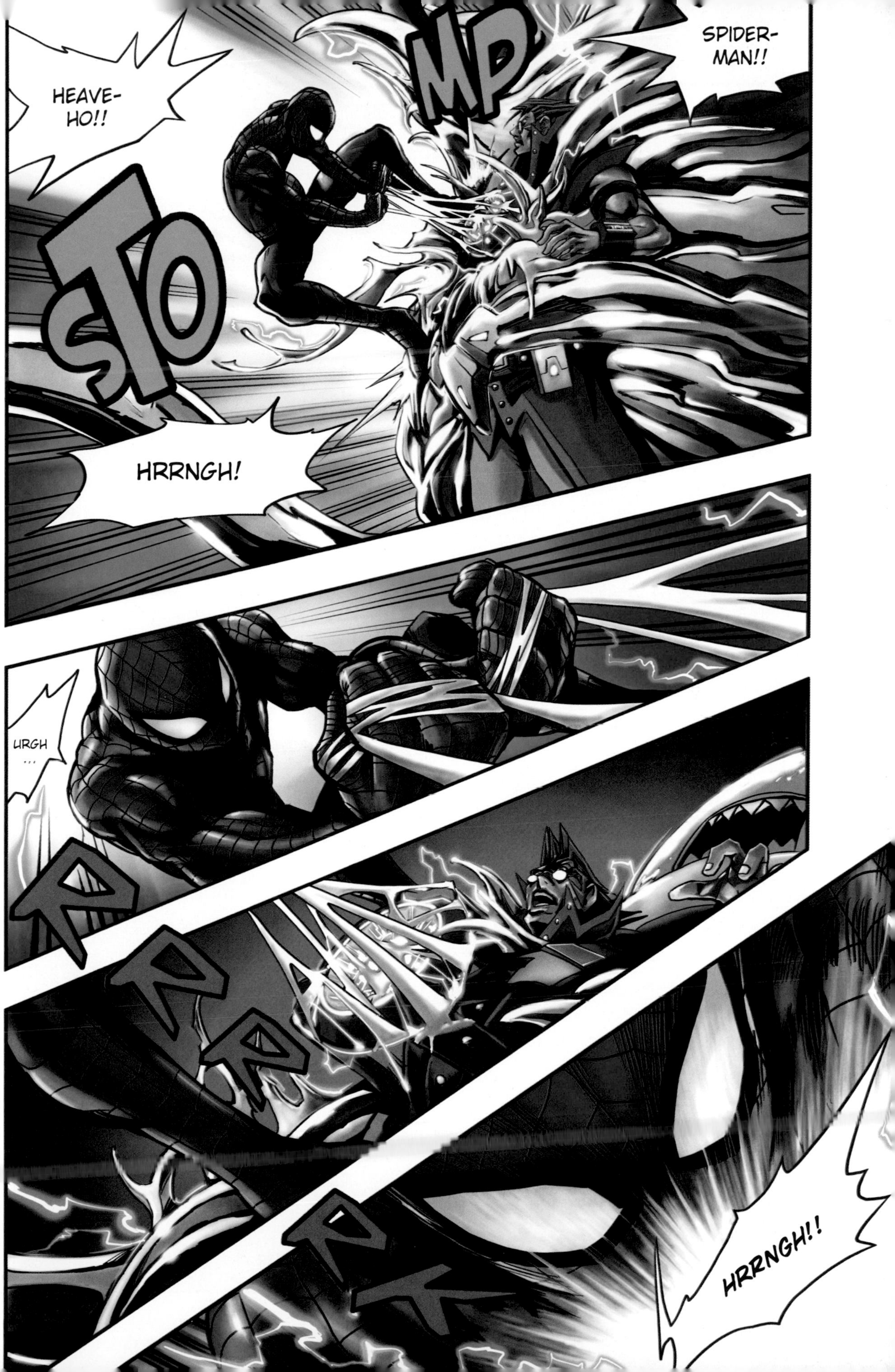
SPIDER-MAN!!
HEAVE-HO!!
STOMP
HRRNGH!
URGH...
RRRRK
HRRNGH!!

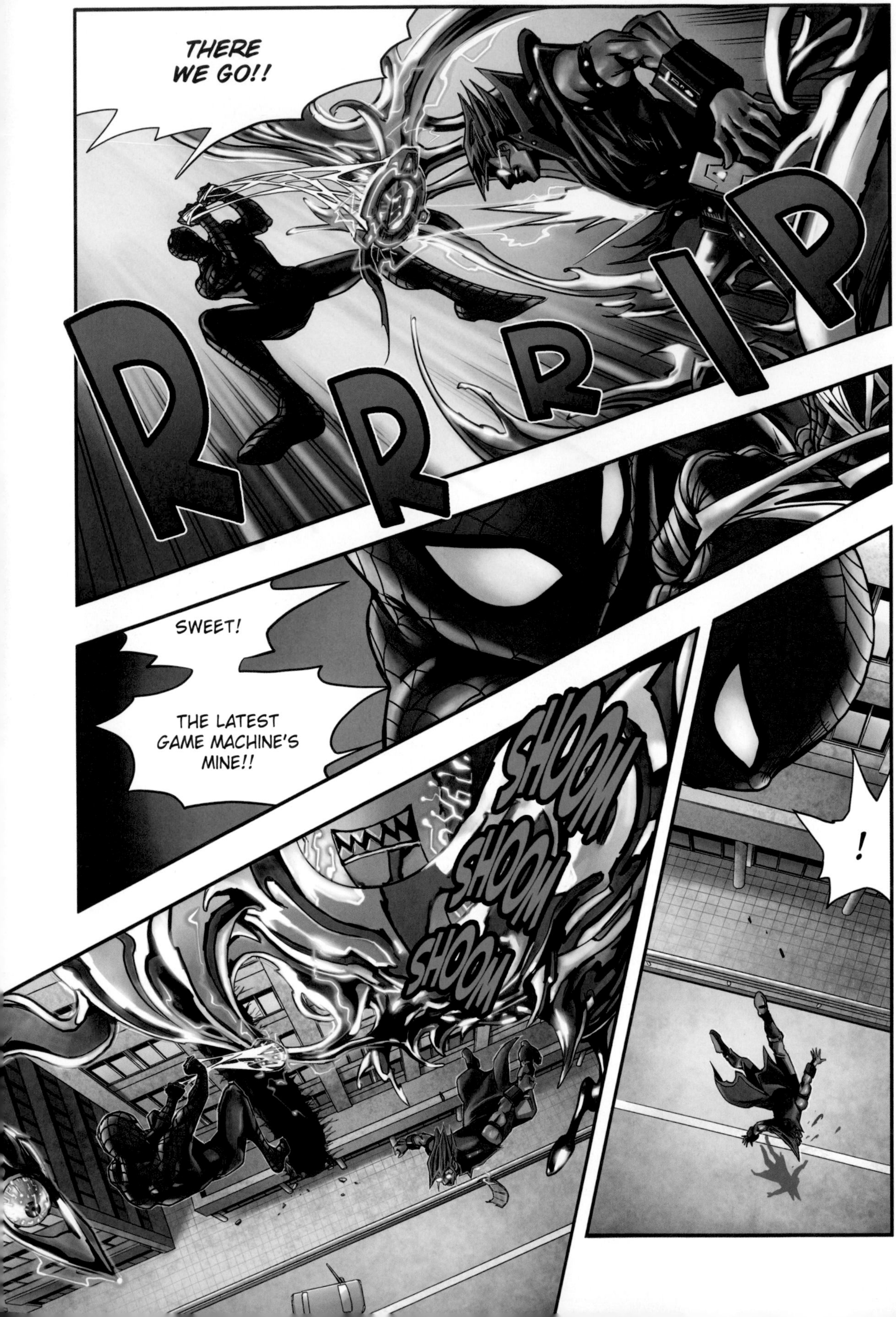
THERE WE GO!!
RRRIP
SWEET!
THE LATEST GAME MACHINE'S MINE!!
!
SHOOM SHOOM SHOOM SHOOM

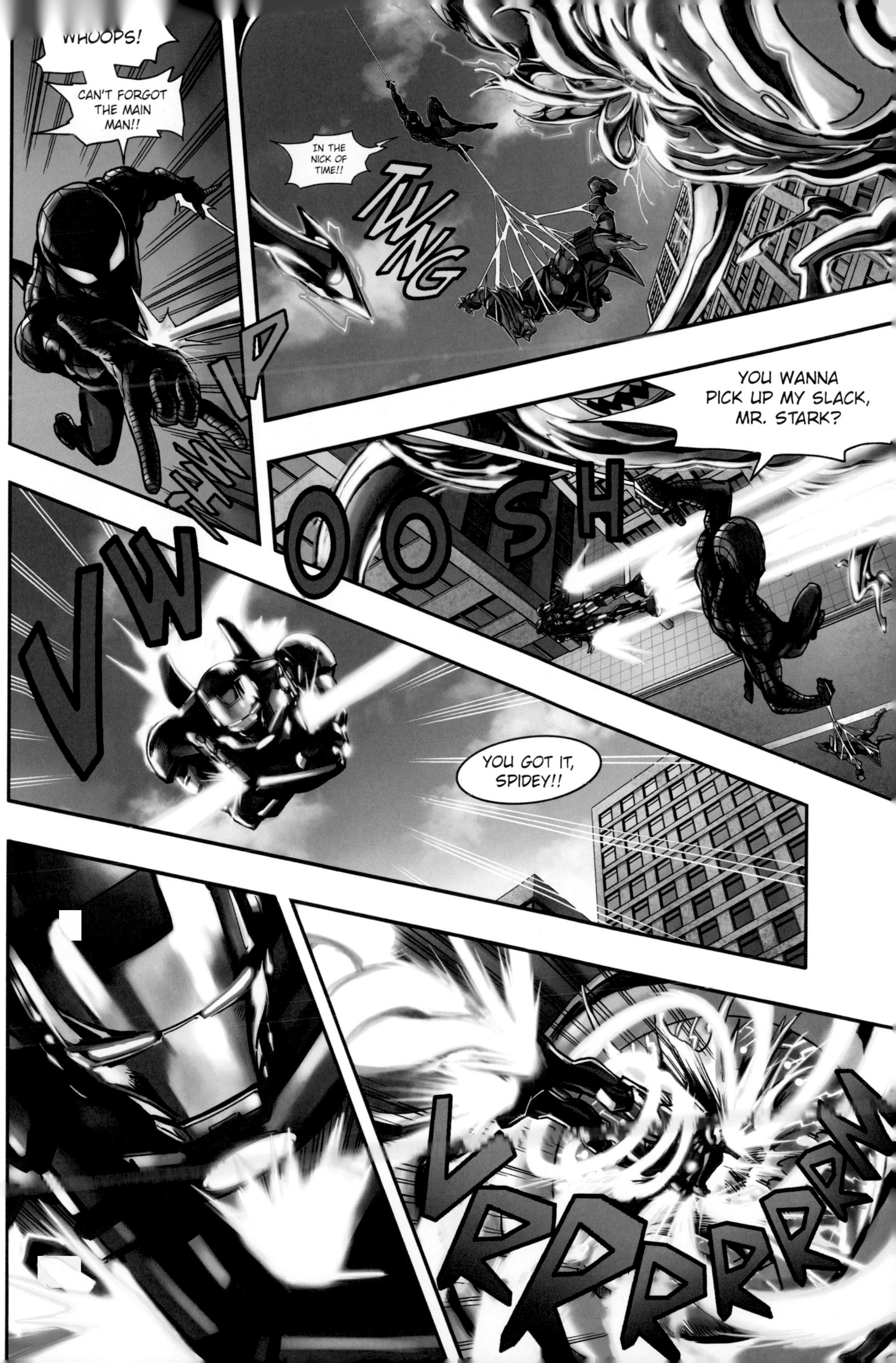
WHOOPS!
CAN'T FORGOT THE MAIN MAN!!
THWIP
IN THE NICK OF TIME!!
TWNG
YOU WANNA PICK UP MY SLACK, MR. STARK?
VWOOSH
YOU GOT IT, SPIDEY!!
VRRRRRRM

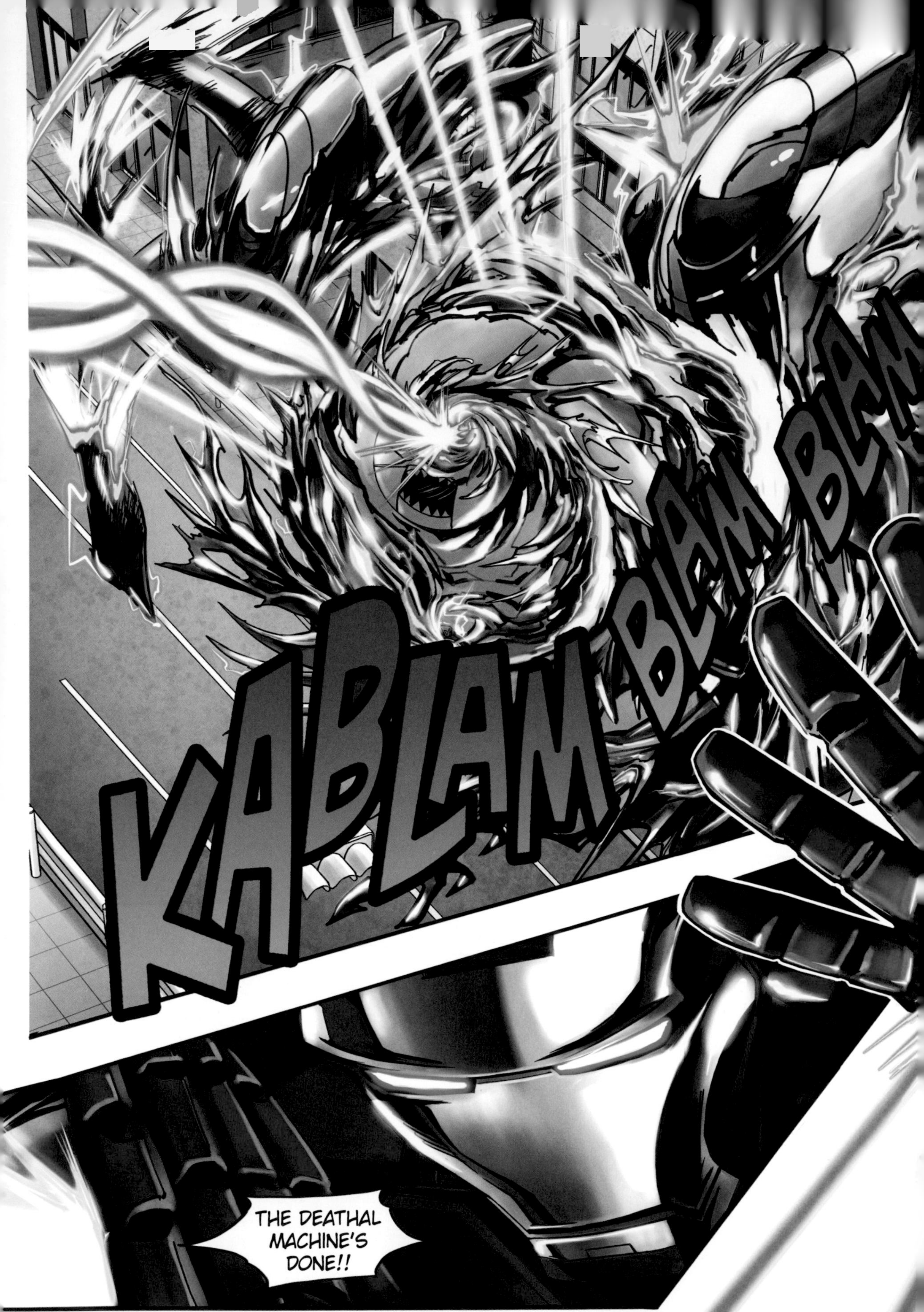
BLAM BLAM BLAM
KABLAM
THE DEATHAL MACHINE'S DONE!!

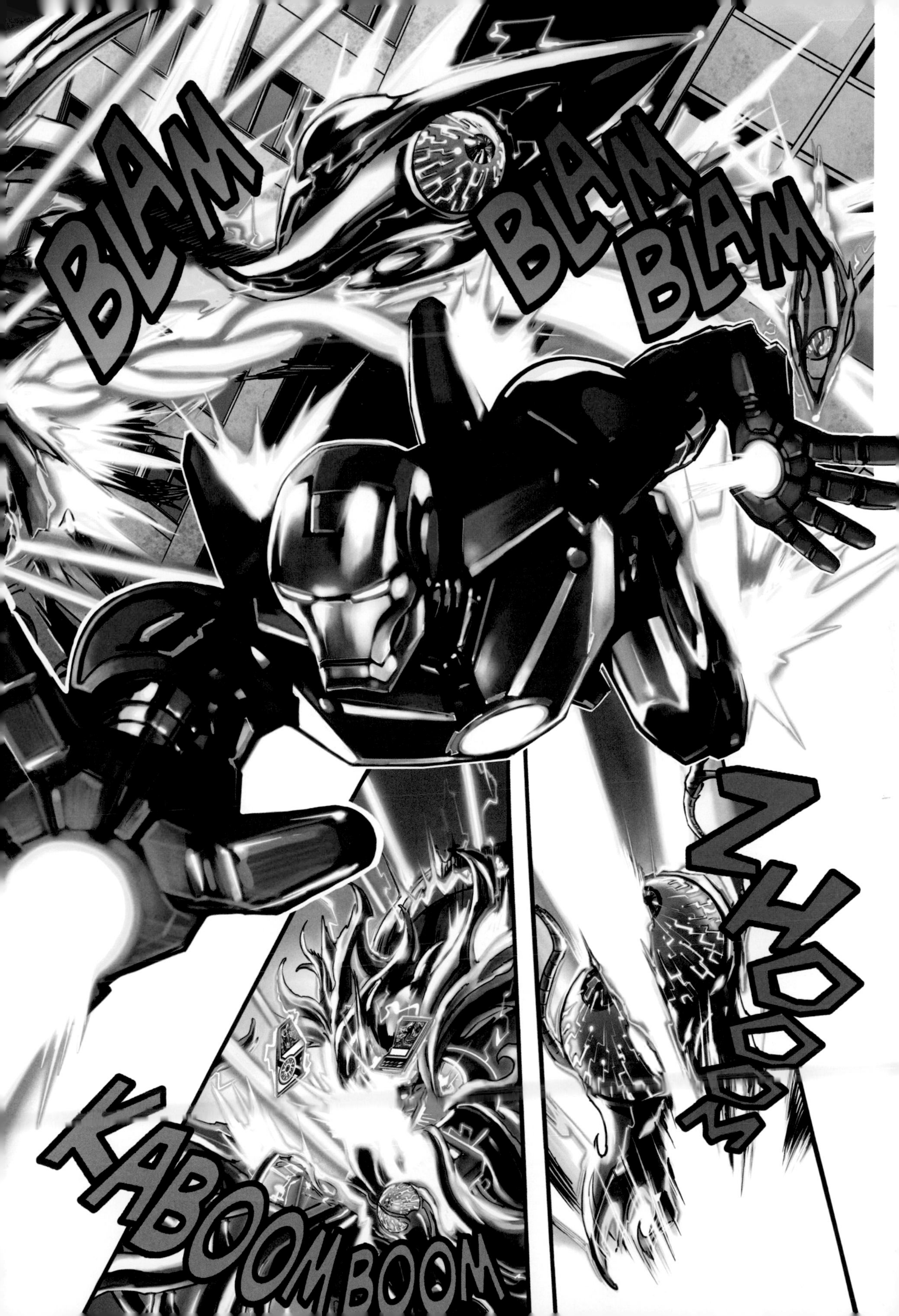

BLAM
BLAM
BLAM
ZHOOOOM
KABOOM BOOM

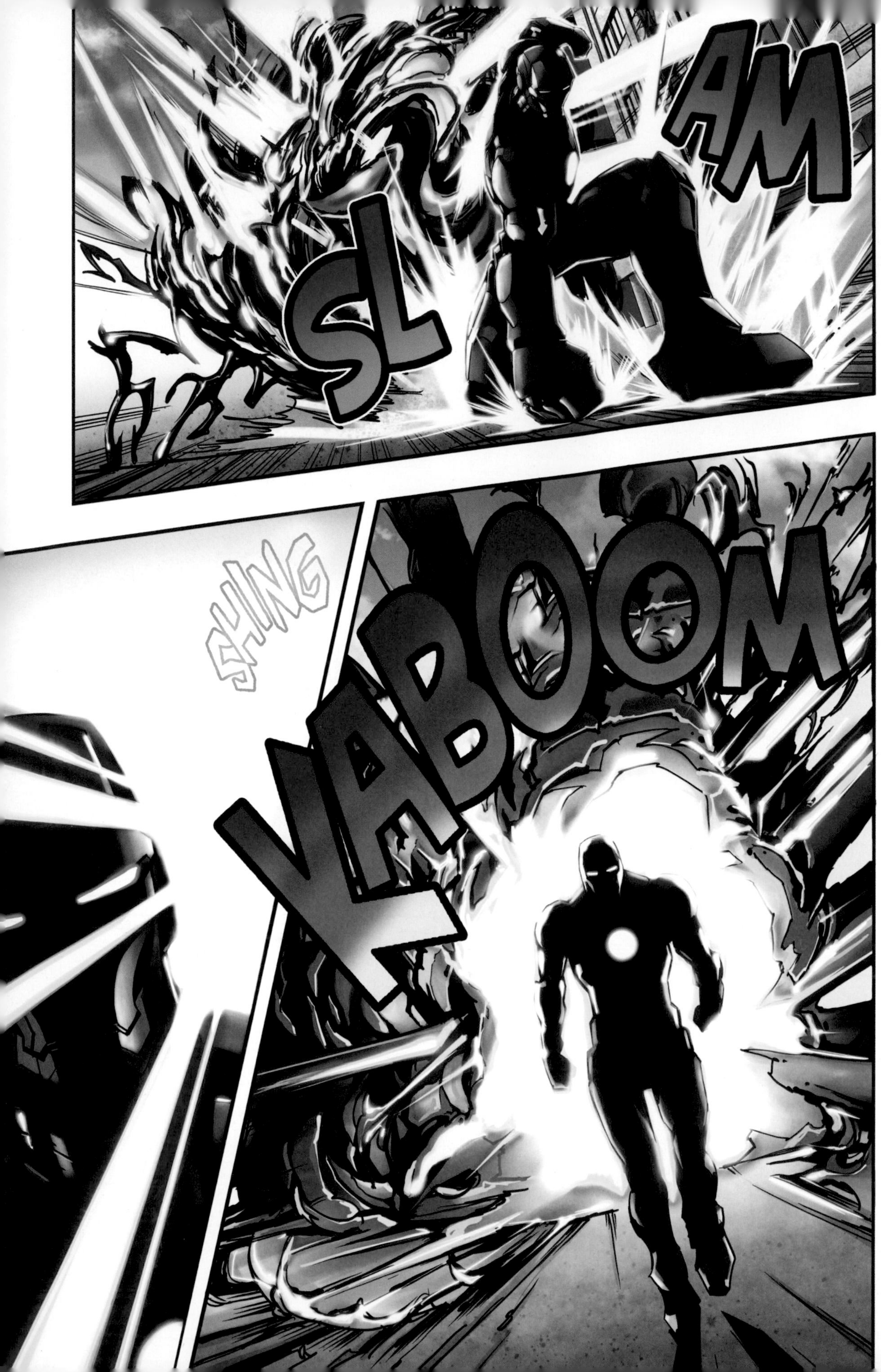
SLAM
KABOOM
SHING

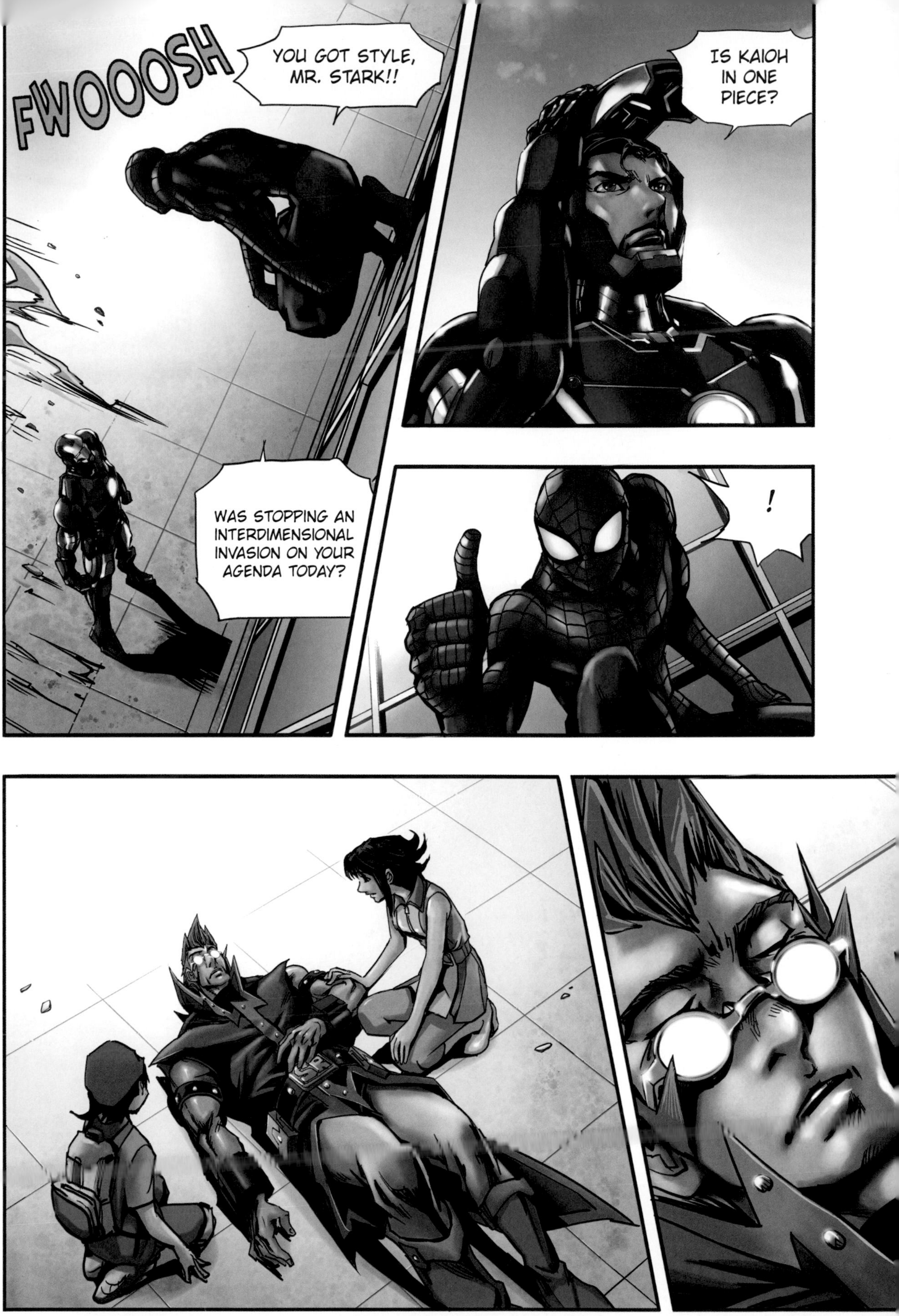
FWOOOSH
YOU GOT STYLE, MR. STARK!!
WAS STOPPING AN INTERDIMENSIONAL INVASION ON YOUR AGENDA TODAY?
IS KAIOH IN ONE PIECE?
!

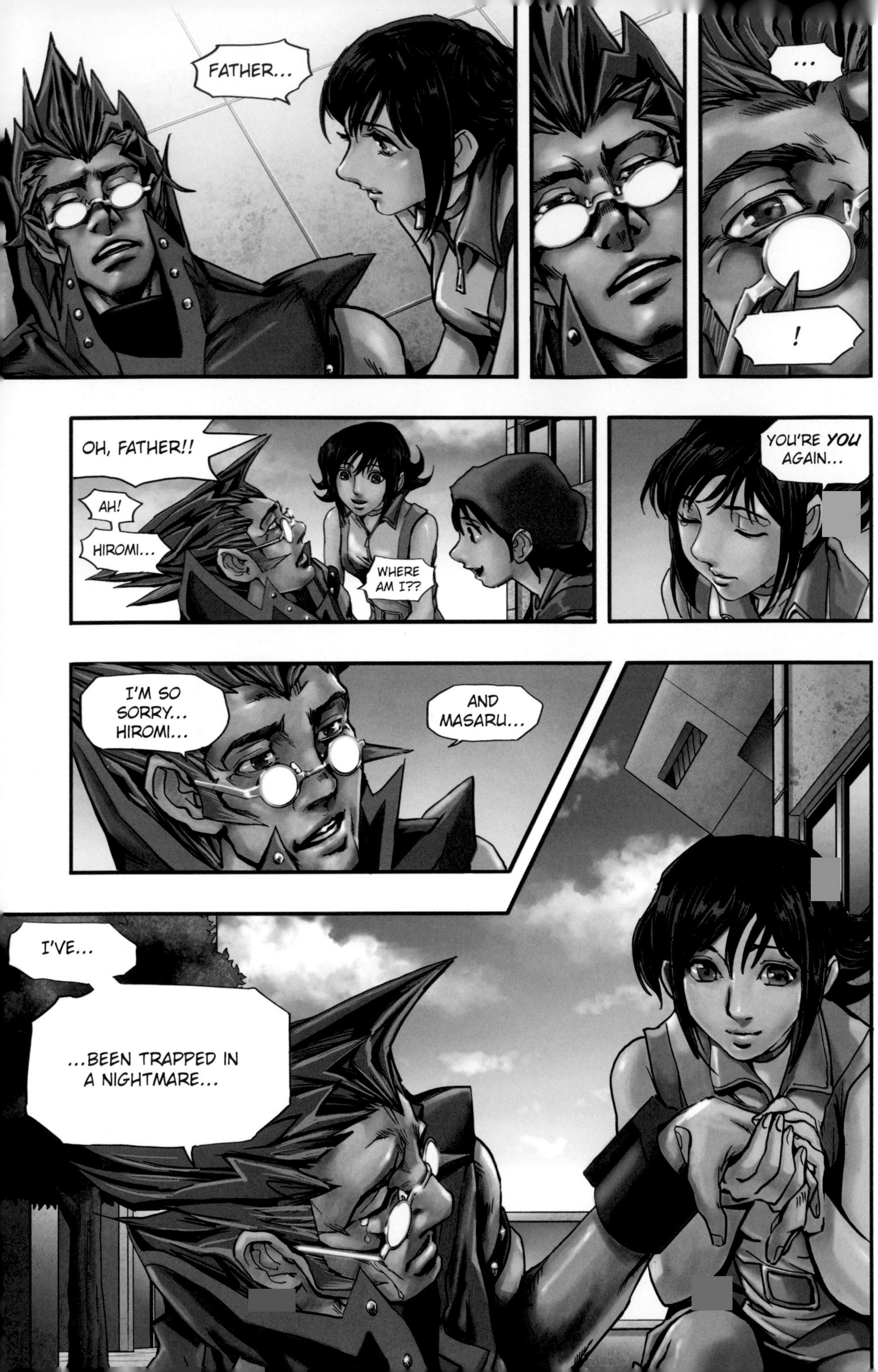
FATHER...
...
!
OH, FATHER!!
AH!
HIROMI...
WHERE AM I??
YOU'RE *YOU* AGAIN...
I'M SO SORRY... HIROMI...
AND MASARU...
I'VE...
...BEEN TRAPPED IN A NIGHTMARE...

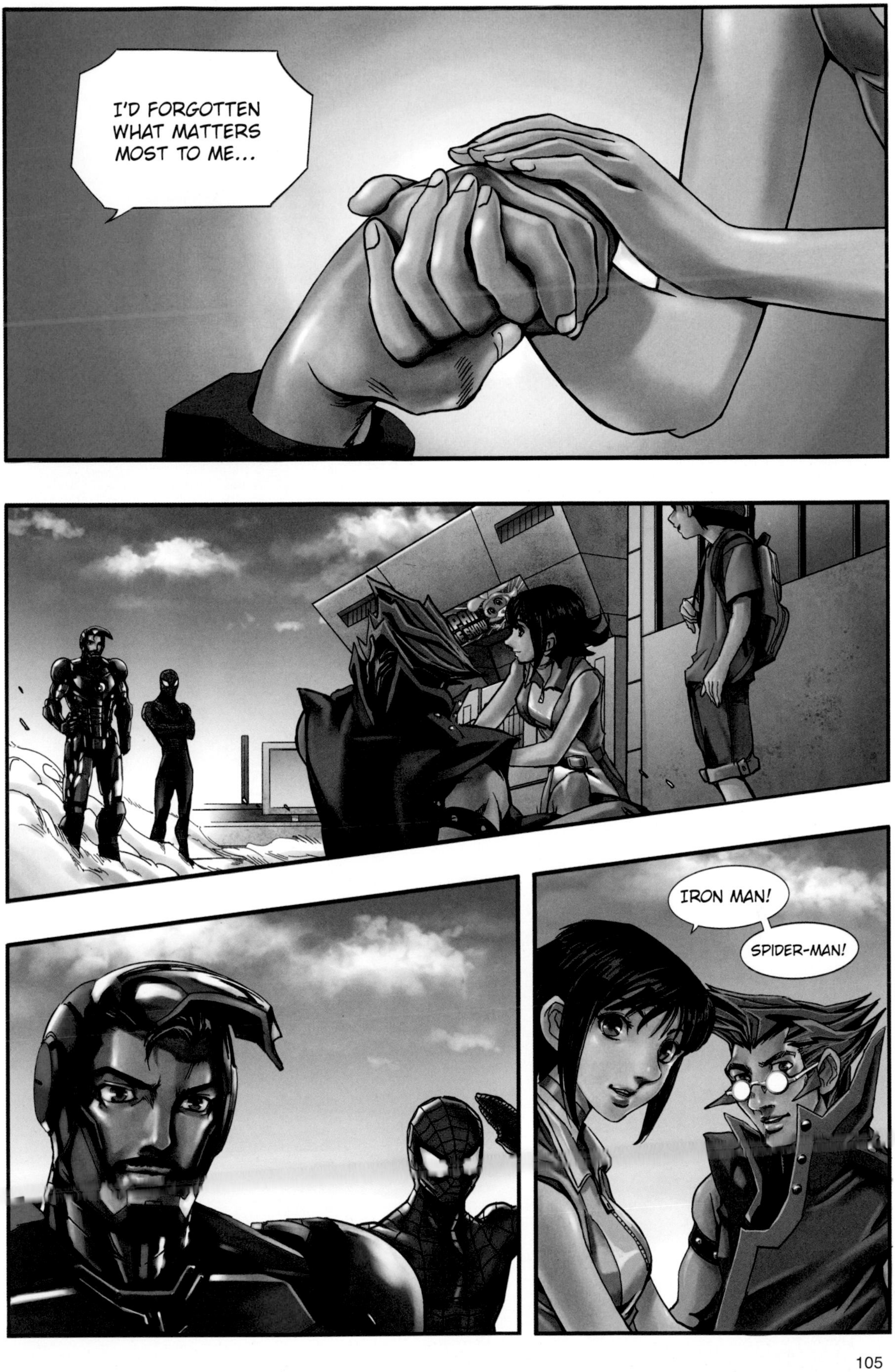
I'D FORGOTTEN WHAT MATTERS MOST TO ME...
IRON MAN!
SPIDER-MAN!

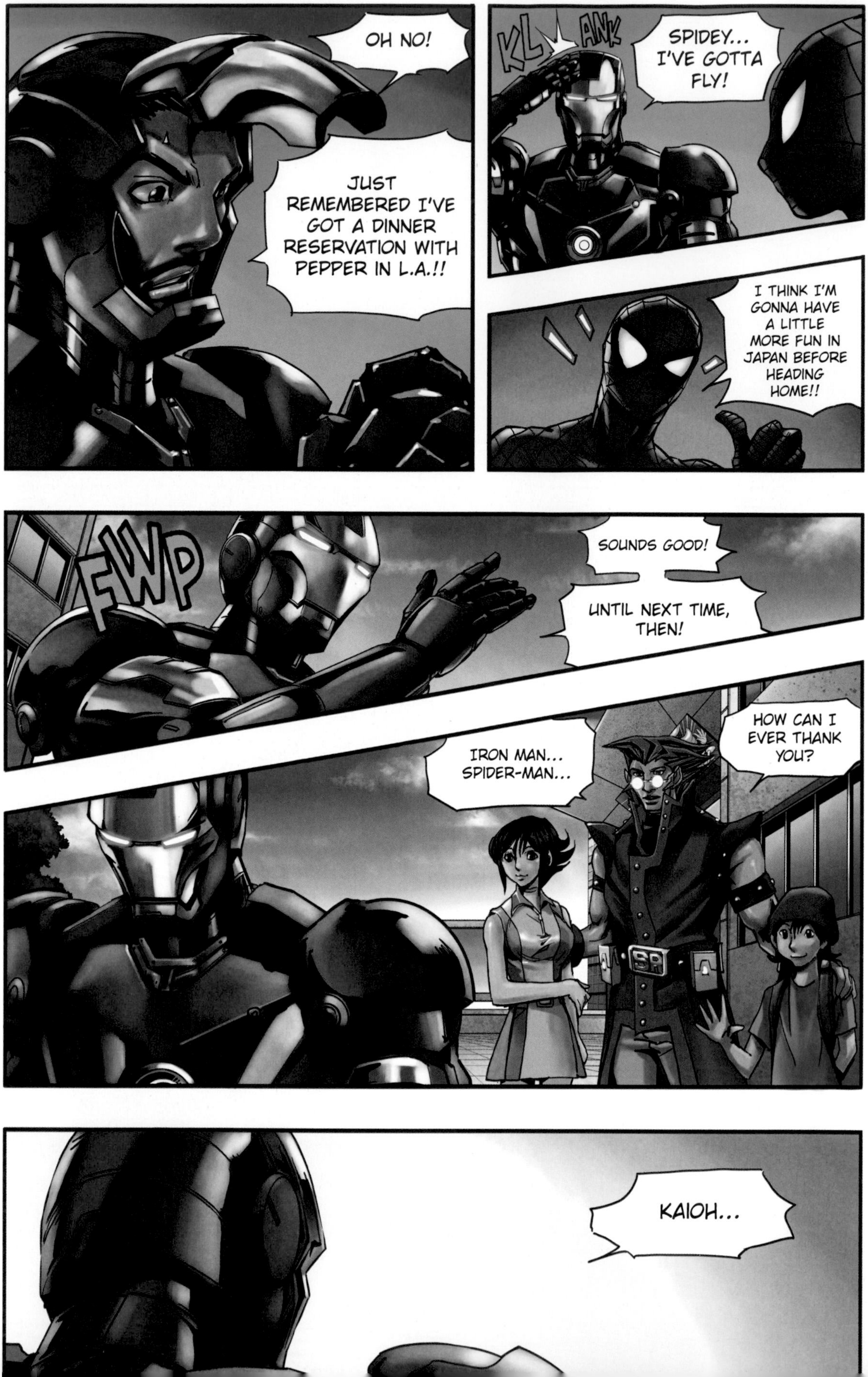
OH NO!
JUST REMEMBERED I'VE GOT A DINNER RESERVATION WITH PEPPER IN L.A.!!
KLANK
SPIDEY... I'VE GOTTA FLY!
I THINK I'M GONNA HAVE A LITTLE MORE FUN IN JAPAN BEFORE HEADING HOME!!
FWP
SOUNDS GOOD!
UNTIL NEXT TIME, THEN!
IRON MAN... SPIDER-MAN...
HOW CAN I EVER THANK YOU?
KAIOH...

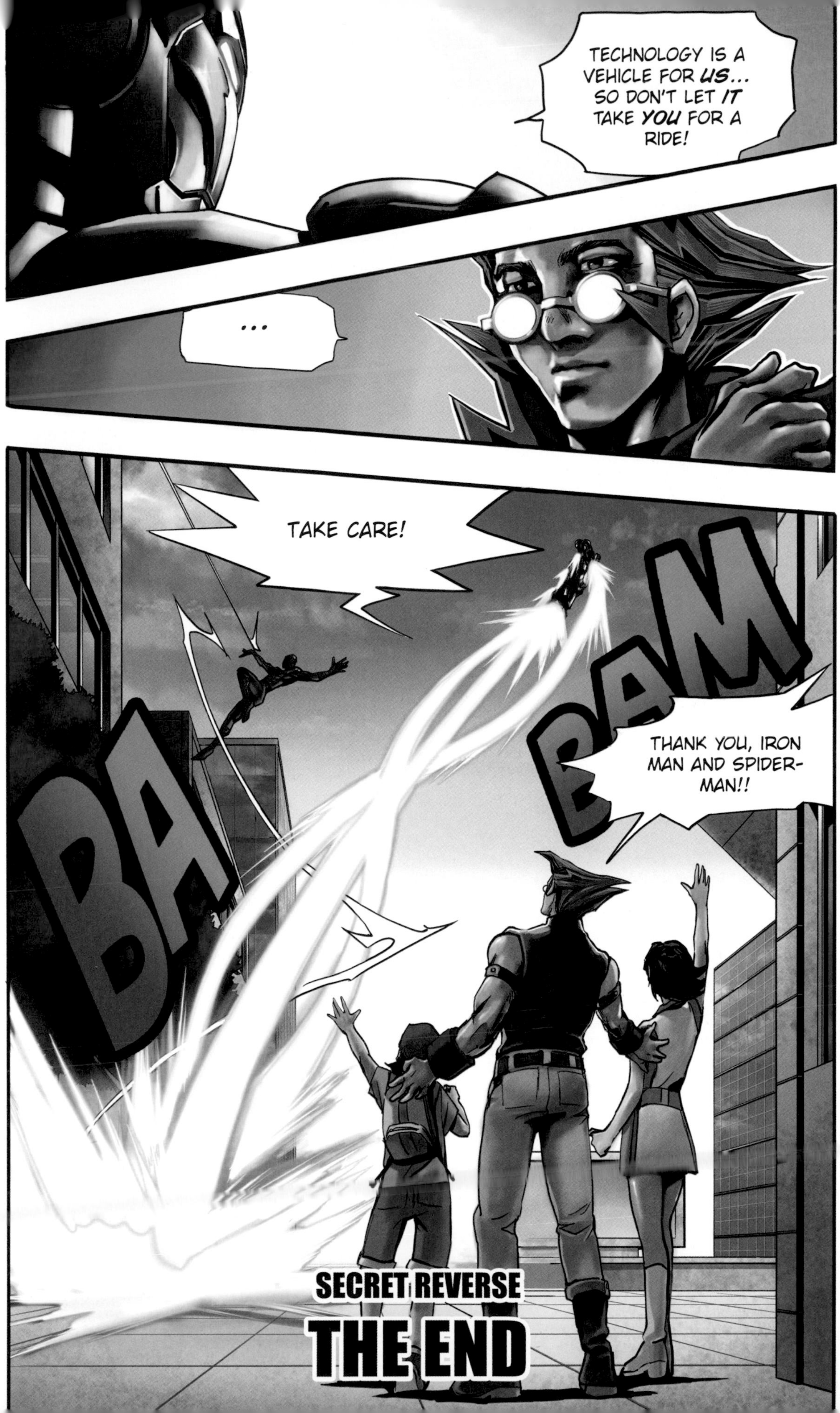
TECHNOLOGY IS A VEHICLE FOR US... SO DON'T LET IT TAKE YOU FOR A RIDE!
...
TAKE CARE!
BAM
BA
THANK YOU, IRON MAN AND SPIDER-MAN!!
SECRET REVERSE
THE END

FOR PART 1'S PUBLICATION VIA JUMP+

SEPTEMBER 4, 2019

"I want to try making a Western-style comic!!"

That's been a long-held dream of mine!

Around the end of last year, Marvel came to me, via Shueisha, and asked if I'd like to do a comic for them. I nearly leapt out of my seat at the offer, and I accepted so fast it probably made their heads spin!

What's more, they gave me—a fan—the freedom to portray my favorite heroes from the Marvel Universe, so that's exactly what I did!!

Iron Man!! And Spider-Man!! Two of Marvel's headliner heroes!!

Kaz 2019

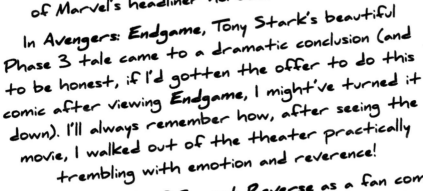

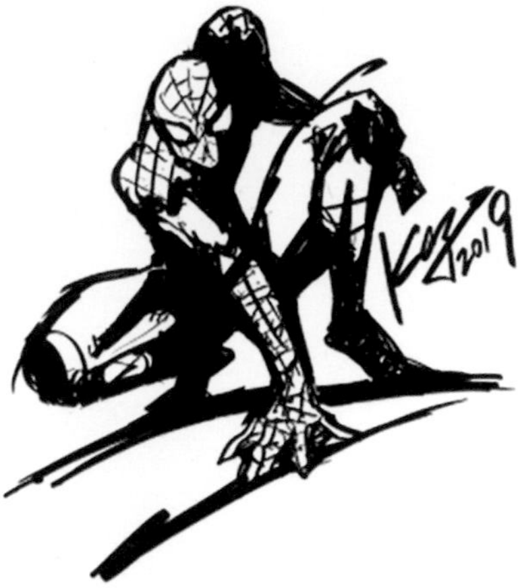

In *Avengers: Endgame*, Tony Stark's beautiful Phase 3 tale came to a dramatic conclusion (and to be honest, if I'd gotten the offer to do this comic after viewing *Endgame*, I might've turned it down). I'll always remember how, after seeing the movie, I walked out of the theater practically trembling with emotion and reverence!

So just think of *Secret Reverse* as a fan comic, packed with all my love for Marvel! I hope you love it!! on that note...

Marvel rocks!!

-Kazuki Takahashi

8/18/2019

DISPLAYED AT TOKYO COMICON 2019

NOVEMBER 22-24, 2019

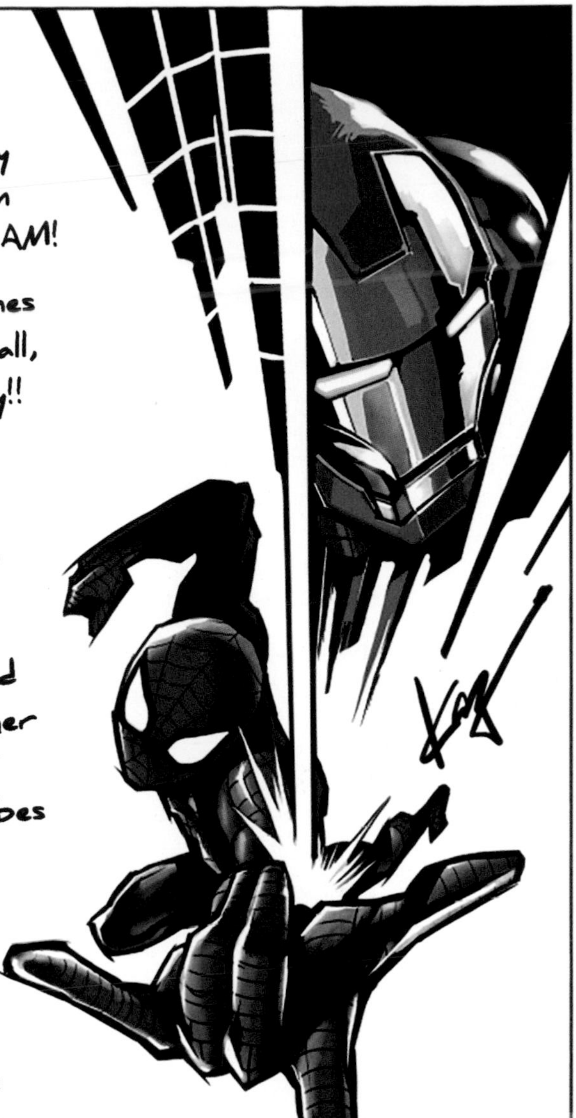

Hello there!

I'm happy to present a very special collaboration between Marvel and Shonen Jump!! BABAM!

A chance like this probably comes about once in a lifetime, if at all, so I couldn't let it pass me by!!

All of which is to say, I got to draw some Marvel heroes in a Western-style comic, coming to Jump+ on November 27!!

Since this is a Jump collab, I had to create a new world altogether that combines the energy of the Marvel Universe with the vibes of Yu-Gi-Oh!

I had such a blast drawing my favorites—Iron Man and Spider-Man!

I'm forever grateful to both Marvel and Shonen Jump for this incredible opportunity!

I hope everyone gets to read it!! Thanks!

-Kazuki Takahashi

11/11/2019

© 2022 MARVEL

SECRET REVERSE
VIZ MEDIA EDITION

Story & Art **Kazuki Takahashi**

Original Series Design **Ryoji Abe/Banana Grove Studio**

Translation **Caleb Cook**
English Adaptation **Molly Tanzer**
Touch-Up Art & Lettering **Evan Waldinger**
Design **Francesca Truman**
Editor **Joel Enos**

Special thanks to **C.B. Cebulski, Yu Kusano, Toshie Fukakasu**

FOR MARVEL PUBLISHING

VP Production & Special Projects **Jeff Youngquist**
Associate Editor, Special Projects **Sarah Singer**
VP, Licensed Publishing **Sven Larsen**
Manager, Licensed Publishing **Jeremy West**
SVP Print, Sales & Marketing **David Gabriel**
Editor in Chief **C.B. Cebulski**

First published in Japan in 2020 by SHUEISHA Inc., Tokyo.
English translation arranged by SHUEISHA Inc.

The stories, characters, and incidents mentioned in this publication are entirely fictional.

Printed in China

Published by VIZ Media, LLC
P.O. Box 77010
San Francisco, CA 94107

10 9 8 7 6 5 4 3 2 1
First printing, June 2022

viz.com

PARENTAL ADVISORY
MARVEL SECRET REVERSE is rated T for Teen and is recommended for ages 13 and up. This volume contains violence.

Original *Yu-Gi-Oh!* creator KAZUKI TAKAHASHI first tried to break into the manga business in 1982, but success eluded him until *Yu-Gi-Oh!* debuted in the Japanese *Weekly Shonen Jump* magazine in 1996. *Yu-Gi-Oh!*'s themes of friendship and competition, together with Takahashi's weird and wonderful art, soon became enormously successful, spawning a real-world card game, video games, and six anime series (two Japanese *Yu-Gi-Oh!* series, *Yu-Gi-Oh! GX*, *Yu-Gi-Oh! 5D's*, *Yu-Gi-Oh! Zexal*, and *Yu-Gi-Oh ARC-V*).

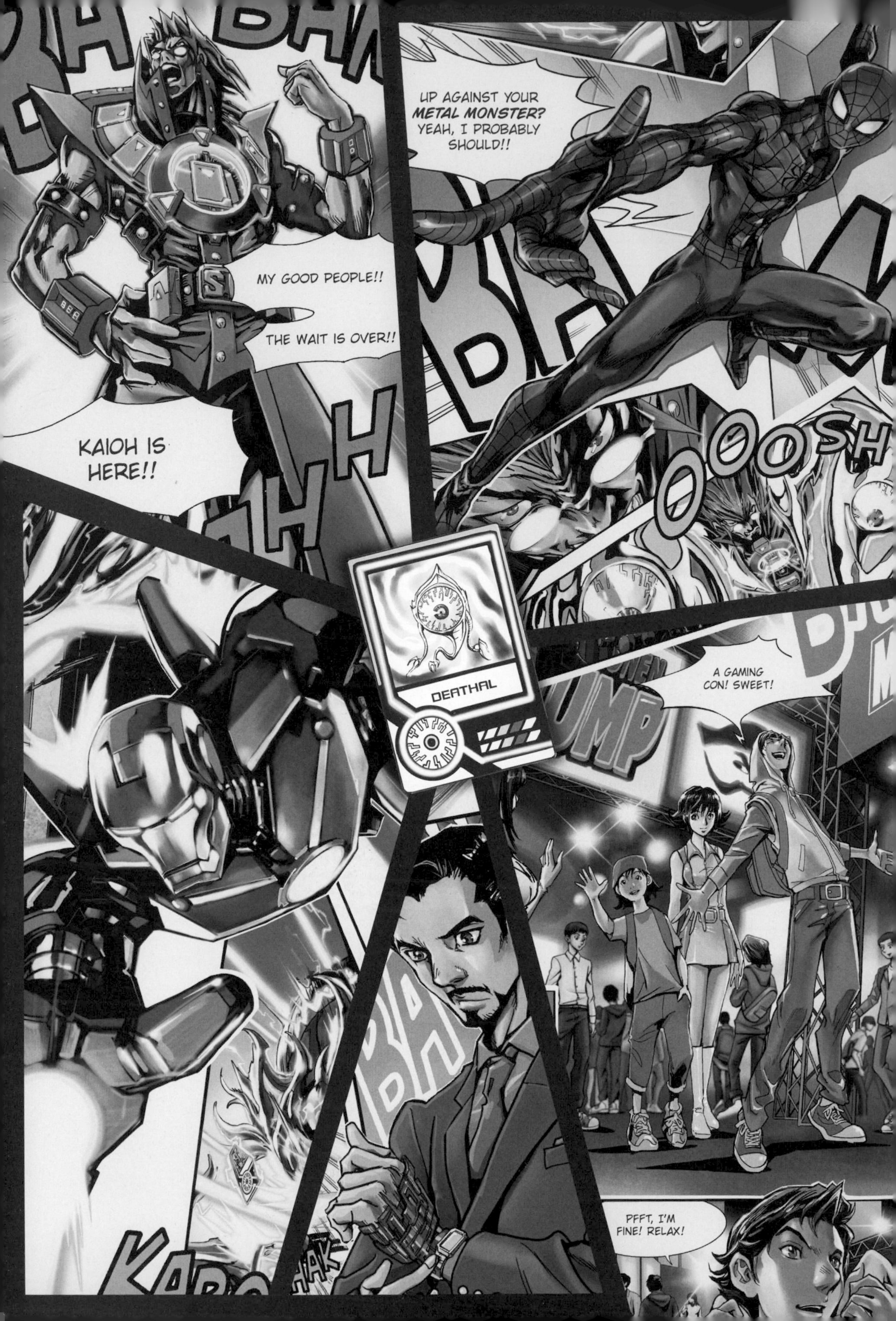
UP AGAINST YOUR *METAL MONSTER?* YEAH, I PROBABLY SHOULD!!
MY GOOD PEOPLE!!
THE WAIT IS OVER!!
KAIOH IS HERE!!
DEATHAL
A GAMING CON! SWEET!
PFFT, I'M FINE! RELAX!